Ibadi Muslims of North Africa

The Ibadi Muslims, a little-known minority community, have lived in North Africa for over a thousand years. Combining an analysis of Arabic manuscripts with digital tools used in network analysis, Paul M. Love Jr. takes readers on a journey across the Maghrib and beyond as he traces the paths of a group of manuscripts and the Ibadi scholars who used them. Ibadi scholars of the Middle Period (eleventh–sixteenth centuries) wrote a series of collective biographies (prosopographies), which together constructed a cumulative tradition that connected Ibadi Muslims from across time and space, bringing them together into a "written network." From the Mzab valley in Algeria to the island of Jerba in Tunisia, from the Jebel Nafusa in Libya to the bustling metropolis of early modern Cairo, this book shows how people and books worked in tandem to construct and maintain an Ibadi Muslim tradition in the Maghrib.

Paul M. Love Jr. is Assistant Professor of North African, Middle Eastern, and Islamic history at Al Akhawayn University, Morocco. He received his Ph.D. from the University of Michigan, is a former Fulbright scholar, and received three prestigious Critical Language Scholarships from the United States Department of State. His research has been funded by the Council for American Overseas Research Centers, the Social Sciences Research Council, the American Institute for Maghrib Studies, and the Woodrow Wilson Foundation.

Cambridge Studies in Islamic Civilization

Other titles in the series are listed at the back of the book.

Ibadi Muslims of North Africa

Manuscripts, Mobilization, and the Making of a Written Tradition

PAUL M. LOVE JR.
Al Akhawayn University, Morocco

CAMBRIDGE
UNIVERSITY PRESS

CAMBRIDGE
UNIVERSITY PRESS

University Printing House, Cambridge CB2 8BS, United Kingdom

One Liberty Plaza, 20th Floor, New York, NY 10006, USA

477 Williamstown Road, Port Melbourne, VIC 3207, Australia

314-321, 3rd Floor, Plot 3, Splendor Forum, Jasola District Centre, New Delhi - 110025, India

79 Anson Road, #06-04/06, Singapore 079906

Cambridge University Press is part of the University of Cambridge.

It furthers the University's mission by disseminating knowledge in the pursuit of education, learning and research at the highest international levels of excellence.

www.cambridge.org
Information on this title: www.cambridge.org/9781108459013
DOI: 10.1017/9781108560498

First published 2018
First paperback edition 2020

A catalogue record for this publication is available from the British Library

Library of Congress Cataloging in Publication data
Names: Love, Paul M., Jr., 1985– author.
Title: Ibadi Muslims of North Africa : manuscripts, mobilization, and the making of a written tradition / Paul M. Love Jr., Al Akhawayn University, Morocco.
Description: New York : Cambridge University Press, 2018. | Includes bibliographical references and index.
Identifiers: LCCN 2018024669 | ISBN 9781108472500
Subjects: LCSH: Ibadites – Africa, North.
Classification: LCC BP195.I3 L68 2018 | DDC 297.8/330961–dc23
LC record available at https://lccn.loc.gov/2018024669

ISBN 978-1-108-47250-0 Hardback
ISBN 978-1-108-45901-3 Paperback

For my parents, Paul and Stephanie.

And to my wife, Sarra.

Contents

Figures

Tables

Acknowledgments

***

This book has its origins in my doctoral thesis from the University of Michigan, and I am delighted to be able to offer my thanks and gratitude to those who helped me on the journey from dissertation to book—although I am terrified of forgetting someone.

During my time in Ann Arbor, I benefited from training in the Department of Near Eastern Studies. I thank my advisor, Michael Bonner, and my internal committee members, Alexander Knysh and Raymond Van Dam, for their support throughout the process of writing the thesis as well as for their guidance on how to turn it into a book in the future. Michael Brett from the School of Oriental and African Studies graciously agreed to serve as an outside committee member, and my project benefited in important ways from his advice, questions, and criticism. My colleagues in NES all shaped my project in ways I did not expect. Conversations with my friends Noah Gardiner and Maxim Romanov led me to a dual interest in manuscripts and digital humanities, respectively. Evyn Kropf, Near Eastern Studies Librarian at the University of Michigan, has for years been a teacher and guide on the journey to learn more about manuscripts and the study of paper. I benefited tremendously from her knowledge and patience. Emma Park and Andrés Pletch deserve special thanks for being excellent friends, good cooks, and helpful critics. My colleagues and students at my new institutional home, Al Akhawayn University, have been a pleasure to work with and I have enjoyed working in such a supportive environment. Special thanks to Eric Ross for creating the map for the book.

Other friends and colleagues both inside and outside the academy helped me on the road from finishing the thesis to writing the book, including Cyrille Aillet, Susan Abraham, Sami Bargaoui, Kelsea Ballantyne, Mohamed Bennani, Jonathan Bloom, Zach Bloomfield, Ali Boujdidi, Frank Castiglione, Laryssa Chomiak, Martin Custers, Yacine Daddi Addoun, Moez Dridi, Derek Elliott, Adam Gaiser, Elisabeth Gilles, Ersilia Francesca, Amal Ghazal, Mehdi Houachine, Grazyna Jurendt-Paruk, Nancy Linthicum, Valerie Hoffman, Renata Holod, Mohamed Hasan, Ali Hussain, Ryan Hunton, Yanay Israeli, Augustin Jomier, Gina Konstantopoulos, Cheng-Wei Lin, Massaoud Mezhoudi, Roberto Merlin, Soufien Mestaoui, James Miller, Antonella Muratgia, Ouahmi Ould-Braham, Karim Ouaras, Fatima Oussedik, Robert Parks, Virginie Prevost, Amanda Propst, Roman Pysyk, Valeriy Rybalkin, Karim Samji, Rachida Smine, Werner Schwartz, Zouheir Tighlet, Slimane Tounsi, Irina Yaremchuk, and Katja Žvan-Elliott.

Most of my research could never have happened without the support of my colleagues and friends from the Maghribi Ibadi community, many of whom opened the doors of their libraries to me. In Jerba, many thanks to Said El Barouni, Farhat Djaabiri, Ahmad Muslah, Naji Bin Yaʿqub, and Samir the taxi driver who put me in touch with the Bin Yaʿqub family. In Algiers and the Mzab, special thanks to ʿUmar Busaʿada, Mohamed Hadj Said, Ahmed Abanou, Mustapha Bendrissou, Elias Bouras, Daoud from the Maktabat Irwan in Ateuf, Noah El-Bechir, and Muhammad and Salih Siusiu for their help at the Maktabat al-Qutb and great conversations about manuscripts. In Oman, many special thanks to Abdulrahman Salimi. I owe additional thanks to all those from the Ibadi organizations and libraries who helped me with research, including Jamʿiyyat al-Turath, Jamʿiyyat al-Shaykh Abi Ishaq Ibrahim Atfayyish; Maktabat ʿAmmi Saʿid, Maktabat al-Qutb, Maktabat al-Hajj Salih Laʿali, Maktabat al-Istiqama, Maktabat At Khalid, Maktabat Al Yadr, Maktabat Al Fadl, Maktabat Irwan, Maktabat al-Hajj Masʿud Babakr, Association Djerba Ettwasol, Ibadica, and Jamʿiyyat al-Manar.

Funding for the research on which the book is based came from the University of Michigan's Department of Near Eastern Studies, the UM African Studies Center, the UM Rackham Graduate School, the UM International Institute, the Council of American Overseas Research Centers, the Social Sciences Research Council, the American Institute for Maghrib Studies, the Woodrow Wilson Foundation, and the Islamic Manuscripts Association. I also had the opportunity to present many of these ideas in public forums, where I received valuable feedback. Special thanks to the participants of the "Roots and Routes 2014, Translation, Mediation, and Circulation: Digital Scholarship and the Pre-Modern Mediterranean" workshop at the University of Toronto, Scarborough (Toronto, 2014), "The International Conference on Ibadi Studies" at Cambridge University (Cambridge, 2014); "Workshop on Ibadi History and Bibliography" at the University of Illinois (Urbana-Champaign, 2014); presentations at the Centre d'études maghrébines à Tunis and the Centre d'études maghrébines en Algérie (Tunis and Oran, 2015); "Arabic Pasts: Histories and Historiographies" workshops at the Aga Khan University (London, 2015 and 2017); the "Islamic Studies Program Symposium on 'Vernacular Islam'" at the University of Michigan (Ann Arbor, 2016); and the participants and attendees of the panel on "Ibadi Archives" at the annual meeting of the Middle East Studies Association (Boston, 2016). Additional thanks go to Maria Marsh and Abigail Walkington from Cambridge University Press and the two anonymous readers, whose helpful comments and criticisms helped me to improve the original manuscript. Despite all this help, any mistakes or shortcomings remain my own.

Finally, I owe the greatest thanks to my family, especially my parents Paul and Stephanie, whom I miss so much. My sister Lauren and nephew Xavier are always a source of fun and support, even from so far away. My in-laws in Tunis and Jerba make sure I always feel at home in both places and regularly offer their help and support in research. My wife Sarra astounds me every day with her intelligence, kindness, and patience. Her support for me in all things keeps me going and pushes me to try to be better at everything. Our daughter Sophia, who joined us while I was writing this book, has brought me more happiness than I can describe.

Thanks, everyone!

Ifrane, 2018

Note on Transliteration and Dates

***

Transliterations from Arabic throughout the book follow a modified version of the system of the *International Journal of Middle East Studies* (*IJMES*). Throughout the main body of the text, I have not included the diacritical marks while still retaining the ʿ and ʾ symbols to represent the Arabic letters ʿayn and hamza, respectively. For the notes and the bibliography, I have included all diacritical marks. For secondary sources and published editions that follow systems of transliterating Arabic in languages other than English (Italian, French, German), I have modified the titles to conform to the *IJMES* system. I have followed the conventional English spellings for well-known Northern African toponyms, such as Jebel Nafusa, Jerba, Sedrata, and Mzab.

The transliteration of Berber (Amazigh) names and toponyms follows the Arabic system, since all the primary sources discussed here are originally in Arabic script. Although there are several variations in how Berber names are transliterated in late medieval Arabic, I have tried to be consistent. Unless otherwise noted, all dates in the main body of the text are provided in Common Era (CE) equivalents of their Islamic *hijri* (AH) originals.

List of Library and Archive Abbreviations

ANOM	Archives Nationales d'Outre Mer	Aix-en-Provence, France
BnF	Bibliothèque Nationale de France	Paris, France
BnT	Bibliothèque Nationale de Tunisie	Tunis, Tunisia
Ivan Franko	Ivan Franko National University of Lviv	Lviv, Ukraine
Jag.	Library of the Institute of Oriental Studies Jagiellonian University	Kraków, Poland
Naples Or.	L'Università degli Studi di Napoli l'Orientale	Naples, Italy
Makt. al-Bārūnī	al-Maktaba al-Bārūniyya	Jerba, Tunisia
Makt. Bin Yaʿqūb	Maktabat al-Shaykh Sālim b. Yaʿqūb	Jerba, Tunisia
Makt. Āl Khālid	Makatbat Āl Khālid	Benisguen, Algeria
Makt. Āl Faḍl	Āl Faḍl	Benisguen, Algeria
Makt. Āl Yaddar	Āl Yaddar	Benisguen, Algeria
Makt. Irwān	Irwān	Ateuf, Algeria
Makt. al-Istiqāma	al-Istiqāma	Benisguen, Algeria
Makt. al-Ḥājj Saʿīd	al-Ḥājj Saʿīd Muḥammad Lakhbourat	Ghardaia, Algeria
Makt. al-Ḥājj Sāliḥ Lʿalī	Maktabat al-Ḥājj Sāliḥ Laʿalī	Benisguen, Algeria
Makt. Bābakr	Maktabat al-Ḥājj Masʿūd Bābakr	Ghardaia, Algeria

(cont.)

Makt. al-Khalīlī	Maktabat al-Shaykh Aḥmad al-Khalīlī	Muscat, Oman
Makt. al-Quṭb	Maktabat al-Quṭb	Benisguen, Algeria
Makt. al-Shaykh Ḥammū	Maktabat al-Shaykh Ḥammū Bābā wa Mūsā	Ghardaia, Algeria
Makt. ʿAmmī Saʿīd	Makatabat ʿAmmī Saʿīd	Ghardaia, Algeria
UBL	Library of the University of Leiden	Leiden, the Netherlands

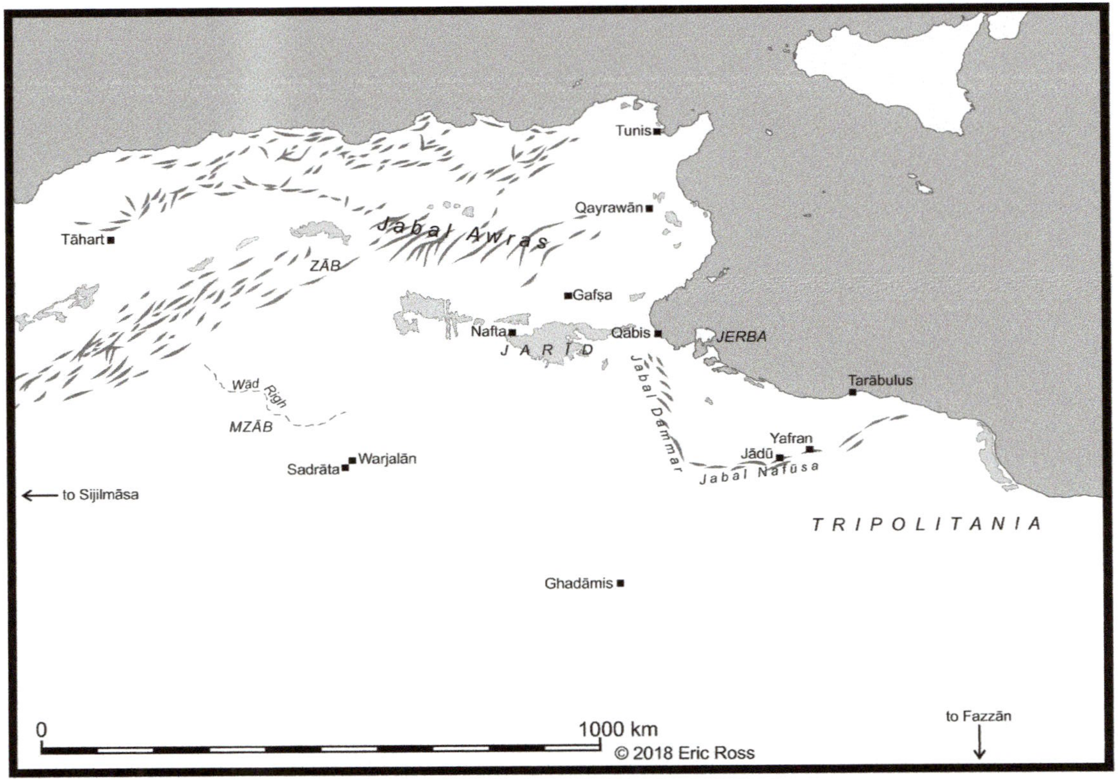

FIGURE 1: Northern Africa in the Middle Period (eleventh–sixteenth centuries). Map created by Eric Ross.

Prologue: Tunis, 2014

***

On 31 October 2014 I walked into the entry hall of the Madinat al-ʿUlum ("City of Sciences") complex in the northern suburb of Ariana just outside downtown Tunis. A large crowd had gathered, drinking juice, eating sweets, and discussing the books and manuscript facsimiles on the display tables in the center of the room. This event marked the beginning of the first annual conference on the "Ibadi Books of *Siyar*" (*Kutub siyar al-Ibadiyya*). The *siyar* were works of literature compiled from the eleventh to the sixteenth centuries in Northern Africa by Ibadi Muslims, a minority religious community whose adherents have lived in the region since the eighth century CE.

It was a large conference of perhaps two hundred people. In addition to regional participants from Tunisia, Algeria, and Libya, the event had attracted a large group of scholars from Oman, where most of the world's Ibadi Muslims live today. These latter stood out in their stark white *dishdasha* robes, elegant headgear, and long beards. Their Maghribi counterparts mostly wore suits, although some also dressed in white robes (often with button-down dress shirts underneath), had short beards, and a few donned small white hats. Many of the Omani students and scholars who had come were women, identifiable in their all-black attire that contrasted in its uniformity with that of other female attendees from Northern Africa and elsewhere dressed in a variety of styles. While the language of the conference was Modern Standard Arabic, the discussions took place in a variety of regional dialects of Arabic, as well as Tumzabt and French.

These two regional Ibadi communities had come together to discuss what they regard as some of the most important sources for understanding their shared past: the books of *siyar*. The meeting was especially symbolic for the Ibadi community because it was held openly in Tunis, which as more than one presenter noted would have been scarcely conceivable prior to the Tunisian revolution in January 2011. In the past, Ibadi communities in Tunisia had kept a relatively low profile, preferring not to attract the attention of the government. Nearly four years later, this conference was advertised throughout the city and on the internet. The Omanis had even brought a full production crew to film the conference. The event marked an open effort by the Tunisian Ibadi community to link their past and that of their coreligionists to the present. This was a public claim by both Northern African and Omani Ibadis that they belonged to the same religious community.

Panels discussed the genre, specific books and themes, as well as differences between the "eastern" (i.e. Omani) Ibadi meaning of *siyar* and its "western" (i.e. Maghribi) equivalent. In the east, the term *siyar* has historically referred to compilations of letters and opinions exchanged among Ibadi scholars. By contrast, in the Maghrib the *siyar* were books containing anecdotal and biographical information about individuals. Ibadis in late medieval Northern Africa never developed a genre of chronicle-style history (*taʾrikh*) as did their contemporaries in western Asia. Instead, the *siyar* played that role, telling the story of the community's past by bringing together anecdotes and biographies of its members from across time and space. In this way, the Ibadi *siyar* functioned as prosopographies, collective biographies in which stories about individual members come together to form a biography of the community. Through the inclusion or exclusion of individuals, these prosopographies drew the boundaries of the community and constructed an Ibadi tradition in Northern Africa.

Having come to Tunisia to search for manuscript copies of the Ibadi prosopographies and trace their history, I was struck by the immediate relevance and central importance of this corpus of late medieval books to this contemporary Ibadi audience. Through the conference, the participants were claiming a shared history not only between Northern Africa and Oman but also between Ibadis of the past and those of the present. For its participants, this conference was a continuation of the centuries-long maintenance of the prosopographical tradition in the region.

The event brought together widely dispersed members of the community to generate scholarly discussion and, crucially, to establish connections among them—to create a network of otherwise discontiguous actors. Despite differences in dress and language, through their participation and attendance the individuals at the conference asserted their ties with the broader Ibadi community. In drawing a straight line between past and present, these participants were also claiming membership in a much older network that had been constructed by the prosopographies themselves.

But this seamless move from past to present, this vision of a shared history that links the medieval Ibadi communities in both Northern Africa and Oman with those of today, belies a long history of tradition building characterized by as much discontinuity as continuity. The Ibadi communities of today are not identical to those of the eighth century any more than were those of the sixteenth. Building this tradition and creating the illusion of a seamless connection through time required centuries of inclusion and exclusion of individuals and groups, the restructuring and reconceptualization of power and leadership, the compilation and transmission of texts, and the constant movement of peoples and books.

How had these the Ibadi *siyar* constructed and maintained the late medieval Ibadi tradition in Northern Africa? Why did their importance extend beyond the sixteenth century, when the tradition ended? What was the conference eliding, overlooking, or silencing by presenting the history of community in this way? How did these medieval books, which for the conference participants lay at the center of their shared history, come to occupy such a place of prominence in the twenty-first century? After attending the conference, these were the issues I decided to address and the questions for which I sought answers. The journey led me to follow circuits of people and paper across the Sahara and the Mediterranean. The result is this book, which accompanies the Ibadi books of *siyar* on their travels and traces their role in the construction and maintenance of the Ibadi tradition through the constantly changing landscapes of Northern Africa over nearly a millennium.

Introduction: Mobilizing with Manuscripts

***

When the eleventh-century Ibadi Muslim scholar Abu al-Rabiʿ Sulayman b. Yakhlaf al-Mazati was asked by his student whether he should consult a book of legal opinions attributed to older generations of scholars, he responded: "Of course! How have we associated with so many of those pious scholars who came before us if not through books?"[1]

Both the question and its answer reveal the growing power of manuscript books in Northern Africa by the beginning of the Middle Period (eleventh–sixteenth centuries) to bring together scholars of different times and places, incorporating them into the same community. For a religious minority like Ibadi Muslims in the late medieval Maghrib, books complemented the webs of personal relationships connecting students and teachers. Ibadis, a Muslim minority community following neither the Sunni nor the Shiʿi traditions of Islam, lived throughout the earlier medieval centuries (the eighth–tenth centuries) in towns and villages across the southern Maghrib stretching from Sijilmasa in what is today southern Morocco to the mountains of the Jebel Nafusa in what is today northwestern Libya. In the early medieval period their communities had flourished, especially through their participation in Saharan trade. But by the eleventh century Ibadis had begun their steady numerical decline in the region. Their numbers dwindled as Arabic-speaking Sunni communities spread into regions where Berber-speaking Ibadis had previously made up the majority. Ibadi scholars responded to this existential threat through literal and literary mobilization.

Itinerant students and scholars traveled widely and met together in small study circles, drawing personal and intellectual connections among different centers of learning in Northern Africa. A longstanding tradition of Saharan trade facilitated travel, and its routes provided the

[1] Abū al-Rabīʿ Sulaymān al-Wisyānī, *Kitāb siyar al-Wisyānī*, ed. ʿUmar b. Luqmān Būʿaṣbāna (Muscat: Wizārat al-Turāth wa-ʾl-Thaqāfa, 2009), 692.

links among different Ibadi towns and villages. Out of these interactions among students and scholars, a formalized system of education and an accompanying large body of texts emerged over the next few centuries. One specific genre, collective biographical texts or "prosopographies" (Ar. *siyar*), both recorded this process and represented the second method of mobilization among Ibadi scholars of the Middle Period. Each prosopographical text comprised anecdotes and biographies of exemplary Ibadis from the collectively imagined beginnings of the community in the early centuries of Islam nearly up to its compiler's lifetime. The prosopographies determined which stories survived as well as which scholars belonged to the Ibadi community and its history. Unconstrained by the lifetime or memory of an individual, these books drew connections among scholars of multiple generations and constructed the Ibadi tradition in the Maghrib by marking its boundaries.

As Abu al-Rabiʿ al-Mazati suggested in the response to his student's question, the perceived value of books extended beyond their capacity to create a narrative of the community's history. The prosopographies also connected the scholars of the present to those of the past. In doing so, these books at once cloaked them in the mantle of the authority of their predecessors and drew the boundaries of the Ibadi community through the inclusion or exclusion of certain individuals or groups. The prosopographical tradition expanded and adapted to the circumstances of the community, with each iteration reflecting the historical experience of the Ibadi community in the Maghrib during the period of its compilation. Each century from the eleventh to the sixteenth witnessed the compilation of a new work of Ibadi prosopography, and each new work of *siyar* absorbed many of the stories of its predecessors—adopting and adapting them to suit the compiler's purposes. Through books, as Abu al-Rabiʿ said, each new generation of Ibadi scholars associated with those that came before it.

A WRITTEN NETWORK

This book tells the story of the compilation, adaptation, and circulation of this late medieval Ibadi prosopographical corpus. I argue that the history of this corpus exemplifies the long-term process of the construction and maintenance of an Ibadi tradition in Northern Africa. The books themselves serve as the main actors in this story, although the scholars whose lives they chronicled and who created and used them play important supporting roles.

Constructing and maintaining the Ibadi tradition in the Maghrib and its boundaries occurred on two distinct but closely interrelated levels. On the narrative level, the Ibadi prosopographies connected several generations of individuals across time and space. When they appeared as friends, colleagues, or fellow travelers in stories, Ibadi scholars became linked to one another. Likewise, even in those cases where hundreds of years separated two or more individuals, their inclusion in the same prosopographical text brought them into a single historical and religious community. I have called this narrative web of connections and associations among Ibadi scholars, constructed and maintained by the prosopographies, a "written network."

The second component relates to the manuscripts themselves and the constellation of links among people, places, and books. I argue here for the importance of examining the physical, material history of these and other Ibadi manuscripts in Northern Africa. Ideas and memory did not move throughout the Sahara and the Mediterranean littoral solely inside the heads of people. As object-actors, manuscript copies of the Ibadi prosopographies proved as important as individuals in the transmission of the tradition in the long run. Manuscripts allowed for the continuation of the tradition through the Middle Period and well beyond. Moreover, the late medieval and early modern transmission of the *siyar* in manuscript form explains the survival of these texts up to the present day.

Manuscript books and people traversed the same paths, moving in tandem along the circuits that connected the geographic hubs of Ibadi intellectual and commercial activity in Northern Africa. While the Ibadi written network appears in the synchronic iterations of the *siyar*, behind it lie dense circuits of the continuous movement of people and books. As a complement to the written network, I follow the manuscript copies of the Ibadi *siyar* as they move along often elliptical trajectories. Since both Ibadi scholars and their books often returned to their point of departure, whether in their original form or as a new copy or other textual vestige, I refer to these journeys and their trajectories as "orbital" (discussed further below). The orbits of the Ibadi prosopographies provide the dynamic complement to the written network they helped create and maintain.

MADHHABIZATION: HISTORICAL CONTEXT(S) FOR THE PROSOPOGRAPHICAL CORPUS

The written network of the Ibadi prosopographies and its orbit emerged out of two interrelated contexts. First were the historical circumstances specific to the Ibadi community in the Maghrib, while the second was the broader historical context of the Middle Period in which Ibadis lived.

As for the first, the *siyar* were not of course the only books Ibadis were writing or circulating from the eleventh to the sixteenth centuries, nor were they the first. Texts produced by identifiably Ibadi Muslim authors represent some of the earliest works of literature by autochthonous Northern Africans. For example, the *Kitab badʾ al-islam wa-sharāʾiʿ al-din* by Ibn Sallam al-Ibadi (ninth century) may well be the earliest work of historiography by a Muslim author from the Maghrib. Ibadi epistles on theology, and especially *responsa* literature between the Ibadi Imams of the Maghrib and their communities, also long predate the prosopographical tradition. Many texts from the ninth and tenth centuries survive in much later manuscript copies, and the Ibadi prosopographical tradition without doubt built off older textual traditions in the Maghrib. But by the eleventh century, circumstances had changed for the Ibadi communities in the region (see Chapters 1 and 2). In numerical decline and pushed to the edges of the Maghrib, this new context contributed to the formation of a genre of literature, distinct in form and purpose from that which preceded it.

The Ibadi prosopographical corpus developed alongside larger efforts toward community construction from the eleventh century forward. John Wilkinson has called this process Ibadi "madhhabization," from the Arabic term *madhhab*, used to refer to different schools of thought and law in Islam. He and other historians of both eastern and western Ibadi communities have pointed to similar moves toward the formalization of Ibadi theology, hadith, law, and political theory in this same period.[2]

[2] John Wilkinson, *Ibāḍism: Origins and Early Development in Oman* (Oxford: Oxford University Press, 2010), 413–37. The same period has been highlighted as important for the formation of Ibadi theological, intellectual, historical, and legal traditions in both the Maghrib and the Mashriq. See, e.g. Pierre Cuperly, *Introduction à l'étude de l'ibāḍisme et de sa théologie* (Algiers: Office des publications universitaires, 1984); Elizabeth Savage, *A Gateway to Hell, a Gateway to Paradise: The North African Response to the Arab Conquest* (Princeton: Darwin Press, 1997); Ersilia Francesca, "Early Ibāḍī Jurisprudence: Sources and Case Law," *Jerusalem Studies in Arabic and Islam* 30 (2005): 231–63; Adam Gaiser, *Muslims, Scholars, Soldiers: The Origins and Elaboration of the Ibāḍī Imamate Traditions* (Oxford: Oxford University Press, 2010).

Perhaps the clearest instance of this process took place in the realm of hadith. While the "science of hadith" tradition had formed by the ninth century or so in the east, before the twelfth century Ibadi scholars did not follow in that tradition.[3] The preoccupation of Sunni scholars with the chains of transmission (sing. *isnad*) of sayings of the Prophet Muhammad that helped lead to some of the most impressive prosopographical literature of the Middle Period in western and central Asia was almost entirely absent from Ibadi circles. Ibadi hadith compendia did exist long before the twelfth century, including most famously *al-Jami' al-ṣaḥīḥ*, attributed to the Ibadi Imam in Basra al-Rabi' b. Habib al-Farahidi (d. 791).[4] But Ibadi scholars approached these compendia with the assumption that their very transmission in the community assured their authenticity, and so chains of transmission only appear on occasion. As Adam Gaiser has noted, this suggests that Ibadi scholars followed a much older approach to hadith, but also that their tradition "increasingly diverged from Sunni and later Shi'i norms."[5] This situation persisted all the way until the twelfth century, when Northern African Ibadi scholar Abu Ya'qub Yusuf b. Ibrahim al-Warjalānī (d. 1174/5) composed his *Tartib al-musnad*, which brought the Ibadi tradition of hadith in line with Sunni standards, including attention to chains of transmission.[6]

Like hadith, the Ibadi prosopographical tradition belonged to this much broader process of madhhabization. Compared to the number of other texts from different genres compiled in the Middle Period, the prosopographies represent only a small part of the larger written corpus. Out of all proportion to its size, however, this corpus has maintained its importance because these works chronicled the lives and relationships among Ibadi scholars, marking the boundaries of the community itself. As such, I argue that the *siyar* represent the most explicit, sustained effort at the larger process of the construction of the Ibadi tradition in Northern Africa.

[3] First discussed in John Wilkinson, "Ibadi Hadith: An Essay on Normalization," *Der Islam* 62 (1985): 231–59.

[4] On al-Rabī' b. Ḥabīb and the prominence of his hadith collection in the written tradition, see Martin H. Custers, *al-Ibāḍiyya: A Bibliography*, 2nd edition (Hildesheim: Georg Olms Verlag, 2016), vol. I, 427–40.

[5] Adam Gaiser, "Ḥadīth, Ibāḍism," in *Encyclopedia of Islam, THREE* (hereafter *EI3*), available at http://referenceworks.brillonline.com/entries/encyclopaedia-of-islam-3/hadith-ibadism-COM_30165.

[6] Printed as Abū Ya'qūb Yūsuf b. Ibrāhīm al-Warjalānī, *al-Jāmi' al-saḥīḥ musnad al-Imām al-Rabī' b. Ḥabīb b. 'Umar al-Azdī al-Baṣrī*, ed. Maḥmūd 'Ayrān (Damascus: al-Maṭba'a al-'Umūmiyya, 1968). See discussion in Custers, *al-Ibāḍiyya* (2016), vol. II, 493 and 497–499.

The second context out of which the written network emerged was the larger world in which Ibadis lived during the Middle Period. Highlighting this context helps demonstrate some of the ways in which this book connects to other studies in Islamic history, in terms of both historical context and methodology. In terms of historical context, the Ibadi *siyar* were not the only works of prosopography produced by Muslims in Middle Period, but their use of the term *siyar* itself, as Chase Robinson has pointed out, distinguishes Ibadis early on from other Muslim communities.[7] The term became associated primarily with either the archetypal biography of the Prophet Muhammad (*al-sira al-nabawiyya*) or biographies of individuals.[8] Ibadis, by contrast, employed the term in slightly different ways. In the east, Ibadis continued for centuries to use the term *sira* for religious epistles, while those in Northern Africa used the term for prosopographies.[9]

For other Islamic traditions, however, different genres served similar functions to the Maghribi Ibadi *siyar*, including so-called biographical dictionaries (works of *tabaqat* and *muʿjam*), which appeared quite early in the ninth century. While universal, chronologically driven histories (*taʾrikh*), a tradition exemplified by al-Tabari's (d. tenth century) *Taʾrikh al-rusul wa-ʾl-muluk*, were absent from the Ibadi tradition in the Maghrib, the *siyar* played a similar role in preserving the community's past.[10]

The Ibadis were thus not unique in developing literature that fulfilled the function of community building in the Middle Period. Not only were they drawing inspiration from existing Sunni traditions of *tabaqat* and *taʾrikh*, they were writing at precisely the same time as their Sunni contemporaries were witnessing major transformations in the historiographical tradition, including "an explosion of contemporary history."[11] These centuries saw the composition of some of the most exhaustive and remarkable local or community-based prosopographies and histories in the larger Islamic tradition. Chase Robinson has argued that it was a move away from traditionist-minded (i.e. hadith transmitter) approaches

7 Robinson was more specifically discussing the eastern (Omani) use of the term to mean "religious epistles." See Chase F. Robinson, *Islamic Historiography* (Cambridge; New York: Cambridge University Press, 2003), 64.

8 On which see Wīm Raven, "Biography of the Prophet," in *EI3*.

9 On Omani *siyar*, see Abdulrahman Al Salimi, "Themes of the Ibadi/Omani Siyar," *Journal of Semitic Studies* 54, no. 2 (2009): 475–514; Abdulrahman Al Salimi, "Identifying the Ibadi/Omani Siyar," *Journal of Semitic Studies* 55, no. 1 (2010): 115–62.

10 For a full overview of the different categories of historiography and the larger tradition into which they fit, see Robinson, *Islamic Historiography*, chapter 4, 55–79.

11 Robinson, *Islamic Historiography*, 101.

to historiography that led to this major shift.[12] Fascinatingly, Ibadi scholars were moving in the opposite direction in this same period. As noted above, the process of madhhabization meant that Ibadi scholars of hadith adopted Sunni norms at the same moment that Sunni "secretaries and bureaucrats" broke with older approaches to history writing.[13] In either case, however, a growing sense of locality and community helped push the development of historiography, including prosopography, forward. Although equally propelled by their increasing marginalization and numerical decline, Ibadis also belonged to this much larger transformation to Islamic historiography in the Middle Period.

Beyond connecting Ibadis to other Muslim communities and their traditions of historiography, alongside my argument about the formation of the Ibadi tradition in Northern Africa sits a methodological intervention that I believe could be of use to historians of other traditions. In the story of the Ibadis I see potential parallels regarding the construction and maintenance of different Muslim communities and their written traditions. Previous studies have examined similar genres of literature like those discussed above and how they functioned in much the same way to help build a sense of community.[14] Yet too little attention has been given to the ways in which various communities in the history of Islam have often relied on the interplay between the movement of people and texts for both their crystallization and long-term vitality. The two complementary

[12] See full discussion in Robinson, *Islamic Historiography*, 83–102.

[13] Robinson, *Islamic Historiography*, 100–01.

[14] This is especially true of work on *ṭabaqāt* literature. The classic study of the *ṭabaqāt* genre is Ibrahim Hafsi, "Recherches sur le genre Tabaqat dans la littérature arabe [1]," *Arabica* 23 (1976): 227–65; Ibrahim Hafsi, "Recherches sur le genre Tabaqat dans la littérature arabe [2]," *Arabica* 24 (1977): 1–41; Ibrahim Hafsi, "Recherches sur le genre Tabaqat dans la littérature arabe [3]," *Arabica* 24 (1977): 150–86. For a more recent take on the genre and a literature review see "An overview of the Ṭabaqāt genre" in Kevin Jacques, *Authority, Conflict, and the Transmission of Diversity in Medieval Islamic Law* (Leiden; Boston: Brill, 2006), 10–16. Cf. Kevin Jacques, "Arabic Islamic Prosopography: The Tabaqat Genre," in *Prosopography Approaches and Applications: A Handbook* (Oxford: Occasional Publications, 2007), 387–414. The best-known studies on Islamic biographical literature include Richard W. Bulliet, *The Patricians of Nishapur: A Study in Medieval Islamic Social History* (Cambridge, MA: Harvard University Press, 1972); Carl Petry, *The Civilian Elite of Cairo in the Later Middle Ages* (Princeton: Princeton University Press, 1981); Michael Chamberlain, *Knowledge and Social Practice in Medieval Damascus, 1190–1350* (Cambridge; New York: Cambridge University Press, 1994); Michael Cooperson, *Classical Arabic Biography: The Heirs of the Prophets in the Age of al-Ma'mūn* (Cambridge; New York: Cambridge University Press, 2000). The genre and recent studies are surveyed in Michael Cooperson, "Biographical Literature," in *The New Cambridge History of Islam, vol IV: Islamic Cultures and Societies to the End of the Eighteenth Century*, ed. Robert Irwin (New York: Cambridge University Press, 2010), 458–73.

and interdependent networks—one written, one human—work together to draw the limits of religious community. Moreover, these networks bore the responsibility of making that community into a tradition, in its literal sense of "passing" or "delivering" it from one generation to the next. This is precisely what I mean in emphasizing both the construction and the maintenance of the tradition over time. As such, the argument I make here about Ibadis seems to me equally applicable to the medieval textual corpora of jurists or traditionists in Baghdad or Damascus, Sufi communities in South Asia, or poets in al-Andalus. The relationships among community, texts, and identity in different subsets of Islamic societies also conforms to the idea of "textual communities" developed by Brian Stock for late medieval Christianity in Europe. Moreover, it deserves note that it was in precisely this same period (eleventh–twelfth centuries) that Stock described this transformation.[15] The key underlying idea is that the Middle Period witnessed a change in which the very creation of texts ended up altering the way the community was understood.

Indeed, in presenting this idea of the construction of the Ibadi prosopographical tradition to other historians of Muslim communities I have at times been told that the argument is almost intuitive, if not obvious. Of course, these kinds of texts do the work of drawing the boundaries of the community. I find this response encouraging. The growing consensus seems to be that prosopographies and biographical texts do the work of tradition building and community construction. But neither the texts nor the people who use them, I argue, could have built or maintained a tradition without the other. Perhaps most importantly, demonstrating how texts worked alongside the people who used them proves not nearly as easy as taking this relationship for granted. I offer here an example of how books and people draw the boundaries of community and I hope that this model proves useful for thinking about similar processes in the history of other Muslim communities.

THE PROMINENCE OF THE *SIYAR* CORPUS

My discussion of this process of tradition building centers on five prominent Ibadi prosopographies in Northern Africa, with each representing about one century of the history of the community in the region (see

[15] "Textual Communities," in Brian Stock, *The Implications of Literacy: Written Language and Models of Interpretation in the Eleventh and Twelfth Centuries* (Princeton: Princeton University Press, 1983), esp. pp. 88–91.

Chapter Outlines below). Beyond their chronological arrangement, I have chosen these specific books for several reasons. The first stems from their prominence in the Maghribi Ibadi tradition itself. Long before the contemporary importance of the *siyar* described in the prologue, these five books occupied a distinguished place in the pre-modern Ibadi tradition, evidenced especially by their circulation in manuscript form (discussed in Chapter 8). Other pre-modern *siyar* existed, but the circulation of manuscript copies of similar works, such as Muqrin b. Muhammad al-Baghturi's (d. early thirteenth century) book known as the *Siyar al-Baghturi* or *Siyar maskhayikh Nafusa*, paled in comparison to the five works I examine here. Moreover, modern works of *siyar* such as Sa'id b. 'Ali b. Ta'arit's (d. 1936) *Risala fi ta'rikh Jarba* or Abu al-Yaqzan Ibrahim's (d. 1973) *Mulhaq al-siyar* explicitly situate themselves as continuations of these prosopographical works of the Middle Period.[16]

A second reason for choosing these five books comes from their prominence in modern historiography on the Ibadis. Some of these works were among the first to be printed in lithograph form by Ibadi print houses in late nineteenth-century Cairo.[17] This made them far more accessible to European scholars than their manuscript equivalents, housed in private libraries throughout Northern Africa. When manuscript copies of the Ibadi *siyar* did become available to European orientalists, it was in the context of colonialism. French and to a lesser extent Italian colonial-era officials, travelers, and historians privileged the *siyar* from an early date, due in part to the utility of knowledge about the Ibadi past for serving colonial interests in the Mzab valley, the island of Jerba, and the Jebel Nafusa.[18] Perhaps the most prominent author on Maghribi Ibadi communities in the twentieth century, the Polish historian Tadeusz Lewicki

[16] The *Siyar al-Baghṭūrī* (also *al-Bughṭūrī*) exists in very few manuscript copies (perhaps only two). See Muqrīn b. Muḥammad al-Baghṭūrī, *Siyar mashāyikh nafūsa*, ed. Tawfīq 'Iyād al-Shuqrūnī ([online edition]: Tawalt, 2009), www.tawalt.com/wp-content/books/tawalt_books/siyar_nafousa/siyar_nafousa.pdf. The *Risāla fī tārīkh Jarba* by Sa'īd b. 'Alī b. Ta'ārīt exists in manuscript form in the private library belonging to the family of Shaykh Sālim b. Ya'qūb (d. 1991). I was provided with a photocopy of the manuscript from one of Bin Ya'qūb's notebooks by 'Alī Boujdidi. On the *MulḤaq al-siyar* by Abū al-Yaqẓān Ibrāhīm b. 'Īsā, see Custers, *al-Ibāḍiyya* (2016), vol. II, 31.

[17] On Ibadi printing in Cairo, see Martin H. Custers, *Ibāḍī Publishing Activities in the East and in the West, c. 1880–1960s: An Attempt to an Inventory, with References to Related Recent Publications* (Maastricht: n.p., 2006).

[18] On the colonial context of these works, see Paul M. Love, "The Colonial Pasts of Medieval Texts in Northern Africa: Useful Knowledge, Publication History, and Political Violence in Colonial and Post-Independence Algeria," *Journal of African History* 58, no. 3 (2017): 445–63.

(d. 1992) published dozens of articles based on manuscript and lithograph copies of the prosopographies at his home institution (first in Lviv and later in Kraków). These books had been acquired through a combination of travel in northern Africa by his teacher, Zygmunt Smogorzewski (d. 1931), and the purchase of manuscripts from the personal library of the French colonial interpreter Adolphe Motylinski (d. 1907).[19] Another well-known scholar who worked on the *siyar*, the Italian orientalist Roberto Rubinacci, based his research on Ibadi lithographs and manuscripts acquired following the Italian invasion of Tripolitania in 1912–13.[20]

In the wake of Maghribi independence from colonial control in the 1950s and 1960s, Ibadi historians engaged with colonial-era work on their community's history. In some cases this involved rectifying what Ibadi scholars viewed as the errors of colonial historiography. Continuing interest in and attention to the five prosopographies examined here later led to several new print editions of each of them, edited and published in both Northern Africa and Oman in the late twentieth and early twenty-first centuries. This combined pre-modern, colonial-era, and post-independence interest and research on the five works of prosopography discussed here has contributed to their unparalleled importance in modern historiography on the Ibadis.[21]

PROSOPOGRAPHICAL NETWORKS: A NEW METHODOLOGICAL APPROACH

Although these five books have long served historians as the main sources for Ibadi history in the Maghrib, in this book I approach them from a very different perspective. The traditional method of using these texts has assumed that they represent interrelated yet separate and distinct collections of biographies and anecdotes about the Ibadi community. By

[19] Krzysztof Kościelniak, "The Contribution of Prof. Tadeusz Lewicki (1906–1992) to Islamic and West African Studies," *Analecta Cracoviensia: Studia Philosophico-Theologica Edita a Professoribus Cracoviae* 44 (2012): 241–55.

[20] See Roberto Rubinacci, "Il 'Kitāb al-Jawāhir' di al-Barrādī," *Annali dell'Istituto Universitario Orientale di Napoli* 4 (1952): 95–110; Roberto Rubinacci, "La professione di fede di al-Gannawuni," *Annali di Istituto Orientale di Napoli* 14 (1964): 552–92; Roberto Rubinacci, "Bibliografia degli scritti di Roberto Rubinacci," in *Studi arabo-islamici in onore di Roberto Rubinacci nel suo settantesimo compleanno*, XIII–IX (Naples: Universitario Orientale, 1985).

[21] For an example of the ways in which post-independence historians engaged with colonial-era historiography on the Ibadis, see Love, "The Colonial Pasts of Medieval Texts," 458–61.

contrast, I follow the initial suggestion of Elizabeth Savage in treating these works as a corpus of prosopographies resulting from a centuries-long "cumulative process of tradition building" by Ibadis in Northern Africa. That is, these works must be approached as a cumulative and interconnected textual tradition rather than as separate and disparate sources for telling the history of the community.[22]

In approaching these five books and their history as a corpus, I adopt some methodological tools from the field of network analysis. "A network," writes Mark Newman, "is, in its simplest form, a collection of points joined together in pairs by lines. In the jargon of the field the points are referred to as vertices or nodes and the lines are referred to as edges." The study of networks assumes a priori that the relationships among nodes constitute an item worthy of inquiry and analysis. This focus on the structure of the relationships means that network analysts have an interest in identifying patterns underlying the formation, growth, and sometimes the destruction of these relationships. I use network analysis in this book as a tool for understanding the relationships among people and manuscripts because these relationships can reveal something important about the structure and maintenance of the Ibadi tradition in Northern Africa. In a way, my point is just that: the relationships *are* the tradition.

The very idea of a prosopography lends itself to network analysis. As in a network, a prosopography provides structure and meaning to a web of relationships among individuals. As Chase Robinson has succinctly put it: "prosopographies make individuals members."[23] Understanding the relationships among nodes (i.e. individual scholars) and the "links" or "edges" (i.e. relationships) among them draws a picture of the structure of the Ibadi prosopographical texts and the community they created. Furthermore, the language of "edges" emphasizes the role of these texts in marking the boundaries of the Ibadi community through the inclusion and exclusion of individuals.

IDENTIFYING RELATIONSHIPS IN THE *SIYAR*

Applying the tools of network analysis to these texts required a model for identifying relationships among individuals. A unique structure underlies each text, although they share the feature of telling the biography of the community through stories, anecdotes, or narratives about individuals.

22 Savage, *A Gateway to Hell, a Gateway to Paradise*, 2.
23 Robinson, *Islamic Historiography*, 66.

Actors interact in many ways in these texts, and their relationships do not remain static. Relationship types included: teacher–student, student–student, father–son, siblings, cousins, travel partners, and fellow scholars. But students who finish their studies and take on their own students no longer have the same relationship with their former teachers.

No model (at least none that I could devise) could take account of the full spectrum of relationships among Ibadi scholars and how they changed over time. Instead, I elected to focus on the most salient feature of these relationships in the texts: instances of in-person interaction. Whenever two individuals encountered one another in an anecdote or a biographical sketch, I noted that relationship in a spreadsheet. The two columns represented the two individuals mentioned in the story. Likewise, in encounters among more than two individuals, those relationships were divided into binaries so that they would fit the model (Figure 0.1).

When an individual appeared in an anecdote alone, without any obvious connection to someone else, I placed their name in both columns (called a "self-loop") to ensure that their presence in the text was recorded.

Having compiled these interactions in a spreadsheet, I then imported them into a network mapping software called Gephi.[24] The software produces network graphs based on the relationships in the spreadsheet. Any two individuals whose names appear side by side in the spreadsheet appear on the graph with a link between them. The larger the number of

1	أبو الخطاب عبد الأعلى بن السمح المعافري	عبد الرحمان بن رستم
2	أبو الخطاب عبد الأعلى بن السمح المعافري	عاصم السدراتي
3	أبو الخطاب عبد الأعلى بن السمح المعافري	أبو داود القبلي النفزاوي
4	أبو الخطاب عبد الأعلى بن السمح المعافري	إسماعيل بن درار الغدامسي
5	عبد الرحمان بن رستم	إسماعيل بن درار الغدامسي
6	عبد الرحمان بن رستم	عاصم السدراتي
7	عبد الرحمان بن رستم	أبو داود القبلي النفزاوي
8	عاصم السدراتي	أبو داود القبلي النفزاوي

FIGURE 0.1: A sample network map spreadsheet.

[24] *Gephi: An Open Source Software for Exploring and Manipulating Networks*, version 0.9.2, 2018, https://gephi.org. While developing this project, I originally used version 0.8.2 in 2014–15. While revising the data, and preparing this manuscript in 2016–18, I redrew some of the graphs using the version 0.9.2. On *Gephi*'s development and structure, see M. Bastian, S. Heymann, and M. Jacomy, "Gephi: An Open Source Software for Exploring and Manipulating Networks," 2009, available at gephi.org/publications/gephi-bastian-feb09.pdf.

links an individual has (called the "degree"), the larger their name appears in the graph. For example, the spreadsheet for a network consisting of one teacher and her five students, none of whom know each other, would look like Figure 0.2.

Gephi would then take those data and visualize them in as in Figure 0.3.

In this example, the teacher appears much larger because she possesses five links, while each of the students appears equal in size because they have only one. Turning to an example from the Ibadi prosopographies, the network graph of the first part of the first work in the corpus, the *Kitab al-sira*, appears in Figure 0.4.

In this book I use these network graphs not as exact numerical measurements of relationships among individuals, but rather as heuristic devices for investigating the structure and aims of each text, as well as how it compares to those that preceded it. Many individual scholars appear multiple (sometimes dozens) of times in the same prosopography. For

1	SOURCE	TARGET
2	Teacher	Student 1
3	Teacher	Student 2
4	Teacher	Student 3
5	Teacher	Student 4
6	Teacher	Student 5

FIGURE 0.2: Simple teacher–student network sheet.

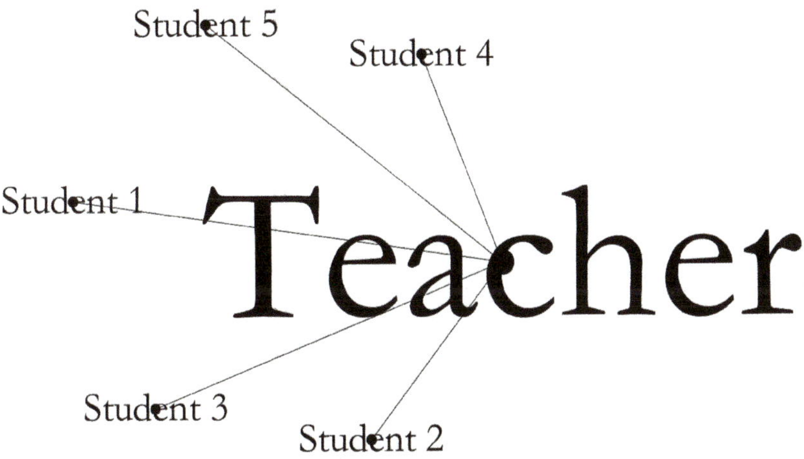

FIGURE 0.3: Sample teacher–student network based on the data in Figure 0.1.

FIGURE 0.4: Sample graph from the first part of the *Kitab al-sira*.

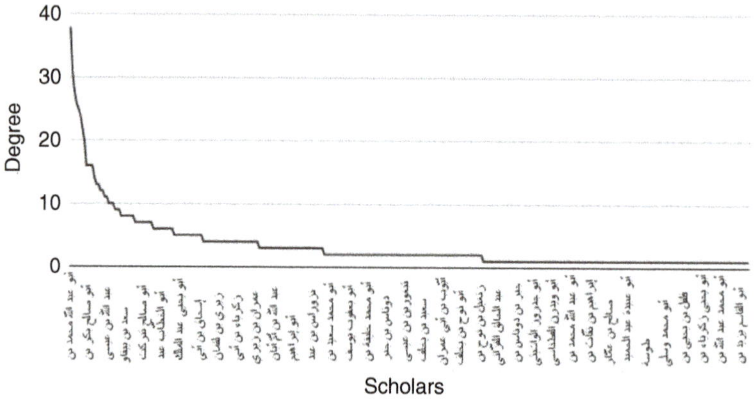

FIGURE 0.5: Degree-distribution graph for parts 1–3 of the *Siyar al-Wisyani*.

example, Abu ʿAbdallah Muhammad b. Bakr (no. 1 in Figure 0.4) stands out in the example above as a central node in the network.

Visualizing these relationships revealed the structure of the texts. The centrality or marginality of certain figures often surprised me, and led to new ways of thinking about the prosopographies. Sometimes, I knew in advance which scholars would have the highest degrees. Often, however, a name would appear much smaller or larger than I had expected, based on the individual's prominence in the wider Ibadi written tradition. That required explanation.

In addition, once I had created these maps I could use other tools from Gephi to examine the structure of the network. For example, calculating the average degree (number of links among scholars) of the network indicated the relative importance of an individual. If the average degree was 3.5, an individual with 29 connections stood out as an especially central character in the network. Specific numbers matter far less in the grand scheme of things than the proportions. Another, related, tool of network analysis called "degree distribution" plots out the numbers of connections each scholar has in a histogram. For example, Figure 0.5 shows the degree distribution for the second prosopography in the corpus, the *Siyar al-Wisyani.*

This graph demonstrates that a very small number of individuals possess far more links than the average. Using network maps, I had to think through why or how certain individuals came to play such key roles in the texts. Reading this type of network graph is as much an interpretive art as a science, and it still requires a thorough understanding of the context and content of the text from which it is drawn.

Finally, the network graphs convey in visual form another key component of my argument. Namely, that the Ibadi prosopographies construct a community and tradition by linking generations of scholars across time and space. In using these network graphs, I am not suggesting that the late medieval compilers or readers of these works would have visualized these relationships among scholars in the same way as the graphs depict them. Nevertheless, the narrative framing of the prosopographies suggests that scholars did understand that connections mattered, and that among the most important types of connections were those with prominent individuals from the past. The edges (or links) among individual scholars in the network graphs represent the limits of community. Through their inclusion or exclusion of certain individuals or groups, the Ibadi prosopographies drew the boundaries of Ibadi Islam in Northern Africa. The network graphs serve to visualize this process of tradition building.

ORBITS: NETWORKS OF MANUSCRIPTS AND PEOPLE

Network analysis provided a useful toolbox for studying the relationships within the texts. When I tried to do something similar with the extant manuscript copies themselves, however, I encountered several setbacks. First of all, any attempt to trace genealogies of copying stood little chance. Most copies lacked paratextual evidence such as detailed colophons or ownership statements that might have permitted me to identify the provenance of a given manuscript. Moreover, I began to realize that this biological metaphor for textual traditions overlooks the much more interesting (and messy) history of texts as they are transformed, summarized, borrowed from, and abbreviated over several centuries. Secondly, although the extant corpus of manuscripts of the five prosopographies was not numerically small (112 extant copies), when I took the span of time and space separating them into account, I grew more disheartened. The clear majority of extant manuscript copies of the Ibadi prosopographies dated to after the end of the tradition in the fifteenth century, and most were from the seventeenth to nineteenth centuries. In short, the fanciful idea of drawing some kind of network map connecting the different copies quickly disintegrated.

Out of this frustrating realization, I developed an approach to the manuscript copies of the *siyar* that in the end proved complementary to their contents. One of the fundamental problems with network maps like those I analyze here is that they reduce relationships to static and unchanging lines between names. Behind those lines and names, of course, lies a complex web of dynamic interactions that constantly changed. The lives and peregrinations of the manuscript copies of the Ibadi prosopographies and the scholars who produced and used them served as witnesses to the constant movement of peoples, texts, and ideas that allowed for the maintenance of the written network described in the texts.

And as I began investigating the histories of these manuscripts and the people who used them, I noticed a few locations that kept reappearing. Fragmentary evidence drawn from colophons, ownerships statements, watermarks, and other manuscript data allowed me to identify the principal circuits along which they moved. Drawing inspiration from John Wansbrough's study of diplomatic correspondence in Mediterranean, I refer to these elliptical circuits connecting different hubs from the fifteenth to the twentieth centuries as orbits.[25] These orbits of people and books from the fifteenth century forward, comprising several sites of intellectual activity and manuscript production throughout Northern Africa, accounted for the maintenance of the written network well beyond the end of the prosopographical tradition of the Middle Period. As a result, the structure of the book mirrors its argument: that the Ibadi prosopographical corpus—both its contents and its extant physical remains in the

[25] "Orbits," in John E. Wansbrough, *Lingua Franca in the Mediterranean* (Richmond: Curzon Press, 1996), 1–75. The concept was more recently applied to medieval Maghribi history in Michael Brett, "The Diplomacy of Empire: Fatimids and Zirids, 990–1062," *Bulletin of the School of Oriental and African Studies, University of London* 78, no. 1 (2015): 149–59.

form of manuscripts—bears responsibility for the construction and long-term maintenance of the Ibadi tradition in Northern Africa.

CHAPTER OUTLINES

Chapter 1 introduces the readers unfamiliar with Ibadi Muslims in the Maghrib to the traditional version of the history of Ibadi communities in the early medieval period. It begins by relating the story of the semi-legendary arrival of the community in Northern Africa in the eighth century. This includes a discussion of how this story became useful to later writers of the ninth and tenth centuries. The primary purpose of the chapter is to set the historical stage for the development of the Ibadi prosopographical tradition in the Middle Period (eleventh–sixteenth centuries). In particular, I describe the historical moment of the mid-eleventh century in the Maghrib, and how the tradition emerged out of the political and religious landscape of the period.

Chapter 2 demonstrates how the first work of Ibadi prosopography called the *Kitab al-sira* constructed a written network that laid the foundation for an Ibadi tradition in Northern Africa in the eleventh century. The chapter begins by examining the interplay among the work's structure, its intended aims, and the historical context out of which it emerged. It focuses on how the *Kitab al-sira* wove together literary themes to create a historical narrative of seamless transition from the Rustamid dynasty in the eighth century to Ibadi scholars of the eleventh. The chapter then turns its attention to the written network of Ibadi scholars. Employing tools from network analysis and using network maps, it reveals how the *Kitab al-sira* used stories about a handful of individual scholars to create a community.

Using a collection of written traditions compiled in the twelfth century known as the *Siyar al-Wisyani*, in Chapter 3 I argue that the late eleventh and early twelfth centuries witnessed two important steps toward the construction and maintenance of the Ibadi community. The first was a move toward privileging the book and writing as tools for the preservation of the Ibadi past, as well as for establishing and maintaining connections among scholars. The second was the sharpening of the boundaries of that community through an increasingly precise description of both the structure of the Ibadi community and the distinction between them and their non-Ibadi contemporaries. Chapter 4 uses the thirteenth-century Ibadi prosopography called the *Kitab al-tabaqat* by Abu al-ʿAbbas al-Darjini to show that this period witnessed the formalization of the Ibadi prosopographical tradition in several ways. These included the written institutionalization of a council-rule system, the structural arrangement of Ibadi scholars from the past into generations of fifty years (*tabaqat*), the linguistic triumph of Arabic in written scholarship, and a further move toward manuscripts as tools for the transmission of knowledge alongside their oral equivalents. These steps toward formalization likewise mirror the changes in the political and religious landscapes of the Ibadi archipelago out of which the book emerged. Finally, the chapter shows how the written network of *Kitab al-tabaqat* represents a contracted and refined version of its predecessors.

Chapter 5 briefly zooms out to pull together a reoccurring theme of the previous chapters: the spread of the use of and trade in paper throughout Northern Africa. Using examples drawn from the extant manuscripts of the prosopographies, I show that one of the main reasons for the commitment of the prosopographical tradition to paper was that Ibadis in the Middle Period were living at a time when paper was becoming much easier to obtain, even in the remotest areas of the Sahara. This situates Ibadis within a much larger context of written culture in the Mediterranean and Sahara. Likewise, their following this broader trend of committing texts to writing contributes to the formalization of their history in the prosopographical tradition.

In Chapter 6 I turn my attention to the fourth work of Ibadi prosopography, the fourteenth-century *Kitab al-jawahir* by Abu al-Qasim al-Barradi. This book departs radically from its predecessors by extending the written network backward in time all the way to the very beginnings of Islam. Al-Barradi claims for Ibadism some of the earliest companions of the Prophet Muhammad in the seventh century, and retells the history of Islam all the way up to the Rustamid dynasty. I show that this "retroactive" networking allows al-Barradi to present Ibadi history as the history of Islam itself.

In addition to comprising a history of Islam, the *Kitab al-jawahir* also includes a list of books known to its author in the fourteenth century. I conclude the chapter by showing what this book list—comprising eastern and western Ibadi works from several centuries—reveals (and conceals) about Ibadi manuscript collections in the fourteenth century. In addition, I demonstrate that the book list complements al-Barradi's history in linking Ibadi books from both east and west, bringing them together to produce a canonical list of the community's literature.

In Chapter 7 I show how the fifth and final work, the *Kitab al-siyar*, brought the medieval tradition of Ibadi prosopography to a close. I argue that this late fifteenth-century work by Abu al-ʿAbbas al-Shammakhi marks the end of the tradition by compiling all of the biographies of its predecessors into one collection. I demonstrate that al-Shammakhi could do that because he lived in the fifteenth-century Maghrib, where manuscripts and libraries were far more abundant than ever before. In addition, since Ibadis had declined in number significantly, and now studied alongside their Sunni contemporaries, the *Kitab al-siyar* offers its biographies of the Ibadi community as much to non-Ibadis as to Ibadis. As such, I show that the end of the tradition of prosopography in the Middle Period also marked a recognition within the Ibadi community of their minority status as one of many religious traditions in the region.

The network maps of the *Kitab al-siyar* demonstrate how al-Shammakhi crafted his arrangement of the biographies. When read closely, these biographies appear to lack any specific order. Using network analysis to map the text, I reveal that al-Shammakhi divided the written network of relationships into temporal divisions, corresponding to the major divisions of Ibadi history in the Maghrib.

In Chapter 8 I shift the focus of the argument away from the content of the prosopographical texts and toward the physical manuscript copies of them. While creating a relational database of extant manuscripts of the prosopographies, I learned that most of the surviving copies date to well after the end of the tradition itself. As a result, I take the argument beyond the Middle Period. Based on manuscript evidence, I argue that the circulation of these manuscripts from the sixteenth to the twentieth centuries accounts for the survival of the prosopographical corpus well beyond the end of the tradition itself.

But manuscripts did not move alone. The combined effort of people and books, moving in tandem along often elliptical circuits, allowed the prosopographical tradition to continue. I call these circuits of movement the "orbits" of the written network. Individuals or texts would often return to their point of origin, whether in their original form or as a relative, a student, or a textual vestige. The movement described within the texts (the written network) found its complement in the movement of the manuscripts and people along these orbital circuits.

Finally, in Chapter 9 I demonstrate what the extant copies of the Ibadi prosopographical corpus reveal about Ibadi manuscript culture of over the periods discussed in previous chapters. Examples relating to paratexts, watermarks, and bindings show the ways in which Ibadi manuscript culture, like the prosopographical tradition it helped produce, at once reflected circumstances particular to the Ibadi communities of Northern Africa and followed broader trends in the Arab-Islamic manuscript tradition in which they operated.

I

Ibadi Communities in the Maghrib

***

In a way, Ibadis arrived in Northern Africa before Ibadism even existed. Only more than a century after the events they described would later Ibadi writers in the Maghrib look back on the late seventh and early eighth centuries and trace the origins of their community to figures from this early period. Later Ibadi scholars told the story of five missionaries, trained in the eastern city of Basra in the early eighth century, who brought Ibadi Islam to the region. Of course, even for later Ibadi historians these missionaries did not bring *Ibadi* anything—they simply brought the true and righteous form of Islam.[1]

The success of these missionaries in the Maghrib during the mid-eighth century coincided with a period of great turmoil back east. The first great Muslim dynasty in western Asia that had ruled in Damascus since the mid-seventh century, the Umayyads, encountered growing opposition, culminating in its replacement by the Abbasids in 750. Around the same time, Northern African communities erupted in revolt against the Umayyad representatives in the region. The grievance of these peoples, collectively called "Berbers" (*al-barbar*) in the Arabic historical tradition, stemmed at least in part from their mistreatment by their new Arab rulers. Despite their having nominally converted to Islam with astonishing speed in the seventh and early eighth centuries, the autochthonous peoples of the Maghrib remained subject to the taxes owed by non-Muslims and, in

[1] An additional component of the story includes the legendary arrival of Salāma b. Saʿīd and ʿIkrama, two earlier missionaries to Northern Africa in the early eighth century, who represent Ibāḍī and Ṣufrī Islam, respectively. On this see Savage, *A Gateway to Hell, a Gateway to Paradise*, 44.

some cases, to legal enslavement. This has led historians to suggest that this inequality helped push local tribes to rebel against Arab rule.[2]

KHARIJITES AND THE ORIGINS OF THE IBADIS IN THE EAST

This context has also provided a partial explanation for the affinity of autochthonous Maghribi tribes for a particular flavor of Islam. Modern historians refer to the supporters of the Northern African revolts of this tumultuous period collectively as "Kharijites." The word *khariji* (pl. *khawarij*), from the Arabic root *kha-ra-ja* ("to go out"), often served the Arabic historical tradition as an umbrella term for groups deemed dissident. In some cases, pre-modern historians connected Kharijites in the Maghrib to the older Kharijite movements of the seventh and eighth centuries in Iraq. The traditional historical narrative traced the origins of the Kharijites to the famous Battle of Siffin (656 CE) in which the opposing armies of the Prophet Muhammad's son-in-law and cousin ʿAli b. Abi Talib and the governor of Syria, Muʿawiya b. Abi Sufyan, battled for the rule of the Muslim community and the empire it was rapidly creating. When ʿAli agreed to an arbitration agreement, a contingent of his supporters left the field of battle in protest. Their opposition to the arbitration (*tahkim*) and slogan that "there is no judgement except that of God" (*la hukma illa li-llah*) led Arabic historians to refer to them as the *muhakkima*. One understanding has their "leaving" the field of battle as their reason for their being dubbed "Kharijites" (i.e. "those who go out"). More likely, however, is the explanation offered by Patricia Crone, who suggested that the term "is a self-designation" referring to the Qur'an.[3] In any case, this simplified version of the Battle of Siffin long served historians as an origin

[2] On accounts of Khārijite revolts in Northern Africa, see e.g. Savage, *A Gateway to Hell, a Gateway to Paradise*, 44–47; "II. La Résistance Berbère, in" Charles-André Julien, *Histoire de l'Afrique du Nord: des origines à 1830* (Paris: Payot & Rivage, 1994), 360–66; Abdallah Laroui, *L'histoire du Maghreb: un essai de synthèse* (Casablanca: Centre Culturel Arabe, 1995), 89–96; Jamil M. Abun-Nasr, *A History of the Maghrib in the Islamic Period* (Cambridge: Cambridge University Press, 1987), 37–42.

[3] For an overview of the basic historical narrative of the emergence of the Kharijites, see Patricia Crone, *Medieval Islamic Political Thought* (Edinburgh: Edinburgh University Press, 2005), 54–64. Crone and Zimmermann had earlier argued that the use of the term in the Epistle of Sālim b. Dhakwān "is a self-designation, probably coined with reference to Q. 4:100 (*wa-man yakhruju min baytihi muhājiran ilā ʾllāh*, 'he who goes out from his house emigrating to God')": Patricia Crone and Fritz Zimmermann, eds., *The Epistle of Sālim Ibn Dhakwān* (New York: Oxford University Press, 2001), 275.

story not only for the Kharijites but also for the division between Sunni and Shiʿi Muslim communities.[4]

As with most concise origins stories, this version of events belies the complexity of the historical development of these different religious communities. But while historians have demonstrated that Shiʿi and Sunni identities crystalized only after centuries, the boundaries of Kharijite movements and their genealogies have not received the same scholarly attention. Recently, however, Adam Gaiser has shown that the Kharijites and their Ibadi inheritors in the east ought to be situated in their Late Antique and Arabian contexts.[5] Similar studies that could more fully contextualize early Kharijite movements in Northern Africa will no doubt appear in the future. In any case, movements and communities labeled Kharijite do often appear to share an intellectual or narrative genealogy that stretches back to the *muhakkima* movement in the mid-seventh century. From there, Muslim scholars of the medieval "heresiographical" tradition laid out subdivisions of the Kharijites, listing the Ibadis as one of their main branches or schools.[6]

In general, the history of pre-modern Ibadi communities comprises two geographic spheres: one comprising a kind of latitudinal line of geographic pockets throughout Northern Africa; and another centered in the Arabian Peninsula, more precisely in Oman. Both geographic communities traced their origins to the Iraqi city of Basra, where support for the *muhakkima* was quite strong in the decades after the Battle of Siffin. That support took a variety of forms, one of which historians have often referred to as "quietist" Kharijite groups, in contrast to the more active calls for revolt among other groups also labeled Kharijite by their

[4] For recent overviews of historiography on the Kharijites, see Najya Buʿajīla, *al-Islām al-khārijī* (Beirut: Dār al-Ṭalīʿa, 2006); Hussam S. Timani, *Modern Intellectual Readings of the Kharijites* (New York: P. Lang, 2008); Adam Gaiser, "The Kharijites and Contemporary Scholarship," *History Compass* 7, no. 5 (2009): 1376–90; "L'épouvantail politique du khârijisme," in Cyrille Aillet, ed., "L'ibāḍisme, une minorité au cœur de l'islam," *Revue du monde musulman et de la Méditerranée* 132 (2012): 13–36.

[5] Gaiser's first and second books situate Ibadi thought in the much broader context of Late Antiquity by examining the history of the concept of the Imamate and the themes of *shurāt* narratives, respectively. See Gaiser, *Muslims, Scholars, Soldiers*; Adam Gaiser, *Shurat Legends, Ibadi Identities: Martyrdom, Asceticism, and the Making of an Early Islamic Community* (Columbia: University of South Carolina Press, 2016).

[6] These issues are most clearly laid out by Keith Lewinstein in his articles on the Kharijites in heresiography. See Keith Lewinstein, "Making and Unmaking a Sect: The Heresiographers and the Ṣufriyya," *Studia Islamica*, no. 76 (1992): 75–96; Keith Lewinstein, "The Azāriqa in Islamic Heresiography," *Bulletin of the School of Oriental and African Studies, University of London* 54, no. 2 (1991): 251–68.

opponents. Historians have identified the Ibadis with the former, quietist tendency, and trace the earliest history of the community to this late seventh- and early eighth-century milieu in Basra. It is in this milieu that ʿAbdallah b. Ibad lived; later historians and heresiographers would refer to him as the founder of the Ibadiyya, although the nature of this early community has been a topic of debate for historians for decades.[7] John Wilkinson has dubbed these earliest inklings of the Ibadi school in Basra as "proto-Ibadi," which has the benefit of recognizing their influence upon and connection to later communities without making a firm commitment as to the nature of that relationship.[8]

Despite some indications of a relationship between them, the history of Ibadi communities in these two different spheres played out quite differently, and each developed largely independent of the other. Nevertheless, the two do share an intellectual genealogy in the early milieu of the *muhakkima*. Since the late nineteenth century, however, the modern Ibadi historical tradition has passionately denied its historical relationship to the Kharijites, in part because of the modern political potency of the derogatory label *khawarij*. While the early *muhakkima* and their supporters may have used the term *khawarij* with pride in their poetry, by the nineteenth and twentieth centuries the title carried a heavy stigma and Ibadi historians were keen to dissociate themselves from it. This rhetorical distancing of themselves from the *muhakkima*-inspired movements also plays into an effort at a rapprochement with representatives of Sunni

7 This is especially true of the letters attributed to ʿAbdallāh b. Ibāḍ, addressed to the Umayyad ruler ʿAbd al-Malik, on which see Michael Cook, *Early Muslim Dogma: A Source-Critical Study* (Cambridge; New York: Cambridge University Press, 1981), 51–67; Wilferd Madelung, "Abd Allāh Ibn Ibāḍ and the Origins of the Ibāḍiyya," in *Authority, Privacy and Public Order in Islam: Proceedings of the 22nd Congress of L'Union Européenne des Arabisants et Islamisants*, ed. E. Michalak-Pikulska and A. Pikulski (Leuven: Peeters, 2006), 52–57; Wilferd Madelung, "The Authenticity of the Letter of ʿAbd Allāh b. Ibāḍ to ʿAbd al-Malik," ed. Cyrille Aillet, *Revue des mondes musulmans et de la Méditerranée*, no. 132 (2012): 37–43.

8 Wilkinson's work is by far the most comprehensive account of Ibadi origins: Wilkinson, *Ibāḍism*. On his idea of "proto-Ibadis," see pp. 161–83. On the origins of the Ibadi school in the east see also Elizabeth Savage, "Survival through Alliance: The Establishment of the Ibadiyya," *Bulletin of the British Society for Middle Eastern Studies* 17, no. 1 (1990): 5–15; Ersilia Francesca, "The Formation and Early Development of the Ibāḍī Madhhab," *Jerusalem Studies in Arabic and Islam* 28 (2003): 260–77; Virginie Prevost, *Les Ibadites: de Djerba à Oman, la troisième voie de l'Islam* (Turnhout: Brepols, 2010). On the early history of the Ibadi community in the east see Tadeusz Lewicki, *Les ibadites en Tunisie au Moyen Âge* (Rome: Angelo Signorelli, 1958); Savage, *A Gateway to Hell, a Gateway to Paradise*; Virginie Prevost, *L'aventure ibāḍite dans le Sud tunisien, VIIIe–XIIIe siècle: effervesence d'une région méconnue* (Helsinki: Academia Scientiarum Fennica, 2008).

Islam in the twentieth century. Unfortunately, these efforts also contribute to the reification of the historical category of Kharijite, meaning that Ibadi historians have joined the ranks of those who employ the term as an umbrella category for a wide variety of political and religious communities in the formative period of Islamic history.[9]

In any event, Ibadi and non-Ibadi historians (both pre-modern and contemporary) agree that the written Ibadi traditions of Northern Africa and the Arabian Peninsula traced at least some of their past to major figures from among the *muhakkima*.[10] From there, the proto-Ibadi movement crystalized among sympathizers with the *muhakkima* in the diverse religious environment of Basra, especially among recent immigrants from Oman belonging to the Azd tribe. Later Ibadi tradition accords much importance to the early Ibadi Imam there, Abu ʿUbayda Muslim b. Abi Karima al-Tamimi (d. 767/68). Tradition credits him with training several missionaries (*hamalat al-ʿilm*: lit. "bearers of knowledge") to Northern Africa, which provided an important historical link with between Basra and the Maghrib. As later chapters will demonstrate, this connection to the east brought authority to the narrative of Ibadi history in Northern Africa.

IBADIS IN THE MAGHRIB

This book is concerned primarily with this Maghribi tradition of Ibadi Islam and, more precisely, with the later articulation of the boundaries of the Ibadi community in the Middle Period (eleventh–sixteenth

[9] On connections between the two communities in the pre-modern period, see Rajab Muḥammad ʿAbd al-Ḥalīm, *al-Ibāḍiyya fī Miṣr wa-ʾl-Maghrib wa-ʿalāqātuhum bi-Ibāḍiyyat ʿUmān wa-ʾl-Baṣra* (al-Sīb: Maktabat al-Ḍāmirī, 1990); Farhat Djaabiri, *ʿAlāqāt ʿUmān bi-shimāl Ifrīqiyā* (Muscat: al-Maṭābiʿ al-ʿĀlamiyya, 1991). The corpus of Ibadi literature in Arabic arguing for their distinctiveness from Kharijites is large, and extends from Northern Africa to Oman. For an overview and list of works see Valerie J. Hoffman, "Historical Memory and Imagined Communities: Modern Ibāḍī Writings on Khārijism," in *Historical Dimensions of Islam: Essays in Honor of R. Stephen Humphreys*, ed. James E. Lindsay and Jon Armajani (Princeton: Darwin Press, 2009), 185–200. On the use of the term *khārijī* for political purposes in contemporary Northern Africa, see Jeffrey Kenney, *Muslim Rebels: Kharijites and the Politics of Extremism in Egypt* (Oxford; New York: Oxford University Press, 2006).

[10] In referring to the "kharijite" as a historiographic umbrella category, I am not questioning the historicity of these groups' existence, but instead pointing to the imprecision of applying the term to heterogeneous groups, movements, and communities. As noted above (n. 28), the terms *khārijī* and *khawārij* were already being used by the Ibāḍī author Sālim b. Dhakwān in the eighth century, and the term is used by other early authors as well.

centuries CE). The early narrative of Ibadi origins in Northern Africa serves as an important component in the prosopographical (*siyar*) tradition of the Middle Period, and that later tradition no doubt built upon an older one. For example, scholarship on one of the earliest extant Ibadi texts from the Maghrib in the ninth century, known as the *Kitab Ibn Sallam*, suggests that the origin narratives of the Ibadi traditions of the Maghrib were circulating two centuries before formal prosopographies were composed. A detailed study of this early narrative of the Ibadis from the late seventh to early tenth centuries lies beyond the scope of this book. Elizabeth Savage has explored this phase of early Ibadi history up to the Rustamids, and in many ways I pick up where she left off in the eleventh century. In the remainder of this chapter, I present only a skeleton outline of the historical narrative assumed by the later Ibadi prosopographical tradition. In the chapters that follow, I revisit many of these same events in light of their reinterpretations throughout the Middle Period.[11]

The written Ibadi tradition in the Maghrib traced the community's origins to several failed revolts against late Umayyad and early Abbasid rule, but most importantly the revolt and briefly lived Imamate under Abu al-Khattab ʿAbd al-Aʿla al-Maʿafari (d. 761), one of the five missionaries trained in Basra under the Ibadi Imam Abu ʿUbayda Muslim b. Abi Karima. He and his supporters, drawn from several local tribes in Tripolitania, seized control of that region, including Tripoli, before moving eastward to capture Qayrawan. Having established control, he appointed another of the missionaries from Basra, ʿAbd al-Rahman b. Rustam al-Farisi (d. 787/88), as governor of Qayrawan. In her study of this early phase of Ibadi history in the Maghrib, Elizabeth Savage wrote:

> As brief as his Imamate was, a short four years, Abu l-Khattab was seen in the [later] Ibadi tradition as a prototype of the ideal North African Imam. Both he and ʿAbd al-Rahman ibn Rustam had been appointed by Abu ʿUbayda himself and were considered by the chroniclers to be uniquely qualified for leadership due to their training and knowledge.[12]

[11] Elizabeth Savage's work remains the only monograph-length study in English on early Ibadi history in the Maghrib. See especially Savage, *A Gateway to Hell, a Gateway to Paradise*, 29–66. Ibn Sallām al-Ibāḍī, *Kitāb fīhi bad' al-islām wa-sharāʾiʿ al-dīn*, ed. Werner Schwartz and Sālim b. Yaʿqūb (Beirut: Dār Iqraʾ, 1986). Cf. Cyrille Aillet, "A Breviary of Faith and a Sectarian Memorial: A New Reading of Ibn Sallām's *Kitāb* (3rd/9th Century)," in *Ibadi Theology: Rereading Sources and Scholarly Works*, ed. Ersilia Francesca (Hildesheim: Georg Olms Verlag, 2015), 67–82.

[12] Savage, *A Gateway to Hell, a Gateway to Paradise*, 46.

In addition to ideal types, equally important would be the way in which the rebellion of Abu al-Khattab provided later Ibadi writers with a neat genealogy for two geographic poles of Maghrib Ibadis in the early medieval period. To the west, Abu al-Khattab's former governor in Qayrawan, ʿAbd al-Rahman b. Rustam, went on to found the eponymous Ibadi Rustamid dynasty (747–909). The Rustamids, based in the city of Tahart in what is today north central Algeria, remained in power for the next century and a half. In the eastern Maghrib, the descendants of Abu al-Khattab himself served as the Rustamids' largely autonomous governors of the Nafusa mountains in what is today northwestern Libya throughout the ninth century.[13] This tidy version of the history of the Ibadis in Northern Africa comes from the later Ibadi tradition, which crystalized long after the fall of the Rustamids, and conceals the far messier reality of persistent opposition to the Rustamids. Overall, the narrative of Abu al-Khattab brought together two key themes that Elizabeth Savage pointed to at the conclusion of her study: the "post-Rustamid Ibadis" and the prosopographical tradition that they produced would follow "two themes: the continuation of Ibadism as a source of authority, and the geographical extent of Ibadi expansion."[14] Several important changes to the political and religious landscape of the Maghrib from the eighth to the eleventh centuries gave rise to this narrative and the written tradition that would transmit it to later generations.

THE RUSTAMIDS, THE WAHBIYYA, AND THE NUKKAR

The significance of the history of the Rustamids comes largely from later imaginings of it in the Ibadi prosopographies of the Middle Period. One important contemporary chronicle of the dynasty, written by a non-Ibadi known to modern historians as Ibn Saghir (d. late ninth century),

[13] See Muḥammad Ṣāliḥ Nāṣir Bābāʿammī, ed., *Muʿjam aʿlām al-ibāḍiyya (Dictionnaire des hommes illustres de l'Ibadisme, les hommes du Maghreb)*, vol. II (Beirut: Dār al-Gharb al-Islāmī, 2000), 242–43. On the Rustamid dynasty, see Ibrāhīm b. Bakīr Baḥḥāz, *al-Dawla al-rustamīyya* (Algiers: Maṭbaʿat Lāfūmīk, 1985); Savage, *A Gateway to Hell, a Gateway to Paradise*; Virginie Prevost, "L'influence de l'état rustumide dans le Sud Tunisien," *Acta Orientalia* 68 (2007): 113; Chikh Bekri, *L'Algérie aux IIe/IIIe siècles (VIIIe/IXe): quelques aspects méconnus du Royaume Rostémide (144–296/761/2–908/9)* (Paris: Éditions Publisud, 2004); Cyrille Aillet, "Tāhart et les origines de l'imamat rustumide," *Annales Islamologiques* 45 (2011): 47–78; Virginie Prevost, "ʿAbd al-Raḥmān ibn Rustum al-Fārisī: une tentative de biographie du premier imam de Tāhart," *Der Islam* 86, no. 1 (2011): 44–64.

[14] Savage, *A Gateway to Hell, a Gateway to Paradise*, 137.

presented a picture of the Rustamid court and the religiously and ethnically diverse capital city of Tahart. Ibn Saghir also made clear, as would both Ibadi and non-Ibadi writers after him, that the Rustamids had a hard time holding on to power. The dynasty regularly encountered opposition to its rule both in the capital city and the broader region. The eastern regions of the Jebel Nafusa and parts of the island of Jerba, in particular, often opposed Rustamid control. The reign of the second Rustamid Imam, ʿAbd al-Wahhab (r. 788–824), marked an especially troubling period for the Rustamids.[15]

Just as later Muslim historians collectively labeled the Ibadis and other opponents Kharijites, so too the later Ibadi tradition loyal to the Rustamids often lumped the opponents of the dynasty into the category of *Nukkar*, or "deniers." In contradistinction to the Nukkar, the authors of the surviving Ibadi tradition in the Maghrib eventually came to call themselves the *Wahbiyya*, perhaps for their support of the Rustamid Imam ʿAbd al-Wahhab. An equally convincing etymology of the word Wahbiyya traces it to ʿAbdallah b. Wahb al-Rasibi (d. 658), the first elected leader of the *muhakkima*. Due to its dominance in the later prosopographical tradition, "Wahbi" has become synonymous with Ibadi in most historiography on the Maghrib. Meanwhile, the Nukkar and other opposition groups were gradually written out of historical memory.[16]

Despite continued opposition, the Rustamid period (749–909) proved a prosperous one for Ibadi communities in Northern Africa. They gained notoriety and wealth through their involvement in Saharan trade networks in the eighth and ninth centuries. The later written tradition contains numerous anecdotes of Ibadi traders in the medieval kingdoms of Western Africa. Especially prosperous were those merchants involved in

[15] Ibn Saghīr's chronicle has been published as Ibn al-Saghīr, *Chronique d'Ibn Saghir sur les imams rostemides de Tahert*, trans. Gustave-Adolphe de Calassanti-Motylinski (Paris: E. Leroux, 1907); Ibn al-Ṣaghīr, *Akhbār al-aʾimma al-rustumiyyīn*, ed. Muḥammad Nāṣir and Ibrāhīm b. Bakīr Baḥḥāz (Beirut: Dār al-Gharb al-Islāmī, 1986). On opposition to the Rustamids, see Paul M. Love, "Djerba and the Limits of Rustamid Power: Considering the Ibāḍī Community of Djerba under the Rustamid Imāms of Tāhert (779–909 CE)," *al-Qantara 33*, no. 2 (2012): 297–323, esp. 305–14.

[16] Writing in the tenth century, the non-Ibadi writer Ibn Ḥawqal used the terms "Ibāḍiyya" and "Wahbiyya" to distinguish the inhabitants of the Jebel Nafusa, which he explained derived from from ʿAbdallāh b. Ibāḍ and ʿAbdallāh b. Wahb al-Rāsibī. See Abū al-Qāsim Ibn Ḥawqal, *Kitāb ṣūrat al-arḍ*, ed. Michael J. de Goeje, 2nd edition, Bibliotheca Geographorum Arabicorum (Leiden: Brill, 1939), 95. For more on the etymology see discussion in Wilkinson, *Ibāḍism*, 140, 230–31. Cf. discussion in Tadeusz Lewicki, "al-Ibāḍiyya," in *Encyclopedia of Islam* (2nd edition) (hereafter *EI2*); Valerie J. Hoffman, *The Essentials of Ibāḍī Islam* (Syracuse: Syracuse University Press, 2012), 10.

the trade of slaves and gold. The Rustamids enjoyed good relations with the important trade center of Sijilmasa in what is today the Tafilalt oasis in Morocco, ruled by the Midrarid dynasty (750–976), as well as with the Umayyads of Spain. Connections with the eastern Ibadi community during the Rustamid period also appear as a constant theme, at least in later accounts. In these stories, the two communities exchanged letters as well as scholars and traders. As I demonstrate in the next chapter, the eastern connections of the Rustamids, like the missionaries trained in Basra, helped to establish the religious bona fides of the dynasty and its followers for the later tradition.[17]

At the beginning of the tenth century the Rustamids and all their dynastic contemporaries in Northern Africa met an astonishingly quick end. The messianic Shiʿi movement later known as the Fatimids, supported by large contingents of Kutama tribesmen, brought down the Rustamids along with the Midrarids, the Idrisids, and the Abbasid clients, the Aghlabids in Ifriqiya. When Tahart fell to the Fatimids in 909 the last Rustamid Imam and his supporters in Tahart fled south to the Saharan region of Warjalan, and the dynasty effectively ceased to exist. That said, the foundation and subsequent flourishing of the new Ibadi city of Sedrata demonstrated that Ibadis continued to enjoy success as merchants of the Sahara long after the fall of Tahart. Meanwhile, the Ibadi supporters of the Rustamid legacy in the Jarid (southern Tunisia) and Jebel Nafusa made several attempts to revolt against the Fatimids; but, their numbers already weakened by defeat in the Battle of Manu against the Aghlabids a few years earlier in 896, they had little success.[18]

[17] On Ibadi merchants in the Sahara, see Tadeusz Lewicki, "L'état nord-africain de Tahert et ses relations avec le Soudan occidental à la fin du VIIIe et au IXe siècle," *Cahiers d'études africaines* 2, no. 8 (1962): 513–35; Michael Brett, "Ifriqiya as a Market for Saharan Trade from the Tenth to the Twelfth Century AD," *Journal of African History* 10, no. 3 (1969): 347–64; Elizabeth Savage, "Berbers and Blacks: Ibadi Slave Traffic in Eighth-Century North Africa," *Journal of African History* 33, no. 2 (1992): 351–68. On the Midrarids see Paul M. Love, "The Sufris of Sijilmasa: Towards a History of the Midrarids," *Journal of North African Studies* 15, no. 2 (2010): 173–88. For connections between Ibadi communities in the Maghrib and al-Andalus, see Adam Gaiser, "Slaves and Silver across the Strait of Gibraltar: Politics and Trade between Umayyad Iberia and Khārijite North Africa," *Medieval Encounters* 19, nos. 1–2 (2013): 41–70. On the authority of connections with the eastern Ibadi community see Virginie Prevost, "L'ibadisme berbère: la légitimation d'une doctrine venue d'orient," in *La légitimation du pouvoir au Maghreb médiéval*, ed. Annliese Nef and Élise Voguet (Madrid: Casa de Velázquez, 2011), 55–74.

[18] For the accounts of these events in Fatimid historiography, see Heinz Halm, *The Empire of the Mahdi: The Rise of the Fatimids*, trans. Michael Bonner (Leiden; New York: Brill, 1996); Abū Ḥanīfah Nuʿmān ibn Muḥammad, *Founding the Fatimid State: The Rise of*

One famous revolt did come startlingly close to success, however. Beginning in the Jarid, a rebellion led by a man named Abu Yazid Makhlad b. Kaydad managed to garner enough support to push the Fatimids all the way to within the walls of their new city on the Mediterranean coast, Mahdiyya. Naturally, this revolt later commanded the attention of both Fatimid and Ibadi historians. But the story of Abu Yazid is also interesting because its protagonist was not a Wahbi, but rather a Nukkari Ibadi. This revolt marked both the last gasp of Ibadi attempts at regaining political control in the region and the ultimate failure of non-Wahbis to survive in the written tradition. When the tide turned in favor of the Fatimids, the rebels fled, and were ultimately routed. Abu Yazid himself was captured and executed. The failure of Abu Yazid's revolt allowed later (Wahbi) Ibadi scholars to vilify him, although the same scholars recorded anecdotes suggesting the widespread support for his revolt among both Wahbi Ibadi communities and, surprisingly, the Maliki scholars of Qayrawan.[19]

For later Ibadi scholars attempting to understand their past and how they had arrived at their present, the period of the Fatimid conquest and the unsuccessful rebellions of Abu Yazid and other Ibadis was a key moment in their history. As they looked back, the scholars of the Middle Period understood this as a period of transition. With no Imams to guide them and their numbers greatly depleted through failed revolts, widely dispersed Ibadi scholars gradually began establishing connections with each other in the region. As the Fatimids turned their focus to the conquest of Egypt and the foundation of their new capital of Cairo in the later tenth century, the scattered Ibadi communities of Northern Africa took advantage of the relative lull to regroup and reorganize.

Saharan regions like Warjalan and the new city of Sedrata, alongside the traditional centers of Ibadi learning on the island of Jerba and in the Jebel Nafusa, attracted students and scholars. The regular travel of

an Early Islamic Empire: An Annotated English Translation of al-Qāḍī al-Nuʿmān's Iftitāḥ al-Daʿwa, trans. Hamid Haji (London: I. B. Tauris, 2006). Cf. "The Fatimid Revolution," in Michael Brett, *The Rise of the Fatimids: The World of the Mediterranean and the Middle East in the Fourth Century of the Hijra, Tenth Century CE* (Leiden; Boston: Brill, 2001), 29–134. For a comprehensive review of Warjalān and Sedrāta, see Cyrille Aillet, "Le Bassin de Ouargla: foyer ibadite et carrefour du Sahara medieval," in *Sedrata, histoire et archéologie d'un carrefour du sahara médiéval à la lumière des archives inédites de Marguerite Van Bercham*, ed. Cyrille Aillet, Patrice Cressier, and Sophie Gilotte, Collection de la Casa de Velázquez 161 (Madrid: Casa de Velázquez, 2017), 25–85. On the Battle of Manu, see Virginie Prevost, "Les enjeux de la bataille de Mānū (283/896)," *Revue des mondes musulmans et de la Méditerranée* 132 (2012): 75–90.

[19] The most thorough account of the revolt of Abu Yazid is Mounira Chapoutot-Remadi, "Abū Yazīd al-Nukkārī," in *EI3*.

Ibadi scholars and students to and from these different centers created an informal system of training and education. One or more scholars took on the role of instructing a group of students, who would sit in a circle (*halqa*) and study. As Elizabeth Savage has noted, even before the fall of the Rustamids, the Ibadi scholars of the villages and towns of the Maghrib would no doubt have played a leading role in their religious communities. The disappearance of even a nominal central religious authority in Tahart, however, augmented the importance of the scholars in Ibadi communities. As they connected with each other in that early period, this "ever-expanding network of Ibadi shaykhs" and their students laid the groundwork for the subsequent development of a formalized system of education and local religio-political leadership councils in the Middle Period.[20]

The uncontested center of Ibadi learning during the tenth century was the island of Jerba. Thanks to an especially charismatic teacher named Abu Miswar Yasja, the island attracted students and scholars from the nearby Jebel Nafusa but also from the mainland to the west. Abu Miswar had come to the island from the Nafusa mountains, and as such his biography provided a narrative link between the two places. He receives credit for founding the island's most famous Ibadi mosque, known as the Miswariyya, which long served as the center of Ibadi learning there. Abu Miswar's son, Fasil, enjoyed similar prestige. Fasil sent his own sons westward to seek out one of his former students, a man named Abu 'Abdallah Muhammad b. Bakr, and to encourage him to found a study circle (*halqa*) for students on the mainland. Later Ibadi tradition traces a highly formalized *halqa* system back to Abu 'Abdallah in the eleventh century and credits him with establishing study circles throughout Ifriqiya in the Jarid, the Dummar mountains, and even the Mzab valley in what is today Algeria. These figures of the tenth and early eleventh centuries lived in the settlements of the "Ibadi archipelago" in Northern Africa, and their relationships with one another provide neat connections among its components.[21]

20 Savage, *A Gateway to Hell, a Gateway to Paradise*, 138.

21 On Abū Miswar, Faṣīl b. Abī Miswar, and the historical formation of the ʿ*azzaba* system, see Farhat Djaabiri, *Niẓām al-ʿazzāba ʿind al-ibāḍiyya bi-Jarba (L'Organisation des azzaba chez les ibadhites de Jerba)* (Tunis: Institut National d'Archéologie et d'Art, 1975), esp. 153–186; Brahim Cherifi, "La Ḥalqa des ʿazzāba: un nouveau regard sur l'histoire d'une institution religieuse ibāḍite," *Bulletin of the Royal Institute for Inter-Faith Studies* 7, no. 1 (2005): 39–68; Mohamed Hassen, "Peuplement et organisation du territoire dans une région d'implantation ibāḍite: le Jebel Demmer dans le sud-est de l'Ifrīqiya," *Revue des mondes musulmans et de la Méditerranée* 132 (2012): 137–54; Virginie

REGIONAL CHANGES: THE BANU HILAL, ARABIZATION, AND THE SPREAD OF MALIKI ISLAM

Alongside this largely internal process of establishing links among themselves and their different communities, Ibadis faced much bigger transformations in the region's landscape that would leave a lasting impact on Northern Africa up to the present. When the Fatimids relocated from the Maghrib to their new capital city of Cairo, they left a Sanhaja Berber family later known as the Zirid (or Banū Zīrī) dynasty to govern in their place. For most of their period of rule the Zirids paid nominal allegiance to the Fatimids. By the mid-eleventh century, however, various factors including growing local opposition to the Shiʿi religious establishment helped lead the Zirids to renounce their allegiance to the Fatimids in favor of supporting the Sunni Abbasid dynasty in Baghdad.

In response, so the traditional narrative goes, the Fatimid Caliph in Cairo unleashed the nomadic Arabic-speaking tribes of the Banu Hilal and the Banu Sulaym on the Zirids. As they made their way across central Ifriqiya and beyond, these tribes ravished the agriculture of the countryside and brought political chaos to the region. These nomads serve the Arabic historical tradition in a way analogous to the role of the Germanic tribes that overran the Roman Empire several centuries earlier in medieval European historiography. Like the simplified story of the barbarian hordes of Late Antiquity overrunning the Romans, behind the legend of the Banu Hilal and its narrative of chaotic devastation lies the story of a much slower demographic transformation.[22]

Prevost, "La renaissance des ibadites wahbites à Djerba au Xe siècle," *Folia Orientalia* 40 (2004): 171–91; Virginie Prevost, "Genèse et développement de la ḥalqa chez les ibāḍites maghrébins," in *Les scribes et la transmission du savoir*, ed. Christian Cannuyer, Acta Orientalia Belgica 19 (Brussels: Société belge d'études orientales, 2006), 109–24; Virginie Prevost, "La formation des réseaux ibadites nord-africans (VIIIe–XIIe siècles)," in *Espaces et réseaux en Méditerranée (Vie–XVIe siècles)*, vol. II (Paris: Éditions Bouchène, 2010), 167–86. The traditional accounts of these different studies draw from the Ibadi prosopographical tradition. On that version of the foundation of the *ʿazzaba* system see Chapters 2 and 3. The term "Ibadi archipelago" comes from Aillet, "L'ibāḍisme, une minorité au cœur de l'islam," 17.

22 The classic account of the deterioration of Fatimid–Zirid relations and the Banu Hilal invasions is "La Catastrophe : L'invasion hilālienne et la fin du règne d'al-Muʿizz," in Hady Roger Idris, *La Berbérie Orientale sous les Zirides* (Paris: Maisonneuve, 1962), 256–59. See also the much more recent version of the history of Banu Hilal in Suraiya N. Faroqhi, "Demography and Migration," in *The New Cambridge History of Islam, vol. IV: Islamic Cultures and Societies to the End of the Eighteenth Century*, ed. Robert Irwin (New York: Cambridge University Press, 2010), 306–31, at 311. On similar historiographical debates relating to the "Barbarian invasions" of the Roman Empire see Walter Goffart, "Rome's Final Conquest: The Barbarians," *History Compass* 6, no. 3 (2008): 855–83.

By the beginning of the eleventh century both autochthonous and Arabic-speaking tribes from the eastern half of Northern Africa had begun slowly migrating westward. Historians of the later Middle Period (and their colonial-era interpreters of the nineteenth century) related the legend of the Banu Hilal as a neat explanation for some of the important transformations that this long-term migration brought about. First, the longstanding economic center of Qayrawan became a shadow of its former self. Changes to the agricultural landscape of the central Maghrib, Saharan trade routes, and the growing importance of the cities and towns of the Northern African littoral all helped marginalize this former capital city. Nomadic migrations might have spelled the end for certain forms of agriculture in the region as they were replaced with pastoralism, but the traditional account of economic collapse is fictional. Still largely controlled by the Ibadis in the eleventh century, Saharan trade continued unabated, albeit following slightly altered routes.[23]

Yet two other effects of the nomadic migrations did alter Ibadi communities in the region. The first of these was the introduction of Arabic as a spoken and written language in the southern regions of the central Maghrib. The cities of the Northern African littoral, as well as the former capital city of Qayrawan, had long been home to Arabic-speaking populations. But the vast majority of the inhabitants of the Maghrib, including the Ibadis, spoke varieties of Berber languages.[24] With the gradual influx of Arabic-speaking tribes in the eleventh century, areas like the Zab, the Jarid, and the Dummar mountains began a transition from

[23] The collected works of Michael Brett present the most thorough account and critical analysis of the medieval historiography on the Banu Hilal. See articles collected in Michael Brett, *Ibn Khaldun and the Medieval Maghrib* (Aldershot: Ashgate/Variorum, 1999). Brett was not the first to challenge the traditional historiography on the Banu Hilal, however. See Jean Poncet, "Le mythe de la catastrophe hilalienne," *Annales ESC* 22 (1967): 1099–1120; John E. Wansbrough, "The Decolonization of North African History," *Journal of African History* 9, no. 4 (1968): 643–50; Jean Poncet, "Encore à propos des hilaliens: la 'mise au point' de R. Idris," *Annales* 23, no. 3 (1986): 600–662.

[24] While I recognize that the term "Berber" can be taken as derogatory, and that some historians have recently rewritten Ibadi history using the terms "Amazīgh" or "Tamāzigha" in place of Berber, the application of these terms, or the term "Tamazight," to refer to pre-modern Berber dialects is no less problematic. A unified Amazigh identity with its sub-nationalist undertones is a product of recent history, and certainly cannot be applied to pre-modern Ibadi communities. The term "Tamazight" as a catch-all for Berber languages also reflects contemporary attempts to develop a standardized, pan-Amazigh language, and is in this historical context at best misleading. In light of these issues, I have elected to follow the terminology of the pre-modern Ibadi sources themselves, which used the terms *al-barbar* to refer to people and *al-barbariyya* to refer to language.

Berber into Arabic-speaking regions. While earlier written scholarship in Ibadi centers of learning had doubtless been in Arabic, the spread of that language as a spoken language in these regions insured that it would be the primary idiom in which Ibadis transmitted their history from that point onward.[25]

Alongside Arabic, however, came another unexpected consequence of the nomadic migrations: the supplanting of Ibadi Islam by Maliki Islam. The process of "Malikization" had been aided by the earlier numerical decline of the Ibadis in the central Maghrib in the tenth century. By the mid-eleventh century, however, former strongholds of Ibadi Islam like the Zab and Jarid began to witness an influx of non-Ibadi Muslims. The religious affiliations of the usually nameless "nomads" who came from the east defy definition, but they would certainly not have been Ibadis. Those Ibadi tribes that did not flee the region (often southward into the Sahara) gradually began assimilating into the new, primarily Arabic-speaking and non-Ibadi landscape of the central Maghrib. In subsequent centuries, the growing popularity of Sufism would also help speed up this process.[26]

CONCLUSION

The Ibadi communities of late medieval Northern Africa sensed that they had come face to face with the threat of extinction. This threat came not from some sudden invasion but instead from slow demographic transformations in the region. Whereas they had once represented a strong, widespread community of Berber-speaking tribes throughout the region, by the mid-eleventh century the Ibadis were suffering a significant and ongoing numerical decline in response to the steadily changing linguistic,

[25] John Wilkinson notes that the Ibadi scholars of the Maghrib during the Middle Period would have wielded considerable influence as a result of their knowledge of Arabic. See Wilkinson, *Ibāḍism*, 426. This raises the question of *how* different Ibadi communities would have communicated with one another; an interesting suggestion for a later period is the theory of a kind of Ibadi "lingua franca": Vermondo Brugnatelli, "D'une langue de contact entre berbères ibadites," in *Berber in Contact: Linguistic and Socio-Lingusitic Perspectives*, ed. Mena Lafkioue and Vermondo Brugnatelli, Berber Studies 22 (Cologne: Rüdiger Köppe Verlag, 2008), 39–52. Cf. Tadeusz Lewicki, "Mélanges berbères-ibadites," *Revue des Études Islamiques* 3 (1936): 267–85.

[26] Allaoua Amara, "La malikisation du Maghreb central (III/Vie–IX/XIIe siècle)," in *Dynamiques religieuses et territoires du sacré au Maghreb médiéval: éléments d'enquête*, ed. Cyrille Aillet and Bull Tuil Leonetti, Estudios Árabes Islámicos (Madrid: Consejo Superior de Investigaciones Científicas, 2015), 25–50; Sami Bargaoui, "(Ne plus) Être ibadhite dans la régence de Tunis: un processus de démarquage confessionnel à l'époque moderne" [forthcoming].

religious, and political landscape of the Maghrib. Far from coincidentally, this same period witnessed the compilation of the first work of Ibadi prosopography: the *Kitab al-sira*. That book's compiler, Abu Zakariya Yahya al-Warjalani (d. 1078), would provide Ibadi scholars with a cohesive narrative of their history. Reflecting the linguistic transformation taking place at the time, Arabic served as the medium for transmitting the community's past. In addition, the *Kitab al-sira* provided later scholars with a justification for the uncertainty of their future in the Maghrib in the face of the ongoing processes of political and religious marginalization. The *Kitab al-sira* and those works of Ibadi prosopography that followed its lead would use all of these events of earlier centuries to weave together a historical narrative that linked their coreligionists of the past with those of the present. The next chapter turns its attention to this first work of Ibadi prosopography and the formation of a written network of Ibadi scholars in the Middle Period.

2

Writing a Network, Constructing a Tradition

***

Writing in the mid-eleventh century, the compiler of the first major work of Ibadi prosopography in Northern Africa, Abu Zakariya Yahya al-Warjalani, began his *Kitab al-sira wa-akhbar al-a'imma* (The Book of the Lives and Accounts of the Imams) with a hopeful lament:

> When we saw what had disappeared from the traditions and what had been lost from the accounts [of our past], it occurred to us to record the stories of those who came before us from among the shaykhs ... So we wrote of those things ... after having feared for the general populace that they might leave [these stories] behind, causing them to be forgotten.[1]

As their numbers dwindled in the wake of the collapse of the Ibadi Rustamid dynasty in 909 and subsequent failed revolts against their conquerors, the Fatimids, Ibadi Muslims in the Maghrib began to forget their past, to lose their memory. The traditions and accounts of the exemplary members of the community such as the Rustamid Imams and the scholars who came after them marked the contours of that memory. By remembering their stories, the Ibadi community could hold on to its past. Conversely, without them the history of the community risked fading into obscurity. For Abu Zakariya, the solution to this problem lay in committing these traditions to writing. The *Kitab al-sira* not only preserved the Ibadi past but also constructed it by weaving together anecdotes into a narrative of connections: a written network.

How did the *Kitab al-sira* create this written network that laid a foundation for an Ibadi tradition in Northern Africa? To answer this question,

[1] Abū Zakarīyā Yaḥyā ibn Abī Bakr al-Warjalānī, *Kitāb al-sīra wa-akhbār al-a'imma*, ed. 'Abd al-Raḥmān Ayyūb (Tunis: Dār al-Tūnisiyya li-l-Nashr, 1985), 39–40.

I begin this chapter by addressing the interplay among the book's structure, its intended aims, and the context out of which it emerged. I then focus on how the *Kitab al-sira* weaved together literary themes (or *topoi*) to create a seamless historical transition from the Rustamids to the Ibadi scholars of the eleventh century. Finally, I turn my attention to the written network of Ibadi scholars. Employing tools from network analysis, I reveal how the *Kitab al-sira* used stories centered on a handful of individuals whose lives spanned several generations to create a community.

THE *KITAB AL-SIRA*: THEME, STRUCTURE, AND NARRATIVE

Abu Zakariya had good reason to worry that the memory of his predecessors might be fading quickly in the mid-eleventh century. The changes in the political, linguistic, and religious landscapes over the previous century and a half had pushed Ibadi communities to the geographic edges of the region. By Abu Zakariya's lifetime, Ibadis lived in a handful of geographic pockets: the mountains of Jebel Nafusa, the island of Jerba, the southern mountainous regions of the Jebel Dummar, and scattered settlements in the pre-Sahara of what is today central Algeria.

The *Kitab al-sira* grew out of the need to establish ties among these different communities. Its structure and aims stemmed from the increasing marginalization of Ibadis in the region. The basic task of the *Kitab al-sira* was to explain how the community had arrived at this point. With the Rustamids gone and the Ibadis standing no chance of reestablishing political power in the region, the book also had to address the problem of how to hold the community together in the future. The two complementary halves of the *Kitab al-sira*, each with a different structure and purpose, together provided a solution.

The first part of the work is a history of the early Ibadi community in Northern Africa. The account of these early years comprises a string of literary topoi, all of which lead the narrative to the rise of Ibadi scholars as the leaders of the community. This first section begins with two important prefaces that list the merits of the Persians and the Berbers respectively. These two groups act as the key players in the narrative of the early Ibadi community in the Maghrib. The Rustamids claimed Persian descent through their founder, ʿAbd al-Rahman b. Rustam, and virtually all other Ibadis in Northern Africa were autochthonous speakers of Berber languages.[2]

The *Kitab al-sira* then tells the story of a group of missionaries who brought Ibadi Islam to the Maghrib. Trained in secret by the Ibadi Imam in the city of Basra in Iraq, these five "bearers of knowledge" (*hamalat al-ʿilm*) establish a link between the early community in the east and the new community in the west. The text next moves on to detailed descriptions of early revolts led by these missionaries against the two successive eastern dynasties that attempted to control the region, the Umayyads and the Abbasids. Although largely unsuccessful, these revolts of the eighth century function as powerful symbols in the *Kitab al-sira* for the support among Berber tribes for Ibadi Islam. One of the five original missionaries, ʿAbd al-Rahman b. Rustam, flees the city of Qayrawan with his supporters and heads west. There they found a new city, Tahart, which would become the capital city of the new Ibadi polity under the dynasty that took his name: the Rustamids.[3]

Here the *Kitab al-sira* reiterates the ties to the community of the east and the passing of the torch westward. While constructing his new city, ʿAbd al-Rahman receives visitors from the Ibadi community in the east. Having judged him a worthy and capable leader, these visitors deliver a gift of gold to ʿAbd al-Rahman. He humbly accepts the gift and uses it to help build his new city of Tahart. When the visitors return a second time, ʿAbd al-Rahman refuses the gold, saying that Tahart no longer needs it. This foundation narrative serves two purposes. First of all, it establishes ʿAbd al-Rahman's credentials as the humble, pious, and able founder of the dynasty to come. Secondly, the narrative legitimizes the Rustamids by linking them to the Ibadi community in the east while also demonstrating that Tahart can now survive on its own.[4] Both ʿAbd al-Rahman, trained in the east, and his visitors, who come from the east, connect Northern Africa to the origins of the Ibadi community in Basra.

The theme of an eastern connection appears throughout the *Kitab al-sira*. For example, when ʿAbd al-Rahman's son, ʿAbd al-Wahhab, succeeds his father as Imam, some challenge his legitimacy. His opponents

[2] The idea that strings of topoi combined to produce other early narratives of Islamic history belongs to Albrecht Noth: see Albrecht Noth and Lawrence Conrad, *The Early Arabic Historical Tradition: A Source-Critical Study*, trans. Michael Bonner (Princeton: Darwin Press, 1994).

[3] On the early Ibadi community in Basra, see Wilkinson, *Ibāḍism*. On the Rustamids, see Baḥḥāz, *al-Dawla al-rustamīyya*; Prevost, *L'aventure ibāḍite dans le Sud tunisien, VIIIe–XIIIe siècle*.

[4] al-Warjalānī, *Kitāb al-sīra*, 85–90.

object to hereditary succession, saying that the community should be led by its best member, regardless of his background. The controversy eventually leads to open rebellion, and the opponents of the Rustamids receive the title of the Nukkar (deniers) for their refusal to accept the new Imam. Meanwhile, a letter was dispatched to the Ibadi Imam in the east asking for his opinion on the matter. The *Kitab al-sira* reproduces the text of the response, which of course favors ʿAbd al-Wahhab and discredits the Nukkar. While rebellions continue throughout the Rustamid period, this nod from the east establishes the bona fides of the dynasty and its hereditary leadership.[5]

The *Kitab al-sira* also speaks to the success of the Ibadis in Saharan commerce under the Rustamids. Throughout the eighth and ninth centuries Ibadi merchants traversed the desert and established trade connections with the towns and cities of Western Africa as well as with Egypt. Participation in Saharan trade helped Ibadis build connections among individuals across vast distances in Northern Africa. This commercial network established Ibadis as a merchant class and, by the time Abu Zakariya was writing in the eleventh century, Ibadi traders had connections spanning the entire region. Merchants and scholars, often the same individuals, traversed these paths carrying both commercial goods and texts.[6]

The narrative of the *Kitab al-sira* takes a new direction with its discussion of two events, both signaling the end of the Rustamid era. The first was the expansion of Aghlabid control into the Ibadi heartland of southern Ifriqiya and Tripolitania. At the end of the ninth century the Ibadis of those regions ended up caught between two competing spheres of influence: the Aghlabid dynasty to the north and the Tulunid dynasty of Egypt to the east. The Aghlabid army headed south to engage the Tulunids, clashing with a group of Ibadis in 896 at what thereafter became known as the Battle of Manu. The *Kitab al-sira* relates that this crushing defeat was followed by a series of attacks on Ibadi communities throughout southern Ifriqiya, slaughtering scholars and scattering them across the region.[7]

The next crucial turning point in the narrative comes with the arrival of the Fatimid army at the outskirts of the Rustamid capital of Tahart in

5 al-Warjalānī, *Kitāb al-sīra*, 92–103.

6 Lewicki, "L'état nord-africain de Tahert"; Brett, "Ifriqiya as a Market for Saharan Trade"; Michael Brett, "Islam and Trade in the 'Bilad al-Sudan', Tenth–Eleventh Century AD," *Journal of African History* 24, no. 4 (1983): 431–40; Prevost, "La formation des réseaux ibadites nord-africans."

7 al-Warjalānī, *Kitāb al-sīra*, 150–57. Cf. Prevost, "Les enjeux de la bataille de Mānū."

909. With the Fatimid conquest of the city, the Rustamid dynasty came to an abrupt end. The last potential Rustamid Imam, Ya'qub b. Aflah b. 'Abd al-Wahhab, the symbol of religious leadership, flees to the Sahara with his supporters.[8] Here the *Kitab al-sira* repeats the two earlier themes of flight from corrupt powers and the founding of a new city, Sedrata.[9] This time, however, there would be an important difference. Instead of reestablishing the Rustamid Imamate in the desert, Ya'qub b. Aflah declines to lead the community as Imam. With this story, the *Kitab al-sira* passes the mantle of authority from the Imams to the Ibadi scholars.

FAILED REVOLTS: TRANSITIONING FROM THE IMAMS TO THE SCHOLARS

In mid-July 945, an Ibadi scholar and charismatic leader named Abu Yazid Makhlad b. Kaydad and his army stood before the massive stone walls of the seaside city of Mahdiyya. Over the previous year Abu Yazid had rallied support among Ibadis and Sunnis throughout Ifriqiya, and led had a brutal uprising against supporters of the Fatimid Shi'i rulers. The Fatimid Caliph al-Qa'im (r. 934–46) had been forced to flee his inland residence in the city of Raqqada, and now lay besieged behind the walls of this fortress town on the Mediterranean coast. If ever Ibadis entertained hope of reestablishing political power in the Maghrib, this was the moment.

Abu Yazid had routed the Fatimid army and mercilessly slaughtered their unpopular supporters in the region's towns and villages, which won him the support of both Ibadis and Maliki Sunnis. But Abu Yazid did not, according to the later Ibadi or Fatimid sources, belong to the Ibadi tradition that recognized the Rustamid legacy. For that, he earned the moniker "al-Nukkari" in the Ibadi prosopographies. A shroud of sensationalism surrounds most accounts of Abu Yazid's rebellion, but all agree on one thing: it failed. After a year of momentum, Fatimid reinforcements from Tunis and a prolonged siege of Mahdiyya in the summertime led to the flight of Abu Yazid's supporters. It took more than two years of pursuit, but in April 947 the new Fatimid Caliph, Isma'il al-Mansur (r. 946–53),

8 al-Warjalānī, *Kitāb al-sīra*, 178–79.

9 Cyrille Aillet and Sophie Gilotte, "Sedrata: l'élaboration d'un lieu de mémoire," *Revue du monde musulman et de la Méditerranée* 132 (2012): 91–114; Cyrille Aillet, Patrice Cressier, and Sophie Gilotte, eds., *Sedrata, histoire et archéologique d'un carrefour du Sahara medieval à la lumière des archives inédites de Marguerite Van Berchem*, Collection de la Casa de Velázquez 161 (Madrid: Casa de Velázquez, 2017).

captured Abu Yazid, whose stuffed and mutilated corpse he put on public display.[10]

Although it labels him al-Nukkari, the *Kitab al-sira* makes it clear that the revolt of Abu Yazid enjoyed widespread support. In addition, it notes that he had received formal training from Ibadi scholars in Tahart and Sijilmasa. Beginning with the revolt of Abu Yazid, the *Kitab al-sira* describes how, in the absence of the Imams, Ibadi scholars led the rebellions. This narrative shift toward the leadership of the learned continues with the repeated theme of failed revolts. In the tenth century, Ibadi tribal confederations tried several times to defeat the Fatimids. Like the unsuccessful rebellions of the Ibadi-allied tribes in the eighth century that eventually led to the formation of a new system of leadership (the Rustamid Imamate), the failed revolts of the tenth would culminate in the formation of an alternative type of social organization in which scholars would take the lead.

Ibadi scholars also led another spectacularly unsuccessful revolt against the Fatimids at the end of the tenth century. The effort was spearheaded by two key figures of the *Kitab al-sira*, Abu Khazar Yaghli and Abu Nuh Saʿid b. Zanghil. These two gathered supporters together from across southern Ifriqiya, Jerba, and the Jebel Nafusa. The Ibadis met the forces of the Fatimid Caliph al-Muʿizz (r. 953–75) at a place called Baghay. The Fatimid army routed the Ibadis, and both Abu Khazar and Abu Nuh were captured.[11] The failure of these revolts signaled the futility of any attempt to reestablish united Ibadi political control. At the same time, the *Kitab al-sira* made clear that scholars had assumed the role and duties of the Rustamid Imams.

BUILDING SCHOLARLY NETWORKS

This transition from scholars to leaders is reflected in the structure of the *Kitab al-sira*, which lays the foundation upon which the written network of scholars and pious individuals rests, and provides justification for its very existence. The biographical sketches that follow the tragic narrative of the rise and fall of the Rustamids and the failed revolts against the Fatimids set the stage for the early formation of a more localized, council-rule system that eventually came to govern Ibadi communities:

[10] al-Warjalānī, *Kitāb al-sīra*, 168–77. For a thorough account with a full list of sources, see Chapoutot-Remadi, "Abū Yazīd al-Nukkārī."

[11] al-Warjalānī, *Kitāb al-sīra*, 201–11.

the ʿ*azzaba*. The term ʿ*azzaba* (sing. ʿ*azzabi*) would later take on a formal meaning as the title for scholars who had followed a specific path of education that earned them the position of the political and religious guides of the Ibadi community. In the eleventh-century world of the *Kitab al-sira*, the term had yet to take on this meaning, but it already referred to exemplary scholars to whom members of the Ibadi community turned for religious guidance.[12]

The second half of the *Kitab al-sira* turns its attention to these newly minted leaders. This part of the text comprises biographies and anecdotes about individual scholars from different Ibadi communities across Northern Africa, stretching from Sijilmasa in the west to Cairo in the east. Having marked the transition from Imamate to the leadership of the Ibadi scholars, the *Kitab al-sira* outlines the formation of a network of relationships among these individuals. In this new phase of Ibadi history, the scholars and the connections among them become the glue holding the community together.

The *Kitab al-sira* conveniently locates that transition from the rule of the Imam to that of the ʿ*azzaba* in the life of a single individual in the eleventh century: Abu ʿAbdallah Muhammad b. Bakr al-Nafusi. The *Kitab al-sira* situates Abu ʿAbdallah at the center of a network of scholars both past and present. This figure holds a place of great importance in both the *Kitab al-sira* and subsequent Ibadi prosopographies, all of which designate him as the founder of the *halqa* system. In this model, either a single scholar or a group of scholars instructs a group of students in a study circle (a *halqa*). These students then eventually took on the role of instructor in other locations, forming their own *halqa*s. The *halqa* long predated the eleventh century, and was not unique to Ibadis, but beginning with the *Kitab al-sira* the prosopographical tradition presented it as the backbone of the nascent council-rule institution of the ʿ*azzaba*. Later Ibadi prosopographies would formalize the details of how and when Abu ʿAbdallah conducted these *halqa*s, but in the *Kitab al-sira* his activities simply mark a transition. Abu ʿAbdallah remained central to the written network of the *Kitab al-sira* because of his links with both an earlier, well-known generation of scholars and the cadre of his students in the region where he traveled and taught.[13]

[12] For traditional accounts of the ʿ*azzaba* and its formation, see Djaabiri, *Niẓām al-*ʿ*azzāba*; Cherifi, "La Ḥalqa des ʿazzāba"; Prevost, "Genèse et développement de la ḥalqa."

[13] al-Warjalānī, *Kitāb al-sīra*, 252–68.

In the *Kitab al-sira*, Abu ʿAbdallah studies under the shaykhs of Jerba, where Ibadis had made a home early on in the Rustamid period. This connection carries great importance, since through it Abu ʿAbdallah becomes central to the past, present, and future of Ibadi communities of the Maghrib. His teacher, Abu Zakriya Fasil b. Abi Miswar al-Yarasani, was the son of one of the most prominent Ibadi scholars of the tenth century. Abu Miswar Yasja received credit for founding Great Mosque (*al-jamiʿ al-kabir*) in Jerba and ushering a period of stability and intellectual activity there. The juxtaposition of the failed attempts to restore the political power of the Ibadis under the Fatimids and the life of Abu Miswar in Jerba links the two periods, marking the seemingly inevitable transition from the era of Tahart to the later period in which local sites such as Jerba became centers of Ibadi learning.[14]

Born in the Jebel Nafusa in what is today northwestern Libya, Abu Miswar's arrival in Jerba at the end of the ninth or beginning of the tenth century provided a concrete link in the historical narrative between these two older communities of Ibadis in Northern Africa. Many scholars and students like him traversed the paths connecting Jerba and the Jebel Nafusa, creating a regular line of intellectual exchange. His son, Fasil, in turn appears in the text as the initiator of the link between the island and the central lands of Northern Africa. In the *Kitab al-sira*, Fasil sends his two sons and nephew to the mainland in search of his prize pupil, Abu ʿAbdallah Muhammad b. Bakr. He tells them to convince Abu ʿAbdallah to found a series of *halqa*s for the benefit of the Ibadis of the Jarid and surrounding areas. Eventually Abu ʿAbdallah agrees, and from him the *Kitab al-sira* describes the fanning out of his connections among his students as he traveled from place to place establishing *halqa*s and creating new hubs of Ibadi intellectual activity.

Crucial to later Ibadi narratives, the text presents Abu ʿAbdallah as the champion of Ibadi Islam even in the Mzab region and its environs, where he succeeds in converting its inhabitants. By the time of the compilation of the *Kitab al-sira* in the eleventh century, the nearby towns of Warjalan and Sedrata had also become centers for Ibadi learning. Abu ʿAbdallah's story provided the historical explanation for the establishment of Ibadi Islam in the broader region. These places had already been home to Ibadi communities since shortly after the fall of the Rustamids when, like Jerba, Warjalan and then Sedrata became

[14] al-Warjalānī, *Kitāb al-sīra*, 239–51.

home to refugees from Tahart. Abu ʿAbdallah and his generation linked the communities of former refugees, Jerba and the Mzab region, with the longstanding strongholds of Ibadism in the Maghrib, the Jarid, and the Jebel Nafusa.

Just as Abu Miswar linked together the communities of the Jebel Nafusa and Jerba, so too his son Fasil and Abu ʿAbdallah provided the connections between Jerba and the mainland farther west in the Jarid, the Jebel Dummar, Sedrata, Warjalan, and the Mzab, as well as north in the Zab region. In this way, the *Kitab al-sira* describes the formation of a network of individuals over two generations that brought together the principal islands of the "Ibadi archipelago" of Northern Africa. This network comprised individuals who either met in person or knew of the other nodes in the network through personal connections. In addition, however, these individuals provided conceptual and historical links between a fragmented present and an imagined, unified Rustamid past.

But the formation of this network of individuals would have meant nothing had it disappeared with the death of Abu ʿAbdallah, Fasil, and their contemporaries in the tenth and early eleventh centuries. In order for this network to persist, it had to grow. This meant training a new generation of scholars who could transmit knowledge through personal interaction. In addition, it required devising a new method of preserving and transmitting the links between past and present: the production of written works of prosopography.

The transition from oral transmission of knowledge and personal interaction to one in which these traditional forms of connections come to include "written" interactions carries tremendous importance for the formation of Ibadi networks in the Maghrib. While a student's journey to study under well-known scholars still carried much value, the *Kitab al-sira* marks a transition toward connecting with a scholar through his writings. Many subsequent themes of Ibadi prosopographies stemmed from this early transition, especially the growing importance of manuscript book culture in the following century.

The two interrelated reasons for this transition frame the *Kitab al-sira* itself. First, the Imams and scholars of the past represent the pinnacles of learning. With those individuals now gone, the only ways to connect to them are through their students or through stories about them. Second, the compiler frames the work with reference to the imagined and, at times, real threat of disappearance of the community and the annihilation of its collective memory.

ARABS AND BERBERS: NARRATIVE THEMES OF LANGUAGE IN CONTEXT

Abu al-Rabiʿ Sulayman al-Mazati and his students had just finished praying and were breaking off into groups to study when they heard the shouting. Earlier that day they had received word that an Arab tribal leader named Ibn ʿUqayl intended to attack the village of Tamulst, where they were staying. The students grabbed their weapons and ran toward the edge of town in the direction of the shouts. Ibn ʿUqayl had come to the village accompanied by several mounted men. A fight ensued, but when one of the students was killed, the rest fled. They sought safety in a nearby cave, covering the entryway with rocks to protect themselves. Unfortunately, Abu al-Rabiʿ had fallen behind. When the Arabs caught up with him, they stripped him of his clothing and beat him before fleeing.[15]

Stories like this one from the *Kitab al-sira* reflect the dangerous situation in which Ibadis found themselves by the mid-eleventh century. Ibadis lived in the middle of a region that had been undergoing great change in the century and a half since the fall of the Rustamids. The Fatimids had moved to their new capital, Cairo, in the mid-tenth century. When they departed, they left power in the hands of a Sanhaja Berber family later known as the Zirids. Ibadis had a rocky relationship with the Zirids in the late tenth and eleventh centuries, which occasionally escalated to the level of armed conflict. To make things worse, the Ibadis were caught between the Zirids and their Zanata Berber opponents, the Banu Khazrun, who controlled Tripolitania. The *Kitab al-sira* highlights the instability of this period, making note of clashes between the Zirids and the Zanata as well as an attack on the Ibadi fortress town of Darjin.[16]

But the Zirids and the Zanata were not the only threats to Ibadis in this period. The eleventh century witnessed the beginning of a long-term demographic change in the form of a slow but steady westward advance by nomadic tribes from the east along the northern edge of the Sahara. Following their particular reading of Ibn Khaldun, colonial historians of the nineteenth and twentieth centuries long regarded this demographic transformation as a sudden, devastating "swarm of locusts" personified in the Banu Hilal and the Banu Sulaym, Arab tribal confederations unleashed by the Fatimids in Cairo against their rebellious Zirid clients. More recent

[15] al-Warjalānī, *Kitāb al-sīra*, 276.
[16] The most authoritative account of the Zirids remains Idris, *La Berbérie Orientale sous les Zirides*.

studies have argued that this cataclysmic legend had much more to do with gradual changes in demography, the economy of Northern Africa, and historiography than sudden, violent invasion.[17] Nevertheless, many of these migrants were Arabic speakers, and their arrival in the southern regions of the Maghrib and the northern Sahara had long-term effects on their linguistic, political, economic, and religious landscapes. Often overlooked, Ibadi communities lay between these incoming nomads and the warring dynasties and principalities of the cities of the Maghribi littoral. Conflicts, skirmishes, and negotiations with Arabic-speaking and Berber nomads like the story of Abu al-Rabiʿ and his students appear in anecdotes throughout the *Kitab al-sira*. This first work of prosopography, compiled in this period of great upheaval, emerged out of this context of change.

Finally, in contrasting the Ibadis with the Arabs, the *Kitab al-sira* highlights one of the most significant characteristics of Ibadi communities in the tenth and eleventh centuries: language. While the *Kitab al-sira* is written in Arabic, the vast majority of Ibadis would not have been Arabic speakers. Through place and tribe names as well as other linguistic markers, the *Kitab al-sira* describes a community of Berber-speaking Ibadis. For example, when the second Rustamid Imam, ʿAbd al-Wahhab, addressed the community of the Jebel Nafusa in a letter, there was a good reason why he used the phrase "by God" in both Arabic (*billah*) and Berber (*abikish*). The network may have been written in Arabic, but the community it formed spoke Berber.[18]

Despite all this change, people did not stop trading or traveling. The *Kitab al-sira* describes how in the face of threats of robbery and attacks on their communities, two generations of Ibadi scholars traveled regularly among settlements such as Warjalan in the Sahara, the island of Jerba, the Jarid, and the mountains of southern Ifriqiya and northwestern Tripolitania. In the book's narrative, the interactions of these scholars seem especially crucial to the survival of the community. Despite the danger they faced in doing so, Ibadi scholars had to travel and make connections in order to survive. In turn, these ongoing threats to the community spoke to the need to record their connections for posterity.

[17] On these historiographical issues see the articles compiled in Brett, *Ibn Khaldun and the Medieval Maghrib*.

[18] Lewicki, "Mélanges berbères-ibadites"; Mohamed Meouak, *La langue berbère au Maghreb médiéval: textes, contextes, analyses* (Leiden; Boston: Brill, 2015).

ANALYZING THE WRITTEN NETWORK

Until now, I have used the term "network" in a broad and metaphorical sense. But the *Kitab al-sira* represents more than the context from which it emerged in the eleventh century. It also produced that context for use by future generations. In juxtaposing the grand historical narrative of the distant Rustamid past and the interactions among different Ibadi scholars from the more recent past, the *Kitab al-sira* linked these together. The connections it draws among different periods, individuals, and locations constructed a network that can be visualized and analyzed.

While the first part of the *Kitab al-sira* moves chronologically through the collective history of the Ibadis, the second part comprises stories from the lives of individual members of the community. In most cases, specific individuals link to others through in-person interaction in the text. The juxtaposition of individuals in the text represents the goal of establishing connections regardless of their type. That is, the *Kitab al-sira* connects people in a variety of ways with the goal of creating a tightly interwoven community. This underlying structure of connections among individuals is the written network of Ibadi scholars drawn by the *Kitab al-sira*.

In this last section, I turn my attention to visualizing that written network. Following the method outlined in the introduction, each instance of interaction presented in the *Kitab al-sira* amounts to a link between two individuals. As one individual gathers connections (the total number of which is called the degree), his name grows larger in the graph. The first graph (Figure 2.1) represents the resulting visualization of written network of the first part of the *Kitab al-sira*.

Some elements of this graph appear obvious after a careful reading of the text. For example, that Abu ʿAbdallah Muhammad b. Bakr (no. 1) appears as the largest name in the network comes as no surprise. The text situates him at the center because it associates him with the foundation of the *halqa* system. Likewise, the prominence of the second Rustamid Imam, ʿAbd al-Wahhab b. ʿAbd al-Rahman b. Rustam al-Farisi (no. 2), points to the importance of the Rustamid dynasty in the narrative of the *Kitab al-sira*. Yet the graph raises questions about the remaining three largest names in the network. Abu Nuh Saʿid b. Zanghil (no. 3) was one of two leaders of the last major revolt of Ibadis following the fall of the Rustamids. As such, he represents a transition in the text from the Rustamid period to the era of the scholars. His prominence in the graph reflects his key intermediary position in the *Kitab al-sira*. The other two prominent individuals also establish links among different communities

FIGURE 2.1: The written network of the first part of the *Kitab al-sira*. The principal nodes in the network are: (1) Abu ʿAbdallah Muhammad b. Bakr; (2) ʿAbd al-Wahhab b. ʿAbd al-Rahman b. Rustam; (3) Abu Nuh Saʿid b. Zanghil; (4) Abu al-Rabiʿ Sulayman b. Yakhlaf al-Mazati; (5) Abu Zakariya Fasil b. Abi Miswar.

and periods in the *Kitab al-sira*. Abu Zakariya Fasil (no. 5) instigated the *halqa* system when he sent his sons out to encourage his former student Abu ʿAbdallah to establish study circles on the mainland. His regular appearance and connection to other scholars in the text demonstrate Abu ʿAbdallah's links to the generations before him, especially to the well-known scholarly family of Abu Miswar Yasja al-Yarasani in Jerba. Similarly, Abu al-Rabiʿ Sulayman (no. 4) connected Abu ʿAbdallah to future generations on the mainland. These included the contemporaries of the compiler of the *Kitab al-sira*, Abu Zakariya Yahya al-Warjalani, who studied under Abu al-Rabiʿ Sulayman.

The network map of this first part of the *Kitab al-sira* depicts the basic chronological and geographic limits of the Ibadi written network. With Abu ʿAbdallah Muhammad at its center, the map shows how each prominent member of the network links various generations to this central figure. The Imam ʿAbd al-Wahhab (no. 2) represents the Rustamid era, while Abu Nuh Saʿid signals the fall of the Rustamids and the failure of revolt (no. 3). Then, the remaining two figures, Abu Zakariya Fasil (no. 5) from the east and Abu al-Rabiʿ Sulayman in the west (no. 4) connect the two edges of the Ibadi community. By situating Abu ʿAbdallah Muhammad at the temporal and geographic center of the written network, the *Kitab al-sira* signals the transition to an era in which the scholars replaced the Imams.

The second part of the *Kitab al-sira* (Figure 2.2), which takes up the lives of the scholars in the generation following this transition, portrays a much different scholarly landscape. Although Abu ʿAbdallah Muhammad b. Bakr (no. 1) remains a key figure, his contemporaries (nos. 2–4) also hold prominent places in the written network. While Abu ʿAbdallah spent most of his life in southern Ifriqiya, the other individuals represent the eminence of another geographic center: the island of Jerba. Abu Muhammad ʿAbdallah b. Manuj (no. 2), Abu Zakariya Yahya al-Nafusi (no. 3), and Abu ʿImran Musa al-Mazati (no. 4) were all scholars who spent significant amounts of time in Jerba. Their central role in the network also stems from their belonging to a group known as the *ahl al-ghar* (people of the cave) or *ahl amajmaj* (the people of [the cave called] *amajmaj*). Later Ibadi prosopographies claimed that this group composed a multivolume compendium of Ibadi jurisprudence. Their high degrees point to their prominence in the network and to the geographic importance of Jerba by the eleventh century.

When the two graphs are combined (Figure 2.3), together they represent the entire written network of the *Kitab al-sira*. In addition to helping reflect the centrality of different figures and geographies in the tenth and eleventh centuries, this graph also reveals immediately something that

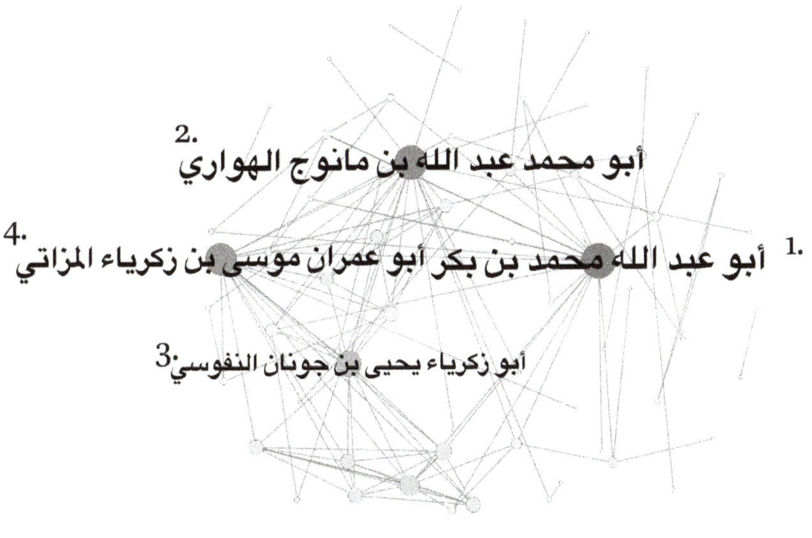

FIGURE 2.2: The written network of the second part of the *Kitab al-sira*. The principal nodes in the network are: (1) Abu ʿAbdallah Muhammad b. Bakr; (2) Abu Muhammad ʿAbdallah b. Manuj al-Hawwari; (3) Abu Zakariya Yahya b. Junan al-Nafusi; (4) Abu ʿImran Musa b. Zakariya al-Mazati al-Dummari.

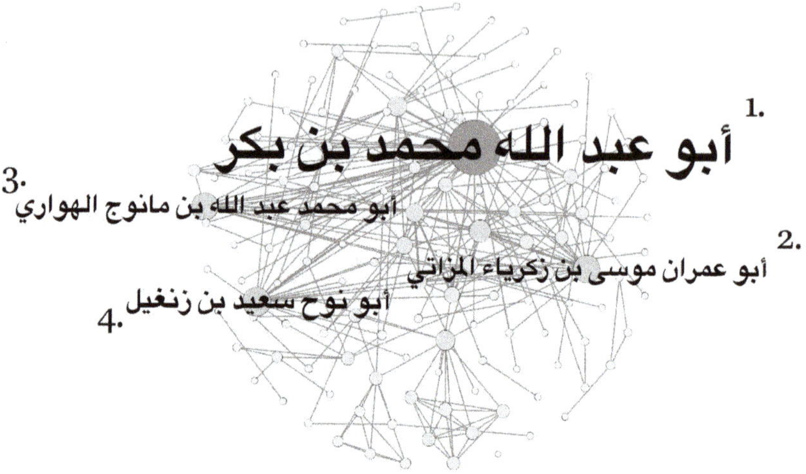

Figure 2.3: The combined written network of the *Kitab al-sira*. The principal nodes in the network are: (1) Abu ʿAbdallah Muhammad b. Bakr; (2) Abu ʿImran Musa b. Zakariya al-Mazati al-Dummari; (3) Abu Muhammad ʿAbdallah b. Manuj al-Hawwari; (4) Abu Nuh Saʿid b. Zanghil.

Figure 2.4: The "ego network" of Abu ʿAbdallah Muhammad b. Bakr. His central position in the written network becomes much more apparent here.

even careful reading of the text might not: the presence of hubs in the network. Hubs are nodes that have a disproportionately large number of links. In networks of relationships between people, this means that some nodes (or "vertices") in the networks have links ("edges") connecting them to many more people than the average.[19]

[19] Mark Newman, *Networks* (Oxford: Oxford University Press, 2010), 9.

Considering that the average degree of the combined written network of the *Kitab al-sira* is 1.692, the fact that Abu ʿAbdallah Muhammad b. Bakr has a degree of 38 demonstrates that he is not simply an important part of the network. Rather, he alone links many of the nodes in the network. The *Kitab al-sira* uses him and hubs like him to link multiple, otherwise unconnected communities and individuals in the network. In addition, hubs also connect to other hubs, and without them many of the existing connections would disappear. Through this handful of well-connected individuals, the written network of Ibadi scholars in the *Kitab al-sira* connects almost every scholar to at least one other individual. In this sense, the network depicted here is nearly complete.

READING THE NETWORK: ON AUDIENCE AND INTENTION

The maps in this chapter serve as heuristic devices for understanding the written network as constructed by the *Kitab al-sira.* As emphasized in the introduction, I borrow tools from network analysis to analyze the prosopographical corpus and to produce the maps of the written network. While these images can and often do reveal important features of the narrative structure of the work, this is not necessarily the way in which either the author/compiler or the users of the book understood the network. Abu Zakariya would not, of course, have had a mental image of the hubs of the written network in the *Kitab al-sira* in mind as he composed and compiled his work. He would, however, have known that there were central figures from the Ibadi past, and that in connecting certain well-known individuals to others, he was drawing them into a single community.

Likewise, the medieval and later readers of the *Kitab al-sira* would not have needed to conceptualize the written network as a map consisting of edges and nodes in order to have understood the process of community building taking place. Readers would have recognized the prominence of particular scholars and how the connections among those scholars and their students represented the boundaries of community. Moreover, as will become clear in later chapters, the expansion of the written network in the following centuries stemmed from this understanding of the community. Both new compilers and their readership understood that connections with older, prominent scholars were important sources of authority. For this reason, the compilers of subsequent iterations of the written network would link their own work to previous prosopographies in an effort to connect both the compiler and the scholars whose lives he linked together with those who came before. This basic form and narrative strategy for constructing the written network began with the *Kitab al-sira*, but it continued to develop over the next few centuries with the cumulative elaboration of Ibadi prosopographical tradition.

CONCLUSION

The opening passage of the *Kitab al-sira* announced to its audience that the book aimed to preserve the memory of a community facing extinction. Approaching this work in the traditional way, with attention to detail and an eye for extraction of historical narratives, the *Kitab al-sira* seems to preserve a memory in fragments that mirrors the fracturing of the Ibadi communities of the post-Rustamid period. Yet looked at from a different perspective, these various fragments combine to form a collective biography of the community—a prosopography—that at once created and defined the limits of the Ibadi tradition in Northern Africa.

Approaching the *Kitab al-sira* as a prosopography that forms a written network reveals how it achieved this result. This approach highlights the book's historical context as well as why this narrative structure proved so enduring in later centuries and why the *Kitab al-sira* served as the basis for those prosopographies that came after it. The *Kitab al-sira* reflects communities of Ibadi scholars in the late tenth and early elevent centuries, separated in space but linked through connections among their hubs. It also shows that by this time the Ibadi communities of the Maghrib had settled into geographic pockets, the islands of the Ibadi archipelago, that would remain spatial hubs of intellectual activity and exchange for centuries.

The narrative structure of the first half of the work—extolling the merits of the Persians, the Berbers, the early community, the Rustamids, and then narrating their downfall—sets the scene for a new phase of Ibadi history in which the scholars and the connections between them became the glue holding the community together. As the network graphs of the *Kitab al-sira* demonstrate, a handful of central individuals tied almost all other figures in the network together, linking the Rustamid past with a new stage in which individual scholars would lead the community. This resulted in the definition of the limits of the community and its leadership in both the past and the present. The *Kitab al-sira* draws the contours of the Ibadi tradition in the Maghrib. No longer would the early Imams of the east or the Rustamid Imams of Tahart need to guide the community and bring it together—although they would remain potent sources of legitimacy for scholars in the future generations. Instead, the *Kitab al-sira* at once creates and proclaims the dawn of the era of the *halqa*, setting the stage for the formalization of a council-rule system and laying the foundation for a tradition of prosopographical literature that would continue to maintain and expand the written network it inaugurated.

3

Sharpening the Boundaries of Community

***

The twelfth-century compilation known as the *Siyar al-Wisyani* tells the story of Abu Muhammad ʿAbdallah al-ʿAsimi and his search for a very important book. Abu Muhammad had been told that a bound copy of a commentary on the Qur'an written by the first Rustamid Imam ʿAbd al-Rahman b. Rustam had gone up for sale in the souk of the fortress town (*qalʿa*) of the Banu Hammad. The Qalʿat Bani Hammad was the center of power for the Hammadids, a rival dynasty to the Zirids throughout the eleventh and early twelfth centuries. Unfortunately, the Ibadis enjoyed as good a relationship with the Hammadids as they did with the Zirids (which is to say, not so good). Nevertheless, Abu Muhammad decided to travel to the town and search for the book. When he arrived in the city, he asked around in the market. A Nukkari Ibadi approached him, informing him that the book had already been purchased.

Having failed to obtain the book, Abu Muhammad decided to stay in town in order to purchase other manuscripts. As it happened, he came upon an Ibadi jurist holding a *halqa* and decided to sit in on it. They were discussing sheep having been brought into the market, which some present thought made doing business in the area illicit for three days. They based this on an opinion laid down by renowned Sunni jurist and founder of an eponymous school of law, Abu Hanifa (d. 767). In response, Abu Muhammad informed the group that according to another scholar's opinion supported by the Ibadis, Abu Hanifa was, among other nasty things, a devil (*shaytan*). It turned out that his opinion was not very popular, and this began a series of uneasy encounters with the people of the city. Nevertheless, Abu Muhammad continued to collect manuscripts and send them back home. When he learned that the Hammadid emir was sending out an army, he gathered his books and left the city with them, eventually fleeing to the south.[1]

The story of Abu Muhammad contains two of the principal themes of the second work of Ibadi prosopography, the *Siyar al-Wisyani*, which frame this chapter. First, manuscript books were growing more important to Ibadi communities in the Maghrib by the twelfth century. Second, the internal and external boundaries of the Ibadi community were growing increasingly defined. Books frame the story. Abu Muhammad seeks out the book of the Rustamid Imam, only to discover from a Nukkari Ibadi that it has already been purchased. He remains in the city to collect books, challenging the opinions of scholars there who uphold the opinions of non-Ibadis. Both components of the story reify the distinction between Ibadis and others in the Maghrib, and each contains a reference to a revered figure of the past.

Focusing on these themes, this chapter turns to a new stage of Ibadi history and prosopography in the Maghrib that corresponds—like the *Siyar al-Wisyani* itself—not to a specific time, place, or written work, but instead to a process. This process included both an augmentation of the tradition of prosopography begun by the *Kitab al-sira* and the maintenance of the Ibadi written network. I argue that this continued construction and maintenance took two important forms in the late eleventh and early twelfth centuries, both of which appear in the story of Abu Muhammad above. The first was a move toward privileging the book and writing as tools for the preservation of the Ibadi past, as well as for establishing and maintaining connections among scholars. The second was the clarification of the boundaries of that community through an increasingly precise description of both the structure of the Ibadi community and the distinction between them and their non-Ibadi contemporaries.

If the *Kitab al-sira* marked the construction of the written network of Ibadi scholars in the late tenth to mid-eleventh centuries, the composite work known as the *Siyar al-Wisyani* reflects changes to both the written network and the Ibadi community in the later eleventh and twelfth. Controversy surrounds the composition and authorship of this work, but what is certain is that the *Siyar al-Wisyani* was compiled over time by multiple individuals. The efforts of philologists and historians to solve the riddle of the transmission and composition of these texts deserve admiration. Here, however, I focus on the collective purpose of the various texts that make up the *Siyar al-Wisyani*, and use network analysis to understand

[1] al-Wisyānī, *Kitāb siyar al-Wisyānī*, 416–17.

what this prosopography accomplishes, rather than who composed it and when.[2]

The *Siyar al-Wisyani* represents both a continuation and an augmentation of the work begun by its prosopographical predecessor, the *Kitab al-sira*. Many of the same scholars and events appear in the *Siyar*, though some of those characters play much more prominent roles in this addition to the prosopographical tradition. Moreover, the *Siyar al-Wisyani* introduces to the written network new scholars from the eleventh and twelfth centuries. I begin here by considering some of the ways that the *Siyar al-Wisyani* presents scholars and the knowledge they carry; namely, the growing importance of books and writing as methods for the transmission of knowledge and the increasingly defined role of the *ʿazzaba*. Next, I demonstrate the utility of stories about nomadic Arabs and the dynastic powers of the eastern Maghrib in helping the *Siyar* to distinguish the Ibadis from their contemporaries. Finally, I examine the changes to and structure of the written network in the *Siyar al-Wisyani*.

THE PURPOSE AND STRUCTURE OF THE *SIYAR AL-WISYANI*

The opening lines of the *Siyar al-Wisyani* situate it squarely in the tradition of prosopography begun by the *Kitab al-sira* by reiterating the importance of books for the preservation of memory:

> I observed the traditions that had been erased and the accounts of the people of our community that had perished. I thus desired to compose for you a book of them, containing that which came down to me, which seemed to correct to me, and in which doubts did not trouble me. In doing so, I sought to follow their method, relying upon what God, King of Kings, permitted me [to do regardless of] my weakness and the paucity of my knowledge[3]

2 On the compilation and authorship of the *Siyar al-Wisyānī* see al-Wisyānī, *Kitāb siyar al-Wisyānī*, esp. 135–80. See also the accounts and perspectives of other studies of these texts, e.g. Mohamed Gouja, "Kitāb al-Siyar d'Abū al-Rabīʿ Sulaymān al Wisyānī (Vie–XIIème): étude, analyse et traduction fragmentaire," Ph.D. thesis (Université de Paris I, 1984); Allaoua Amara, "Remarques sur le recueil ibāḍite–wahbite Siyar al-Mashāyikh: retour sur son attribution," *Andalus-Maghrib* 15 (2008): 31–40; Ouahmi Ould-Braham, "Une chronique ibāḍite à textes berbères: le complexe Kitāb al-siyar de Wisyānī," *Études et Documents Berbères* 29–30 (November 2010): 311–44; Ouahmi Ould-Braham, "Pour une étude approfondie d'une source historique médiévale: une chronique ibāḍite à textes berbères (VIe H/XIIe siècle)," *Études et Documents Berbères* 33 (2014): 7–26; Ouahmi Ould-Braham, "The Case of the Kitāb al-Siyar of Wisyānī (Sixth H/XII Century AD) and its Various Manuscript Copies," in *Today's Perspectives on Ibadi History and the Historical Sources*, ed. Reinhard Eisener (Hildesheim: Georg Olms Verlag, 2016), 161–76.

3 al-Wisyānī, *Kitāb siyar al-Wisyānī*, 228.

But the *Siyar*, like other works in the corpus after it, now also introduces the structure of the book as well as the compilers' debt to the prosopographical tradition that came before it:

> I begin that [task] with the accounts of the people of our community from the people of the Jebel [Nafusa], including what has come to me from our shaykhs—may God have mercy on them—of their stories and virtues. And I desire from whomever sees in [this work] error or distortion that he correct it. And may the mercy of God be upon our shaykh Abu Zakariya [al-Warjalani], for he has precedence in this.[4]

This attention to the written works of predecessors, alongside an indication as to the structure of the work that the compiler lays before the reader, became standard practice in the prosopographies that followed the *Siyar* over the next three centuries. This in itself marks an important change in awareness of authorship and a recognition that books had identifiable, if fluid, boundaries. The connection among the authors and compilers of these prosopographies represents yet another type of link among Ibadi scholars in the network. In acknowledging and in many cases drawing from the writings of their predecessors, the compilers of the Ibadi prosopographies connected themselves to the ever-expanding network of the prosopographical tradition. On the levels of both composition and narrative content, the Middle Period (eleventh–sixteenth centuries) witnessed an increasing reliance on manuscript books and the work they do to augment the tradition of oral transmission via personal interaction among scholars.

The *Siyar al-Wisyani* reflects this growing reliance on written materials in several stories about how and why books were written, compiled, collated, and read. These often include comparison with or correction by oral tradition. In the tenth century, Abu Miswar Yasja and his companion Abu Salih Bakr travel to a village in the Jarid to study from books. When they complete their studies, they return home to their teacher to check the veracity of the information they had gathered in these books. This same Abu Salih has his son recite from three different copies of the same book to determine which of three represents the authentic and correct version. In another story from the eleventh century, Abu ʿAbdallah Muhammad b. Bakr supports his opinion by first quoting an oral source and then a book. This juxtaposition of oral and written knowledge points to the growing importance and presence of written works in this period as well as the interrelationship of oral and written texts.[5]

[4] al-Wisyānī, *Kitāb siyar al-Wisyānī*, 229–30.

[5] al-Wisyānī, *Kitāb siyar al-Wisyānī*, 294, 290, 340; cf. similar anecdotes on 380–81, 411.

Lengthy passages in Berber also point to this interplay of the oral and the written in the *Siyar*. Aside from providing further evidence that the medieval Ibadi communities of the Maghrib would have spoken Berber rather than Arabic, these passages also suggest something about the use of the *Siyar*. The recitation of books would not only have aimed at verifying their contents but also at instruction and discussion of those contents. The extended passages of Berber texts in the *Siyar* suggest that scholars and students would often have read it—like other medieval Islamic texts—aloud rather than in private. The *Siyar* provides no explanation or translation of these passages in Arabic, meaning that the audience understood these passages when read aloud. These Berber quotations throughout the *Siyar* point to the performance of the text and a continuing exchange between oral and written texts.[6]

The *Siyar* also speaks more directly to the composition, copying, and collation of books. Texts were often lecture notes, and could remain for a long time on wooden writing tablets (*alwah*) before eventually being arranged and transferred to paper. That an author often did not pen his work in his own hand is a reoccurring theme of the *Siyar*. Many times, a book was made up of notes taken by the students of the author. Two well-known eleventh-century works of Ibadi law entitled the *Kitab al-wasaya* and the *Kitab al-buyuʿ* were attributed to Abu Muhammad Wislan but comprised *responsa* compiled by his students. In this case, the *Siyar* notes that the book was also recited in Abu Muhammad's presence for his approval:

> The *ʿazzaba* saw in their good judgement that every time Abu Muhammad [Wislan] stood up and left the *majlis*, they would gather together and would write down every response he had given in each *majlis* on wooden tablets (*alwah*) … This went on until they had written what God permitted them to write. They then recited it to Shaykh Abu Muhammad [for verification], who said to them, "Good, good."[7]

[6] Mohamed Meouak recently published a monograph on the use of Berber in the medieval Maghrib, which demonstrates the continuing importance of Berber languages alongside Arabic well beyond the confines of the Ibadi community. On the Berber-language texts by Ibadi authors, see Mohamed Meouak, "Vestiges de la langue berbère dans les textes ibadites du Maghrib," in *La langue berbère au Maghreb médiéval*, 297–360. On the Berber passages in the *Siyar al-wisyani* see Ould-Braham, "Une chronique Ibāḍite à textes berbères"; Lewicki, "Mélanges berbères-ibadites."

[7] al-Wisyānī, *Kitāb siyar al-Wisyānī*, 578. Leaving books on *alwāḥ* boards was a common practice in manuscript culture in the premodern Sahara. See Houari Touati, "Écriture et commerce dans le Sahara précolonial," *Studia Islamica* 107 (2012): 122–31. On Abū Muḥammad Wīslān and his *Kitāb al-waṣāyā wa-ʾl-buyūʿ*, see Bābāʿammī, *Muʿjam aʿlām al-ibāḍiyya*, 448.

While this process of verifying the contents of a text became quite formalized in other late medieval Muslim communities, the Ibadis of the Maghrib appear to have had a less formalized practice. Books were copied and either collated orally in an informal audition with a scholar known to have memorized the work or to have collated it with addition written copies. For example, the eleventh-century copyist Hammu b. Aflah al-Matkudi had a reputation for his fine handwriting, and the *Siyar* describes how he collated ten different books by comparing written versions of the texts. This same Hammu was also regularly employed to finish books with missing sections through a similar practice of copying and collating.[8]

Perhaps most famously, the *Siyar* refers to two important collectively authored works by scholars in the eleventh and twelfth centuries. The first was the eleventh-century compendium (*diwan*) written by the "people of the cave of *amajmaj*." This group, mentioned already in the *Kitab al-sira*, composed an eleven-volume text of jurisprudence (*fiqh*) on the island of Jerba. In the twelfth century, a group of scholars in the Warjalan area composed another compendium known as the *Diwan al-ashyakh* comprising some twenty-five volumes. While the manuscript tradition tracing these two works is unclear and the two are often confused with one another, their composition in the eleventh and twelfth centuries points further to the importance of committing knowledge to writing among Ibadi communities in this period. Moreover, like the *Siyar al-Wisyani*, their multiple authorship emphasizes the collective and cumulative character of the Ibadi literary tradition to which the Ibadi prosopographies belong.[9]

Other stories speak to scholars' desire to purchase, collect, and retain books. These show that the world of the *Siyar al-Wisyani* was one in which manuscripts were appreciated both for their monetary value and for the prestige and pleasure of owning and collecting them. The eleventh-century Ibrahim b. Abi Ibrahim al-Mazati spent some one thousand dinars (!) on books. At the time of his death, he left behind forty sacks (*mikhla*) of them. In another story, a man takes a loan in order to purchase a well-known exegesis of the Qur'an (*tafsir*). When he fails to repay the loan, the debate over ownership of the book escalates to the level of

[8] al-Wisyānī, *Kitāb siyar al-Wisyānī*, 502.

[9] The two collections are often confused. See Virginie Prevost, "Majmāj et les sept savants: la création du Dīwān al-ʿazzāba," *Acta Orientalia* 73 (2012): 35–58. For a full bibliography on the two works see "Diwān al-ashyākh" and "Dīwān al-ʿazzāba," in Custers, *al-Ibāḍiyya* (2016), vol. II, 52–59.

a tribal dispute between the two parties. It finds resolution only when a judge solomonically cuts the book in half with a knife, instructing each side to copy that of the other.[10]

These stories reflect the monetary value of books as well as the lengths to which scholars would go to obtain and collect them. Books were prized for their ability to connect their owners with those who came before them, whether through their legal opinions, their poetry, or stories of their exemplary behavior. The power of books to form associations and bring the community closer together could also prove dangerous, however. The texts of challengers to the Rustamid legacy, called "dissenters" or "dissidents" (*mukhalifun*), appear in the *Siyar al-Wisyani* as potential threats. Debates over whether reading these works constituted grounds for temporary excommunication from the community or even the adverse effects of the physical presence of the manuscripts hold a prominent place in the *Siyar*.[11]

Stories often warn of the dangers of associating with the *mukhalifun* by reading their books. When Abu Muhammad al-Lawwati (d. 1133) purchases a rival legal compendium to the *Diwan al-ʿazzaba*, he is overcome with regret and decides to bury it in the ground. The book is (conveniently) discovered by a man named Nafath b. Nasr, who himself becomes a dissident in the Wahbi tradition. Another story goes a step further, when Abu Muhammad Wislan (d. early eleventh century) instructs his student to burn a book because of the danger inherent in it. The famous eleventh-century scholar Maksin b. al-Khayr (d. 1097) hesitates to accept an offer of twelve books because he believes them to be written by Nukkaris. Ultimately, he is relieved to find out that they are in fact refutations of the arguments of the Nukkaris. The *Siyar* elsewhere associates dissident books with selling used garments (considered ritually unclean) or illicit commercial practices.[12]

The danger that books could spread illicit ideas or draw associations with rival Ibadi communities reiterates the almost total absence of the Nukkaris and other non-Wahbi voices from the written traditions of the Ibadis in Northern Africa. As in the stories above, those communities become unnamed "dissenters," and both they and their books often represent literary motifs rather than specific people. In this way, another

[10] al-Wisyānī, *Kitāb siyar al-Wisyānī*, 738–39, 485.

[11] On the dangers of associating with dissenters and their books is the topic of two sections, see al-Wisyānī, *Kitāb siyar al-Wisyānī*, 507–10, 522.

[12] al-Wisyānī, *Kitāb siyar al-Wisyānī*, 445; on Nafāth's book: 303. On the ritual impurity of these kinds of books see al-Wisyānī, *Kitāb siyar al-Wisyānī*, 721–22.

effect of the move toward the use of manuscript books for the transmission of collective memory was that the Ibadi prosopographical tradition helped write out of existence those communities that competed with it.

Whether as positive agents for connecting Ibadi scholars from different places and times or as dangerous tools for spreading illicit ideas, the *Siyar al-Wisyani* demonstrates that by the early twelfth century books came to complement itinerant scholars in the maintenance of the boundaries of the Ibadi community in the Maghrib. The *Siyar* makes it clear that writing, compiling, collating, and reading books began to take on great importance for the Ibadi community in the Middle Period. Stories describing how scholars composed, transported, read, sought out, copied, coveted, or avoided books reflect a growing role for written works in establishing and maintaining the connections between scholars. As such, books came to serve as agents of communication across time and space alongside the scholars themselves, continuing the process of constructing and maintaining links in the written network. Lastly, stories about illicit books by the Nukkaris and other dissenters in the *Siyar* reflect the power of the prosopographical tradition to create or to destroy those connections.

THE ROLE OF THE *ʿAZZABA*

Who made these decisions as to the licit or illicit nature of books and the ideas they contained? As discussed in the previous chapter, the traditional narrative of Ibadi history in the Maghrib is that the council-rule system of the *ʿazzaba* emerged out of the leadership vacuum left by the fall of the Rustamid Imamate. The *Kitab al-sira* attributed the foundation of the *ʿazzaba* to Abu ʿAbdallah Muhammad b. Bakr, who brought the whole region together through his travels. But the *Kitab al-sira* provided little detailed about the *ʿazzaba* or what they actually did. This is because the system did not yet exist—at least not in the more institutionalized form of later centuries. The *Siyar al-Wisyani*, however, demonstrates the move toward formalizing this system in the late eleventh and twelfth centuries. Stories in the *Siyar* distinguish the larger categories of scholars (*ʿulamaʾ*) or pious figures to be imitated (*sulahaʾ*) from the more specialized category of the *ʿazzaba*.

Passages throughout the *Siyar* associate specific practices and characteristics with the status of *ʿazzabi*. This category of people become associated with certain dietary restrictions, modes of interaction with each other, and even specific ways of wearing clothing. The *Siyar* also relates stories about groups of *ʿazzaba* traveling together. For example, one passage describes the practice of *ʿazzaba* visiting the home of a recently deceased person to offer collective consolation and recite the Qur'an. Other practices include *ʿazzaba* gathering to discuss Qur'anic commentaries and then sending written communiqués to those unable to attend. *ʿAzzaba* also appear as mediators in disputes and protectors of both their students and others. At the same time, the category had yet to take on a political character because the *Siyar* has them in consultation or disagreement with tribal leaders or officials of the Zirid or Hammadid dynasties, in whose spheres of influence they normally lived. Finally, the *Siyar* also suggests that the roles of the *ʿazzaba* included codifying the Ibadi legal tradition in the form of large collective works such as the *Diwan ghar amajmaj* and the *Diwan al-ashyakh*. While the *Siyar* does not offer a precise description of what or who the *ʿazzaba* are, the work reflects an increasingly defined set of standards and practices associated with them by the twelfth century.[13]

As was the case with alternative textual corpora, alternative *ʿazzaba* systems also appear in the *Siyar* as a threat. Similarly, by their very mention these rival illegitimate *ʿazzaba* systems reinforce the legitimacy of the tradition represented by the Ibadi prosopographies. The Nukkaris of Jebel Dummar, for example, took over the region and installed their own *ʿazzaba*. Occasionally, the line separating Ibadis from their Nukkari rivals blurs as it relates to the *halqa*s when Nukkaris appear as participants in debates and discussions among the *ʿazzaba*. In general, however, the *Siyar* provides vignettes and accounts from the lives of scholars in which Nukkaris are identified by that title, distinguishing and excluding them from the community.[14]

The prosopographical tradition took another century to codify the rules and regulations of the *ʿazzaba* and to formalize the memory of their establishment. The *Siyar al-Wisyani* builds upon the foundation narrative laid out in the *Kitab al-sira* with anecdotes pointing to the roles and behaviors associated with *ʿazzaba*. The lines separating scholars, pious figures, and *ʿazzaba* remained blurred, but the move toward formalization had clearly begun by the twelfth century. Just as books began to draw connections among scholars and define the boundaries of the written network, so too the *ʿazzaba* marked the internal limits of authority

[13] al-Wisyānī, *Kitāb siyar al-Wisyānī*, 425–26, 487, 664, 666, 677, 678, 679, 680.
[14] al-Wisyānī, *Kitāb siyar al-Wisyānī*, 413: "ʿuzzāb al-nukkār," 467–68, 295.

and defined the structure of the Ibadi community. At the same time, the *Siyar al-Wisyani* demonstrates that the tradition it helped construct did not stand unchallenged in the Middle Period. Alternative interpretations of Ibadi Islam continued to thrive in the form of both books and rival *ʿazzaba* throughout the region.

IBADIS AND OTHERS: REFINING COMMUNAL BOUNDARIES

When asked about avoiding interaction with Arabs in the Maghrib, the ever-quotable Abu al-Rabiʿ al-Mazati replied that he would advise against it: "They are lawless raiders, insatiable robbers! And they kill in combat, for they are the ones of whom God said, 'They fight against God and His messenger, spreading corruption on the earth.'"[15] If books and the *ʿazzaba* had begun to define the internal parameters of the community, the *Siyar al-Wisyani* also uses anecdotes like this one to mark the external limits of the Ibadi community by distinguishing them from their non-Ibadi rivals and enemies. In some cases these were the same unnamed "Arabs" and other nomads who continued their slow but steady migration into the Maghrib in the late eleventh and twelfth centuries. In other cases these stories describe the dynasties that continued to impose their rule over Ibadis in the region. Both types of interaction with non-Ibadis also indicate the geographical boundaries of the Ibadi community in this period—the Ibadi archipelago of oases, mountain villages, and island strongholds in Northern Africa. Stories with these themes in the *Siyar* provide a clear picture of the context that produced this second prosopography.

The large-scale migration of Arabic-speaking and non-Arabic-speaking tribes in the eleventh century had real effects on Ibadi communities and the whole region by the early twelfth century. By the mid-eleventh century these tribes had ended Zirid influence in all areas except the Mediterranean coast. Qayrawan had been plundered and its economic prominence in the region lost. The western rival dynasty to the Zirids, the Hammadids, occasionally won the allegiance of the larger cities in Ifriqiya but in general the period is characterized by the constant shifting of allegiances, sieges, and small battles. To make things even more complicated, at the end of the eleventh century the Pisans and the Genoese attacked the Zirid stronghold of Mahdiyya, only to be followed a few decades later, in

[15] al-Wisyānī, *Kitāb siyar al-Wisyānī*, 684.

the mid-twelfth century, by the Normans, who took control of the large cities of the coast and ended the Zirid dynasty.[16]

Closer to home for Ibadis in the south, the arrival of the Arabic-speaking tribes had combined with the Zirid crisis in the north to produce a half century of chaos. Different petty dynasties ruled southern Ifriqiya in the mid-to-late eleventh century, normally based in the cities of Gabes (Qabis) or Gafsa (Qafsa). These rulers allied themselves with different nomadic Arabic-speaking tribes—and even the Normans at one point—against Zirid leaders, who desperately tried to reestablish control. In general, Ibadis had a rocky relationship with these nomadic tribes, reflected in the stories of their encounters with them in the *Siyar al-Wisyani*.

As with the *Kitab al-sira*, the *Siyar* relates accounts of nomadic tribes plaguing Ibadi communities with raids and attacks upon villages and travelers. Unnamed Arabs appear throughout the *Siyar*, raiding villages, attacking shepherds, and stealing sheep, goats, or slaves.[17] The compiler(s) devoted an entire chapter to controversies surrounding association with Arabs, ranging from doing business with them to sharing their drinking water. Even things associated with Arab tribesmen such as camel meat or firewood are deemed illicit. Likewise, one scholar encourages disassociation (*baraʾa*) from certain Berber tribes "because they are like the Arabs" in that they made raids against Ibadi villages.[18]

The *Siyar* also distinguishes Ibadis from the forces and supporters of the Zirid and Hammadid dynasties. In addition to defining the shifting geographical boundaries of the Ibadi communities of the region, the regular attacks against the Ibadis by these two dynastic forces reinforce the overall mood in the *Siyar* of a community under constant threat. By the late eleventh century the two dynasties had already separated into their respective realms, the Zirids attempting (and failing) to control the eastern Maghrib and its littoral and the Hammadids struggling to control their fortress stronghold before transferring their seat of power to Bijaya on the coast and attempting to control the areas to their west. Encounters with these dynasties, like those with the nomadic tribes of the south, appear throughout the *Siyar*. Accounts are equally imprecise when mentioning either dynasty, often referring to them by their shared tribal affiliation, Sanhaja. Alongside stories of "Sahaja thieves" and sieges of Ibadi

[16] Michael Brett, "Muslim Justice under Infidel Rule: The Normans in Ifriqiya, 517–55 H/1123–1160 AD," *Cahiers de Tunisie* 43 (1991): 325–68.

[17] For examples of unnamed "Arab" tribesmen or nomads, see al-Wisyānī, *Kitāb siyar al-Wisyānī*, 390, 391, 403, 701.

[18] al-Wisyānī, *Kitāb siyar al-Wisyānī*, 685.

towns, the *Siyar* relates the story of the late eleventh-century destruction by the Hammadids of the Ibadi city of Sedrata, where the last members of the Rustamid dynasty and its supporters had fled at the beginning of the tenth century.[19]

Relations with the Zirids, especially in Jerba, were a bit more complex. The Ibadis of Jerba and the nearby Jebel Nafusa did not have to deal with the nomadic tribesmen moving across the region to the same extent as their mainland coreligionists in southern Ifriqiya and the Zab. Instead, their enemies often came from the north or the sea, as when the Zirids attacked the island at the beginning of the eleventh century. Prior to the attack, however, the *Siyar* gives an account in which Abu Zakariya Fasil b. Abi Miswar receives a letter from the Zirid commander Ibrahim b. Wanmu al-Mazati (who is, by both tribal affiliation and implication in the story, himself an Ibadi). The letter instructs Abu Zakariya to separate his family from members of the Zawagha tribe on the island before the Zirid forces arrive. When they do, several Ibadi scholars die in an attempt to repel the attack—with the notable exception of Abu Zakariya and his Yahrasin clan.[20]

In these different anecdotes and vignettes the *Siyar* points to a volatile period of political change in the Maghrib in the eleventh and early twelfth centuries. Through these often violent encounters with nomadic tribes, the Hammadids, and the Zirids the *Siyar* distinguishes the Ibadis from their non-Ibadi contemporaries. The emerging importance of book culture, the increasingly defined role of the *'azzaba*, and the political and geographic marginalization combined to allow the *Siyar* to mark the internal and external boundaries of the Ibadi community in the Maghrib. Those limits had not remained static in the century following the compilation of the *Kitab al-sira*, and so the *Siyar al-Wisyani* also carried out the important task of expanding membership in the Ibadi community to include new generations of scholars from the late eleventh and early twelfth centuries. The remainder of the chapter shifts focus to how the definition of the community's external boundaries coincided with the ongoing augmentation and maintenance of the written network within the text.

[19] On relations with the Hammadids and Zirids in the *Siyar al-Wisyānī* see pp. 285, 479, 734. See also Djaabiri, "al-'Ahd al-Ṣanhājī," in *Niẓām al-'azzāba*, 297–301. For accounts of the destruction of Sedrata, see Virginie Prevost, "Une tentative d'histoire de la ville ibadite de Sadrāta," *Mélanges de la Casa de Velázquez* 38, no. 2 (2008): 129–47.

[20] al-Wisyānī, *Kitāb siyar al-Wisyānī*, 298, 307–08; Djaabiri, *Niẓām al-'azzāba*, 297–99.

SHARPENING EDGES: THE WRITTEN NETWORK OF THE *SIYAR AL-WISYANI*

In some ways, the network of personal interactions in the *Siyar al-Wisyani* reproduces that of the *Kitab al-sira*. Many of the same principal characters appear, although with different degrees of centrality. In addition, however, the *Siyar* adds new scholars to the written network. As was the case with the *Kitab al-sira*, the written network of the *Siyar al-Wisyani* also reflects its context and sources.

The relative importance of specific geographic locations become much more pronounced in the *Siyar*. Rather than framing the lives of scholars in rough chronological order, the first part of the *Siyar* divides these accounts and anecdotes according to geographic region. While many of these individuals were constantly on the move, Ibadi scholars of the late eleventh and twelfth centuries remained concentrated in an archipelago of oases, rural villages, mountain regions, and the island of Jerba (Figure 3.1).

The absence of a chronological frame in the *Siyar al-Wisyani* means that only the geographic locations and connections among scholars appear defined. Nevertheless, even without chronological markers, the geographic concentrations are striking. The *Siyar* focuses its efforts on describing the lives and interactions among scholars living in a narrowly defined geographic region. Those who might have lived in more distant locations like Sijilmasa or even closer by in Tunis or Qayrawan are left out. In doing so, the *Siyar* complements the conceptual boundaries laid

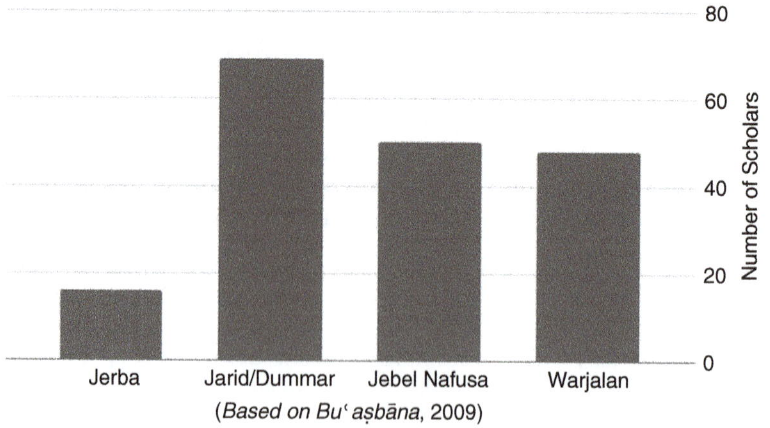

FIGURE 3.1: Geographic distribution of scholars in part 1 of the *Siyar al-Wisyani*.

out in its narrative by drawing geographic boundaries for the Ibadi community in the Maghrib.

In addition to geographic boundaries, the compilers of the *Siyar* also continued the work of the *Kitab al-sira* in defining the limits of community by including and excluding individuals. Figure 3.2 shows those same data from the first part of the *Siyar* visualized as a network of interactions.

The scholars in this graph represent the key figures in the first part of the *Siyar al-Wisyani*. As in the case of the *Kitab al-sira*, the graph reflects both the content of the *Siyar* and the context in which it was compiled. The first noteworthy difference between the two books is the increase in the overall size and complexity of the written network. In this first part of the *Siyar* alone the number of nodes in the network increased from

FIGURE 3.2: Network map of part 1 of the *Siyar al-Wisyani*, representing a significant increase in the number of scholars and connections as well as isolate nodes.

147 to 183, and the total number of edges (relationships) increased from 254 to 286. Although the two prosopographies share many of the same actors, the *Siyar* brings those actors closer together through an increased number of relationships. Another striking difference between the two versions of the network is the appearance of isolates (scholars with no connections) in the *Siyar al-Wisyani*. This first part of the text alone has anecdotes relating to thirty-four people who have no explicit connection to anyone else in the network. Yet by inserting these individuals into the prosopography, the *Siyar* brings even the isolates into the same network of the Ibadi tradition.

The scholars with high degrees also reveal something about the context of the *Siyar*. For example, the largest name, Abu Muhammad ʿAbdallah al-ʿAsimi, served as one of the named oral sources of information for the *Siyar*. To examine the other scholars with high degrees, the map must be simplified. The next network map represents only those scholars with a degree of ten or more (Figure 3.3).

The majority of these well-connected scholars in the map spent the bulk of their lives in Jerba rather than in the Jarid, Dummar, Jebel Nafusa, or Warjalan, as one would expect from the geographic distribution above. This suggests an especially important role in the *Siyar* for the scholars of Jerba in the late tenth and early eleventh centuries and their prominence in a manuscript tradition compiled in the twelfth century. Although a

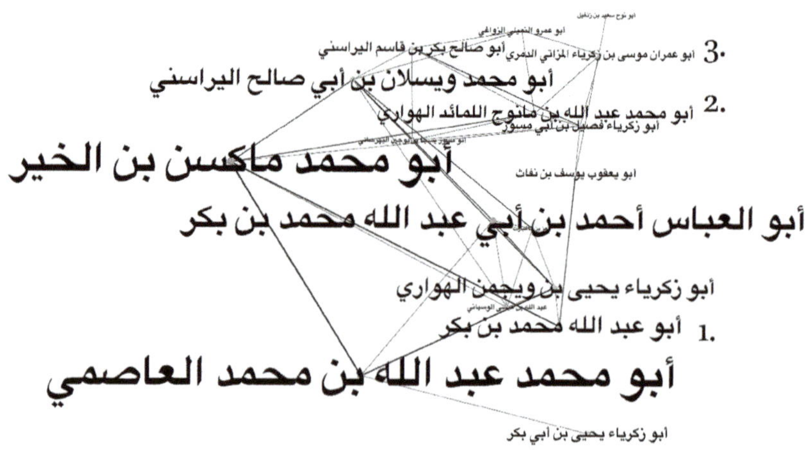

FIGURE 3.3: Network map of part 1 of the *Siyar al-Wisyani*, showing only those nodes with ten or more edges: (1) Abu ʿAbdallah Muhammad b. Bakr; (2) Abu Muhammad ʿAbdallah b. Manuj al-Hawwari; (3) Abu ʿImran Musa b. Zakariya al-Mazati.

larger number of scholars from other regions appear in the *Siyar*, those of Jerba have a much higher degree of connectivity.

The *Kitab al-sira* had already assigned Jerba a prominent place in the written network. Although they discuss individuals from around the same time and period, the two books distribute the centrality or importance of individuals differently. For example, Abu Muhammad ʿAbdallah b. Bakr (no. 1), no doubt the most central figure of the *Kitab al-sira*, has a much lower degree in the first part of the *Siyar al-Wisyani*. While other key figures from the former text like Abu Muhammad b. Manuj (no. 2) and Abu ʿImran Musa al-Mazati (no. 3) still hold an important place, they have far lower degrees in the *Siyar al-Wisyani*.

The second part of the *Siyar al-Wisyani* is usually assumed to have been compiled by one or more of al-Wisyani's students. While the first part of the *Siyar* maintained the written network created by the *Kitab al-sira*, this second part charts the growth of the network to include new members from the late eleventh and early twelfth centuries. The second part shares many of the structural features of the first (hubs, isolates, etc.). However, the complexity of the graph of the second part of the *Siyar* makes it difficult to read. Applying the same filter pushes the principal nodes of the network to the fore (Figure 3.4).

Several things are immediately striking about this map. First of all, Abu ʿAbdallah Muhammad b. Bakr (no. 4) remains a well-connected node. However, his son Ahmad (no. 1) now takes his place as the scholar with the most links. Another fascinating feature of this graph is the prominence of Abu Zakariya Yahya b. Abi Bakr (no. 6), the attributed author of the *Kitab al-sira*. Since connections between scholars in the network

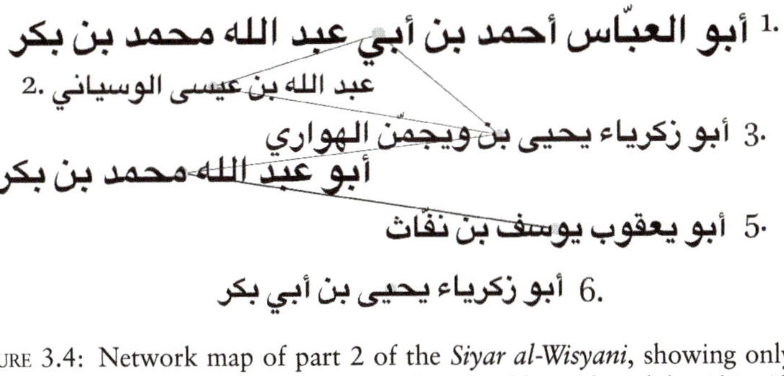

FIGURE 3.4: Network map of part 2 of the *Siyar al-Wisyani*, showing only those nodes with ten or more edges: (1) Abu al-ʿAbbas Ahmad b. Abi ʿAbdallah Muhammad b. Bakr; (2) ʿAbdallah b. ʿAysa al-Wisyani; (3) Abu Zakariya Yahya b. Wijamman al-Hawwari; (4) Abu ʿAbdallah Muhammad b. Bakr; (5) Abu Yaʿqub Yusuf b. Naffath; (6) Abu Zakariya Yahya b. Abi Bakr [al-Warjalani].

do not rely on chains of transmission but rather on instances of personal interaction, by the twelfth century Abu Zakariya had become a key node in the written network he created.

Some historians have argued that the third and final part of the printed edition of the *Siyar al-Wisyani* is the second part of the *Kitab al-sira*. The confusion over the attribution of these texts only reinforces the larger point that the Ibadi prosopographical tradition aimed at bringing Ibadi scholars together across time and space. Whether each part of the *Siyar al-Wisyani* represents a separate manuscript tradition matters little from the perspective of the written network. Indeed, the overlap between the two works supports the idea that Ibadi prosopographies sought to establish links rather than divisions among different parts of the network. Combining all three parts of the printed edition of the *Siyar* reveals an especially dense network in which a key structural feature of the previous two maps, the isolates, has all but disappeared (Figure 3.5).

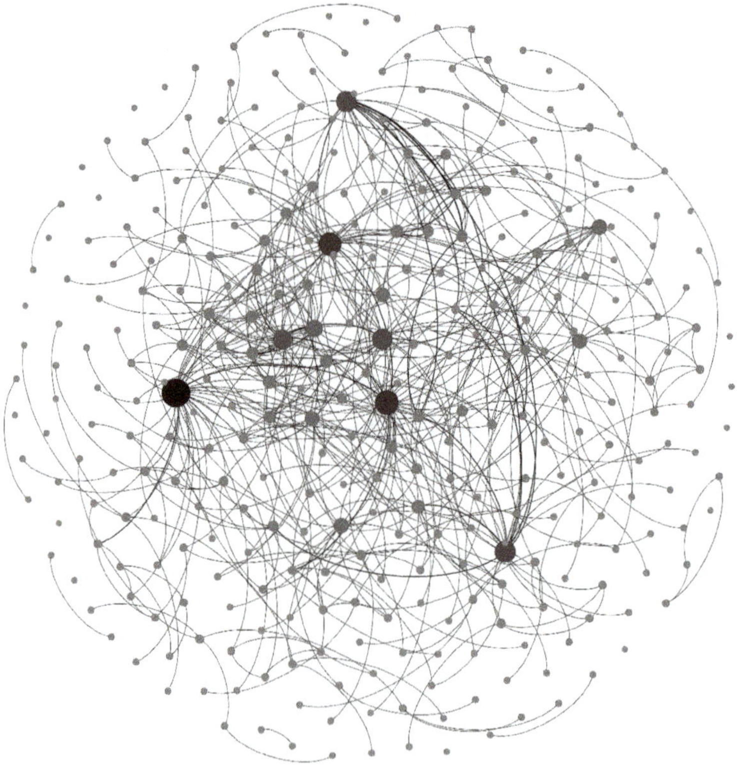

FIGURE 3.5: Network map of parts 1–3 of the *Siyar al-Wisyani*, showing the presence of hubs.

An additional tool of network analysis, degree distribution, offers another way of visualizing the structure of the written network in the *Siyar al-Wisyani*. Degree-distribution charts plot the number of connections for each node (the degree) in a histogram. Like the network maps, the distribution graph demonstrates that a handful of scholars hold far more connections than the average. Arranged according to degree, all scholars from all three parts of the *Siyar* appear in Figure 3.6. These data reveal a fascinating feature of the structure of the written network of the *Siyar*, what network analysists call a power-law distribution.

A power-law distribution suggests that the network is "scale-free," meaning that it has no peak and that a small number of nodes have an unusually high number of connections. This same scale-free structure applies to virtually any real-world network, and examples with the same structure come from fields ranging from computer science to epidemiology.[21] In terms of the "real-world" network described in the *Siyar*, this would mean that a very small number of scholars served as the hubs connecting most other students and scholars to one another. In establishing a link to one of these principal connectors (either in person or through a written network), the *Siyar* inserted a student or scholar into the network of Ibadi scholars in the eleventh and twelfth centuries as well as backward in time. More precisely, this degree distribution reflects the written network constructed by the *Siyar al-Wisyani* in the eleventh and twelfth centuries. The text itself connected the average scholar to this handful of

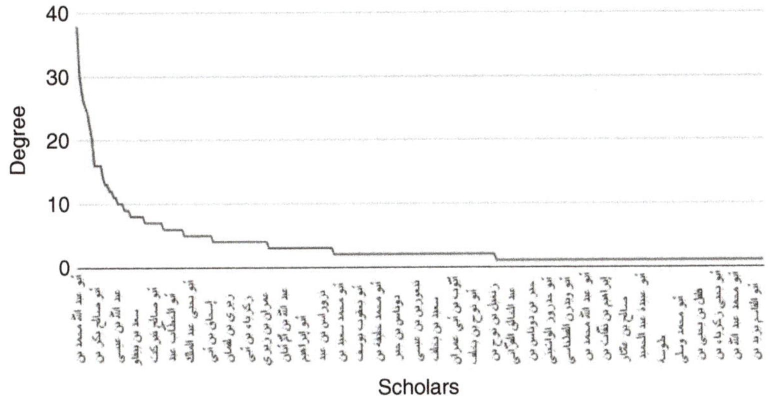

FIGURE 3.6: Degree-distribution graph of the *Siyar al-Wisyani*, demonstrating a "power-law distribution."

[21] Albert-László Barabási and Eric Bonabeau, "Scale-Free Networks," *Scientific American* 288, no. 5 (2003): 52–53.

hubs. Both the "real" and written networks raise the same question: how did this happen?

Although network analysts offer mathematical probability as one possible explanation for the emergence of a power-law distribution, in the case of Ibadi networks of the eleventh and twelfth centuries two additional concepts of network analysis help illustrate its development over time: preferential attachment and homophily. Social scientists studying networks of human relationships use these terms as technical equivalents to the axiom "birds of a feather flock together."[22] In the case of the human relationships under consideration here, homophily applies to Ibadi scholars and students in that they were most likely to associate with other Ibadi—rather than non-Ibadi—scholars (often of the same tribe or living in the same location). This lays the groundwork for the network described in the *Siyar* as a whole.

A companion concept, preferential attachment, clarifies that new nodes in a network had a tendency to associate with those scholars in the network who themselves already had a large number of connections. In the same way as a modern-day agent attempts to obtain roles for her client in films with prominent actors to increase the client's prestige, so too association with prominent scholars enhanced the profile of students. Association with prominent figures also increased the chances that they would go on to attract their own students. Well-known scholars such as Abu ʿAbdallah Muhammad b. Bakr or Abu al-Rabiʿ al-Mazati attracted students, which would in turn reinforce their centrality. This partially explains the large number of students and associations between already-established scholars as the network expanded.

Yet the network in the *Siyar* no doubt represents only a fraction of the Ibadi students and scholars active in the eleventh and twelfth centuries. Explaining the development of these hubs in the written network of the *Siyar al-Wisyani* also means acknowledging that the compilers made the choice to include or exclude certain individuals from the written network. The large number of anecdotes concerning these hubs in circulating oral traditions or other written works led compilers to emphasize connections among them, other lesser-known scholars, and their students. In this way, the compiler of the *Siyar* caused scholars who already had many connections to become even more connected while simultaneously relegating lesser-known scholars—or those deemed dissidents in the eyes of the prosopographical tradition—to obscurity.

[22] "7.13 Homophily and Assortative Mixing," in Newman, *Networks*, 220–26.

Although the intent of the compilers of the *Siyar al-Wisyani* is even more elusive than was the case for the *Kitab al-sira*, the reception and use of the written network remained similar. Here again, the network maps and charts above do not reflect the understanding of the *Siyar al-Wisyani*'s audience, but they do communicate the centrality of particular individuals and their prominence in the written tradition. Those students who read and studied the traditions passed on in the *Siyar al-Wisyani* would have appreciated the importance of the handful of scholars whose names appear prominently in these maps. They would also have understood, as do fledgling actors or graduate students today, that those whom you work with have a big impact on your future. In other words, associations matter.

CONCLUSION

The *Siyar al-Wisyani* expanded and defined the written network of Ibadi scholars in the late eleventh and early twelfth centuries. This composite text achieved that expansion, growing complexity, and definition in several different ways. First of all, the many passages throughout the *Siyar* relating to book culture point to the emerging importance of manuscripts and their power to bring members of the community together. This move toward written works also reflects a much broader trend in the Maghrib toward the production and use of paper for the preservation and transmission of thought. The Berber passages of the *Siyar* simultaneously demonstrate the continuing use of that language among Ibadi communities in the region. Books had the power to bring the community together, but they could also prove dangerous, as case the case with the dissemination of "dissident" texts.

I have also shown here that the *Siyar* marked a trend toward defining the internal and external boundaries of the Ibadi tradition. It drew the internal limits with stories that further defined the role of the *ʿazzaba*, whereas it defined the community's external limits through accounts that distinguished Ibadis from their non-Ibadi contemporaries. Likewise, the exclusion of individuals deemed dissidents by the compilers and audience of the prosopographies also points to the power of these written works to ostracize rivals from the tradition.

The analysis of the written network of the *Siyar al-Wisyani* also mirrored this process of expansion and maintenance. Its compilers augmented the network initiated by the *Kitab al-sira* by introducing new scholars and connecting them to previous generations. Degree distribution in the network suggests a "scale-free" structure, meaning that a handful of individuals in the network served to unite the whole. In addition, degree distribution in the *Siyar* highlights the role of the work's compiler's in shaping the limits of the community through the inclusion or exclusion of individuals as well as the choice to include many anecdotes relating to specific individuals.

The often-silent influence of the compiler would become much more pronounced as the prosopographical tradition changed in later centuries. From the end of the twelfth century the Ibadi prosopographical tradition continued to maintain and augment these trends toward defining the limits of the community and the expansion of the network in response to the changing religious and political landscapes of the Maghrib in the Middle Period.

4

Formalizing the Network

***

Abu ʿAmmar ʿAbd al-Kafi came to Tunis from a village called Tanawut on the outskirts of Warjalan in the Sahara. When he arrived in the mid-twelfth century, Tunis had already replaced Qayrawan as the most important trade hub in Ifriqiya. In addition, most in the region now acknowledged the rule of the Almohads, a dynasty originally from the Atlas mountains in the far west of Northern Africa. Abu ʿAmmar completed his studies under the Ibadi shaykhs of Warjalan before setting out for Tunis to concentrate on his studies. More specifically, however, he had come to the regional hub to surround himself with speakers of Arabic. Berber remained the spoken language of everyday life in southern Ifriqiya and the Sahara, meaning that Ibadi scholars like Abu ʿAmmar had to devote time, energy, and money to perfecting their knowledge of the language of learned circles: Arabic. While in Tunis, Abu ʿAmmar received annually a handsome sum of 1,000 dinars from his family. Half of this amount went to his teacher, while the other half he used to buy clothing, food, and (of course) books.[1]

This early stage in the life of Abu ʿAmmar, who went on to become one of the most famous Ibadi scholars of the Middle Period, typifies the changes to the Ibadi community and the prosopographical tradition from the mid-twelfth through the thirteenth centuries. Aspiring Ibadi scholars like Abu ʿAmmar required a command of Arabic and access to books. Moreover, the need for language skills and access to written materials was not unique to Ibadis. There were broader regional standards for Muslim scholarship, to which Ibadis began to conform in this period.

[1] Aḥmad ibn Saʿīd al-Darjīnī, *Kitāb ṭabaqāt al-mashāʾikh bi-ʾl-Maghrib*, ed. Ibrāhīm Ṭallay (Constantine: n.p., 1974), 486.

The work of Abu ʿAmmar himself served as the model for the next major work of Ibadi prosopography, the *Kitab al-tabaqat* of Abu al-ʿAbbas Ahmad b. Saʿid al-Darjini (d. mid-thirteenth century). The *Kitab al-tabaqat* exemplifies the changes in Ibadi scholarship and scholarly writing in this period. From the mid-twelfth to thirteenth centuries, both the Ibadi community and the written network took on a new, more institutionalized form. John Wilkinson dubbed this process "madhhabization," in reference to the process of Ibadis forming an identifiable Muslim community or school (*madhhab*) according to the standards of their Sunni contemporaries.[2] Perhaps more than any other genre of literature, the prosopographical tradition typifies this process for the Ibadi communities of the Maghrib.

In this chapter I use the *Kitab al-tabaqat* to show how this period witnessed a crucial move in the formalization of the Ibadi prosopographical tradition in several ways, including the written institutionalization of the *ʿazzaba* system, the structural arrangement of Ibadi scholars from the past into generations of fifty years (*tabaqat*), the linguistic triumph of Arabic in written scholarship, and a further move toward manuscripts as tools for the transmission of knowledge alongside their oral counterparts. Finally, these steps toward formalization mirror the changes in the political and religious landscapes of the Ibadi archipelago out of which the book emerged.

STRUCTURES, AIMS, AND THEMES OF THE *KITAB AL-TABAQAT*

"The *Kitab al-tabaqat*," wrote Polish historian Tadeusz Lewicki, "consists of two distinct parts of which the first is merely a reproduction of the *Kitab al-sira* ... of Abu Zakariyya Yahya b. Abi Bakr al-Wardjlani, or rather the first part of this chronicle."[3] The long-held assumption of historians that the first, "less interesting" half of the *Kitab al-tabaqat* amounts to little more than a revised version of the *Kitab al-sira* overlooks all of the important work that al-Darjini did to remake this text into his own.[4] Like the *Siyar al-Wisyani*, the *Kitab al-tabaqat* explicitly identifies Abu Zakariya al-Warjalani as the author of the *Kitab al-sira*. In his introduction, al-Darjini notes that he had been asked to present a revised version

2 Wilkinson, *Ibāḍism*, 413–37.
3 Tadeusz Lewicki, "al-Dardjīnī," *EI2*.
4 Tadeusz Lewicki, "Notice sur la chronique ibāḍite d'ad-Darjīnī," *Rocznik Orientalistyczny* 11 (1936): 146–72, at 154.

of the first part of the *Kitab al-sira*—but he made clear that he had no intention of reproducing this work verbatim:

> Someone whose request must be obeyed and whose interest cannot be ignored ... asked that I compile what was possible for me to gather of the biographies of our predecessors and their accounts and lay them down in an ordered composition (*tasnif*), preserving every account from the book of Abu Zakariya b. Abi Bakr—may God be pleased with him—summarizing and making selections from it ... I thus took to the revision (*tahdhib*) of the aforementioned book, adding to it whatever sermons and little-known poetry were necessary ... And I saw fit to present an introduction as a frame for the book.[5]

Al-Darjini made good on his promise. The *Tabaqat* may contain much of the text of the *Kitab al-sira*, but the work is the product of careful arrangement, augmentation, and transformation at al-Darjini's hand. To begin with, he notes in the introductory pages that he feels obliged to include what amounts to a dictionary of terms (*mustalahat*) associated with the *ʿazzaba* and the *halqa*. One by one, al-Darjini explains not only the meaning of each term but also the roles and functions of each member of the *ʿazzaba*. In doing so, the *Kitab al-tabaqat* formalizes the roles described in anecdotes and stories about the *ʿazzaba* in the *Siyar al-Wisyani*.[6]

The author himself noted that he adapted this section on the duties and characteristics of the *ʿazzaba* from an earlier, late twelfth-century text known as the *Siyar* attributed to the same Abu ʿAmmar ʿAbd al-Kafi who traveled to Tunis to surround himself with Arabic. This text served as the model for both al-Darjini's introduction on the *ʿazzaba* and the *tabaqat* structure of book.[7] Abu ʿAmmar's work described the ideal characteristics of the members of the *ʿazzaba* and gave a list of the earlier generations of Muslims in Mecca and Basra. The appearance of this text sometime in the twelfth century and its influence on the *Kitab al-tabaqat* in the thirteenth together point to the trend toward formalization of both the *ʿazzaba* system and of the method for presenting the history of the Ibadi tradition.

As al-Darjini moved through the text of the *Kitab al-sira* and other sources like the traditions found in the *Siyar al-Wisyani* for composing his own work, he made several remarkable changes to them. Among the more striking features of the *Kitab al-tabaqat* are the rearrangement and omission of as well as the addition of passages to the *Kitab al-sira* and

5 al-Darjīnī, *Kitāb al-ṭabaqāt*, 2–3.
6 "Dhikr alfāẓ mimmā aṣṬalaḥa ʿalayhā ahl al-Ṭarīq," in al-Darjīnī, *Kitāb al-ṭabaqāt*, 3–6.
7 al-Darjīnī, *Kitāb al-ṭabaqāt*, 6. For the printed edition of Abū ʿAmmār ʿAbd al-Kāfī's *Siyar*, see Abū ʿAmmār ʿ Abd al-Kāfī al-Tanāwatī, *Siyar Abī ʿ Ammār ʿAbd al-Kāfī*, ed. *Masʿūd Mazhūdī* (Oman: Maktabat al-Ḍamirī, 1996).

the absence of Berber-language passages that had appeared in the *Siyar al-Wisyani*. As for the first of these, al-Darjini composed the *Tabaqat* in a sophisticated register of Arabic, making heavy use of a style of continuous rhyming prose (*saj'*).[8] Additions, omissions, and changes to the text of the *Kitab al-sira* effectively produced a new work in a higher register of formal Arabic, including standardized sentence structures and rhetorical devices. The second remarkable feature of the *Tabaqat*, the absence of Berber-language passages, stems from the first. Al-Darjini strove to compose a work entirely in a formal register, showcasing his own command of the Arabic language.

Apart from toponyms and onomastic information, al-Darjini chose to replace all quotations from other traditions that had previously appeared in Berber with their Arabic equivalents. This deserves note especially since al-Darjini himself came from a long line of Berber-speaking scholars and poets, evinced by his comments on the meter of Berber poetry and the biographies of his father and grandfather.[9] Berber would have remained the language of instruction during his lifetime, however, especially for novices. For example, al-Darjini relates a story about one Abu Muhammad b. al-Amir attending a session in which an *'azzabi* was reciting the hadith traditions:

> Abu Muhammad said: One day, we were sitting and studying in [the town of] Ajlu. An *'azzabi* man was reciting the [hadith] traditions of al-Rabi' [b. Habib] … I would explain what the *'azzabi* said in the Berber tongue (*lisan al-barbariyya*). Whenever he would mention a chain [of transmission], I would pass over it and not mention it. Instead, I would leave it and communicate only the hadith or the tradition. When I spoke, Abu Zakariya [Yahya b. Wijman] heard us and said, "What's the matter with you? Why do you not mention the name of your Imams?" So I repeated all of what was recited [with the *isnads*].[10]

Al-Darjini's account emphasizes that hadith and the traditions were communicated in Arabic but needed to be translated into Berber (*al-barbariyya*) for the audience. Arabic had come to dominate the field of written scholarship, but Berber remained the spoken language of Ibadi communities in the late twelfth and thirteenth centuries.

Alongside the absence of Berber comes another striking difference between the *Kitab al-sira* in its earlier iteration and the version found in

[8] See remarks in Lewicki, "Notice sur la chronique ibāḍite d'ad-Darjīnī."

[9] Al-Darjīnī offers several biographies of his ancestors, many of whom are renowned for their Berber poetry: al-Darjīnī, *Kitāb al-ṭabaqāt*, 513–21.

[10] al-Darjīnī, *Kitāb al-ṭabaqāt*, 416.

the *Tabaqat*: the explicit citation and use of written sources. Beginning with the *Kitab al-sira*, al-Darjini makes reference to numerous Ibadi works. Throughout the second part of the work he also regularly introduces anecdotes and traditions with "Abu al-Rabiʿ mentioned (*dhakara Abu al-Rabiʿ*)," which al-Darjini himself clarifies refers to passages from the *Siyar al-Wisyani*.[11] At other times the name refers to Abu al-Rabiʿ Sulayman al-Mazati, who served as the main oral source for the *Kitab al-sira*. In addition to his prosopographical predecessors and the *Siyar* of Abu ʿAmmar ʿAbd al-Kafi, al-Darjini drew from many other written Ibadi works of the Maghrib and the eastern Ibadi community.[12]

Al-Darjini's recension of the *Kitab al-sira* also makes use of written sources by non-Ibadi authors. This distinguishes the *Tabaqat* from both of its predecessors, who drew mainly from local oral traditions and, in the case of the compilers of the *Siyar al-Wisyani*, a handful of written Ibadi texts. Al-Darjini explicitly interrupts his revision of the *Kitab al-sira* with a reference to the work of the eleventh-century Andalusi geographer al-Bakri (d. 1094), the *Kitab al-masalik wa-ʾl-mamalik*, in his description of the Rustamid capital of Tahart:

> Shaykh Abu al-ʿAbbas [al-Darjini] said: In the *Kitab al-masalik wa-ʾl-mamalik*, I came across a clearer and longer telling of the building of Tahart. I saw fit that I should place [the account] in this place. If [the account] erred, we corrected it based upon the [accounts of the Ibadi] shaykhs.[13]

Considering the geographical coverage of al-Bakri's work, which addresses the whole of Northern Africa and the Iberian Peninsula, it would also have provided al-Darjini access to numerous historical details on the history of the broader region.

His references to these Ibadi and non-Ibadi works as written and authored books suggest an increase in the circulation of manuscripts in Ibadi communities during the thirteenth century. Al-Darjini composed his work on Jerba, an important hub in the Ibadi intellectual network since the tenth century. The *Tabaqat* contains no indication as to where these sources were held, or any mention of personal or public book collections. Nevertheless, the number of sources he quoted in

[11] al-Darjīnī, *Kitāb al-ṭabaqāt*, 513.

[12] On al-Darjīnī's sources for the *Kitāb al-ṭabaqāt*, see full discussion in Alejandro García Sanjuán, "al-Darjīnī," in *EI3*.

[13] al-Darjīnī, *Kitāb al-ṭabaqāt*, 42–43. The corresponding passage in the printed edition to al-Bakrī's work is ʿAbdallāh b. ʿAbd al-ʿAzīz b. Muḥammad al-Bakrī, *al-Masālik wa-ʾl-mamālik*, vol. II (Beirut: Dār al-Kutub al-ʿIlmīyya, 2003), 248.

creating his recension of the *Kitab al-sira* points to the availability of a much larger number of manuscript works than in the two previous centuries.

In addition to locally available works, by the late twelfth century Ibadi scholars would have encountered manuscript collections as they traveled regularly to Tunis and other cities along the Northern African or in al-Andalus littoral to seek education and training. Already in the eleventh century, Abu ʿAbdallah Muhammad b. Bakr had traveled to Qayrawan to study. The story of Abu ʿAmmar ʿAbd al-Kafi with which the chapter opened illustrates that in the twelfth and thirteenth centuries, study in cities such as Tunis brought Ibadi scholars into contact with many Ibadi and non-Ibadi works in both written and oral form. The travels of Ibadi students like Abu ʿAmmar al-Tanawuti to study and to buy books reflect the increased reliance in the twelfth and thirteenth centuries upon written sources, both Ibadi and non-Ibadi.

FORMALIZING THE ROLE AND FUNCTIONS OF THE *ʿAZZABA*

Modern historians of Ibadi Islam have relied on al-Darjini as a kind of glossary for understanding the *ʿazzaba* system since its "foundation" under Abu ʿAbdallah Muhammad b. Bakr in the eleventh century. However, the *Tabaqat* does not describe this as it existed in the time of Abu ʿAbdallah. Instead, it speaks to the written formalization of this system in the thirteenth century when al-Darjini was writing. This does not mean, of course, that nothing like the *ʿazzaba* existed prior to the thirteenth century. The two previous chapters have noted multiple references to the *ʿazzaba* in the *Kitab al-sira* and the *Siyar al-Wisyani*. Rather, the systematic definition the *ʿazzaba* system as depicted in the *Kitab al-tabaqat* represents only one part of a broader trend toward the written formalization of various aspects of the Ibadi tradition in the late twelfth and thirteenth centuries.

The structure of the second part of the *Kitab al-tabaqat* communicates the formalization of the *ʿazzaba* and an expanded body of written materials from which scholars could draw. Much more than its prosopographical predecessors, this portion of the work fits neatly into the model of other *tabaqat* works in Arabic. More broadly, the *Tabaqat* conforms to what historians of Islam have called the "biographical dictionary," which specifically refers to a work divided into lists of individuals arranged chronologically into chunks of time such as fifty-year generations.[14] Al-Darjini's inspiration for this model, as he stated in his introduction, came from his predecessor Abu ʿAmmar ʿAbd al-Kafi. More generally, however, the choice of this structure by a thirteenth-century historian in the Maghrib suggests that he and other Ibadis had access to similar collections of biographies of scholars in the major cities of Ifriqiya, Egypt, and Syria.[15]

In choosing this *tabaqat* structure, al-Darjini continued the process of marking the boundaries of the Ibadi community in Northern Africa, carefully revising his predecessors' works and adapting them to fit a new model. His arrangement of scholars into fifty-year *tabaqat* provided the written prosopographical network begun in the eleventh century with a solid chronological framework. This structure reinforced links between individuals already present in the *Kitab al-sira* and the *Siyar al-Wisyani*—regardless of whether they interacted—by placing them alongside one another in time. What mattered now was not who someone knew and met, but rather his juxtaposition within the text alongside other Ibadis. Through its chronological and spatial arrangement, the *Tabaqat* formalized the shape of the written network of Ibadis in Northern Africa. At the same time, the choice of the *tabaqat* form for his book demonstrates how al-Darijini followed broader trends in Northern Africa and western Asia. As such, the *Tabaqat*'s form itself serves as a further step toward madhhabization.

INCLUSION AND EXCLUSION

Two remaining features of the *Tabaqat* also deserve attention in considering the structure of this written network and the context out of which it emerged. First of all, the paucity of information on the earliest generations of Ibadis in the east and the Maghrib is remarkable. Al-Darjini notes

[14] Most modern historians have drawn from the detailed study by Tunisian historian Farhat Djaabiri, whose description of the *ʿazzāba* blends the account of al-Darjīnī with early modern and contemporary (1970s) practices in the cities of the Mzab valley. See Djaabiri, *Niẓām al-ʿazzāba*, esp. 181–87.

[15] On studies of biographical collections from the early Islamic and Middle Periods see Bulliet, *The Patricians of Nishapur*; Petry, *The Civilian Elite of Cairo*; Chamberlain, *Knowledge and Social Practice in Medieval Damascus*; Cooperson, *Classical Arabic Biography*; Jacques, *Authority, Conflict, and the Transmission of Diversity*; Konrad Hirschler, *The Written Word in the Medieval Arabic Lands: A Social and Cultural History of Reading Practices* (Edinburgh: Edinburgh University Press, 2012).

that the lives and stories associated with the Prophet Muhammad, the Companions, and the Followers are so well known that he had little need to mention them:

> The first fifty [individuals] from the first one hundred whom I group together are the Companions of the Messenger of God—peace be upon him. Their virtue[,] … their names, and their merits are so famous that we need not list them.[16]

The fame of these early generations may very well have led al-Darjini to omit them. However, he did choose to include a handful of figures from the east adopted by the later Ibadi tradition in his first and second *tabaqat*. These biographies link the early generations of Ibadi scholars in the Maghrib to the eastern community, beginning a process that the later Ibadi prosopographical tradition would complete.

The second remaining feature of the *Tabaqat* is the way in which al-Darjini brought the work up to date by adding newer generations of scholars from the late twelfth and early thirteenth centuries. In discussing these more recent figures, al-Darjini often relies on contemporary oral sources. This is especially true of the history of his own family: his father, grandfather, and great-grandfather enjoy long entries in the *Tabaqat*.[17]

These final chapters also raise questions about what they leave out. The later biographies of the *Tabaqat* focus on the communities west of Jerba, to the exclusion of the scholars on the island and the nearby Jebel Nafusa. Tadeusz Lewicki, who observed this regional focus in the latter part of the *Tabaqat*, suggested that it represented al-Darjini's parochial interest and that these passages had only "local" importance.[18] Certainly, the inclusion of al-Darjini's relatives and fellow tribesmen from the Jarid, Warjalan, and southern Ifriqiya would have been intended to commemorate and to honor these individuals by placing them alongside earlier generations of Ibadi scholars. In al-Darjini's case, he did so with good reason because he came from a prominent scholarly family:

> Like many other Ibadi historians from North Africa, al-Darjini … hailed from a family of learning and wealth: his great-grandfather had been a merchant, his grandfather a jurist, and his father a traditionist.[19]

16 al-Darjīnī, *Kitāb al-ṭabaqāt*, 6.

17 This is especially the case for the eleventh *ṭabaqa*, covering 500–550 AH: al-Darjīnī, *Kitāb al-ṭabaqāt*, 457–523.

18 Lewicki, "al-Dardjīnī."

19 Robinson, *Islamic Historiography*, 162.

As Chase Robinson points out in this passage, al-Darjini's background makes him similar to many Muslim scholars in the Middle Period including the likes of Ibn al-Athir (d. 1233) or Ibn Hajar al-ʿAsqalani (d. 1449). Al-Darjini's background helps explain his conformity in both language and style with the predominantly Sunni genre of *tabaqat* literature. Yet his focus in the *Kitab al-tabaqat* on the western region also relates closely to important changes in the political and religious landscape of the region in the twelfth and thirteenth centuries.

By the mid-twelfth century the arrival of the Almohads, combined with an attack by an Italian confederation on the coastal city of Mahdiyya, had ousted the Normans from the coastal towns of Ifriqiya. Unlike the coast, however, the Zab region, the Jarid, Jerba, and Tripolitania remained regular thorns in the side of the Almohads as they attempted to establish control in Ifriqiya. The Ibadis were not, however, the main opponents to Almohad rule in southern Ifriqiya. Far more troubling to them were the Arabic-speaking tribes that had arrived in the eleventh century, many of whom were allied with the tenacious Banu Ghaniya.[20]

A remnant of the Almoravids, who had come to Northern Africa after having lost control of the Balearic Islands, the Banu Ghaniya moved about southern Ifriqiya fighting the Almohads throughout the late twelfth and early thirteenth centuries. The central and eastern Maghrib in this period comprised several petty principalities, as it would continue to do for the next century before the Hafsid successors to the Almohads succeeded in establishing some semblance of stability in the fourteenth century. Some local leaders allied themselves with the Banu Ghaniya against the Almohads, while others—like the Ibadis—suffered attacks by both them and their allies. Especially symbolic for Ibadis in the region was the final and complete destruction of the city of Sedrata in the mid-thirteenth century by the Banu Ghaniya and their Arab allies. Ibadis of the Jebel Nafusa also faced pressure from the east, where the Ayyubid dynasty of Egypt was increasingly interested in controlling the Libyan desert and Tripolitania. Pressed between these different competing forces, many Ibadi communities of the Zab, the Jarid, and Jebel Dummar took refuge in Jerba or moved farther into the Saharan to the oases of the Mzab valley.[21]

[20] This especially chaotic period of northeastern African history has been studied in detail by Amar S. Baadj, *Saladin, the Almohads and the Banū Ghāniya: The Contest for North Africa (12th and 13th Centuries)* (Leiden; Boston: Brill, 2015).

[21] The classic argument for the increasingly centralized Hafsid power in the fourteenth and especially fifteenth centuries goes back to the still unsurpassed study by Robert Brunschvig, *La Berbérie Orientale sous les Hafsides des origines à la fin du XVième siècle*,

A concomitant result of these multiple points of pressure was either the migration or the "Malikization" of many of Northern Africa's Ibadi communities. Many Ibadi tribes of the Zab region, previously an Ibadi stronghold, became Maliki Sunnis in the twelfth and thirteenth centuries. Al-Darjini himself described another potent force in Northern African history that impacted the Ibadis: the spread of Sufism in Ifriqiya. In one instance, he relates a story about the excitement surrounding the arrival of Sufi shaykh named Abu al-Qasim b. al-Amudi and his students to the town of Nafta, where he debates the Ibadi position toward ʿAli b. Abi Talib with al-Darjini's grandfather, ʿAli. This traveling Sufi shaykh was far from an anomaly. The twelfth and thirteenth centuries marked an especially important period for the history of Sufism in the Maghrib, and its popularity among the Ibadis' northern contemporaries gradually spread to the heartlands of Ibadi Northern Africa. These centuries witnessed the activity of perhaps the three best-known figures of western Sufism: Abu Madyan Shuʾayb (d. 1198), Ibn al-ʿArabi (d. 1240), and Abu al-Hasan al-Shadhili (d. 1258).[22]

As both the political and religious landscapes changed around them, those who remained Ibadi suffered marginalization as political and religious dissidents in the eyes of the Almohads and the Banu Ghaniya, as well as their Arab allies or enemies. In addition, the establishment of Arabic-speaking principalities throughout the region also meant that Berber-speaking Ibadis were gradually to become a linguistic minority. Faced with political, religious, and linguistic marginalization, the Ibadis of the central Maghrib in the twelfth and thirteenth centuries either became Sunnis or relocated to one of the increasingly smaller number of settlements in the Ibadi archipelago.

2 vols. (Paris: Maisonneuve, 1940). More recently, however, Ramzi Rouighi offered a critique of this understanding of the Hafsid era, suggesting that "emirates" correspond more to a historiographical category than a political reality: Ramzi Rouighi, *The Making of a Mediterranean Empire: Ifriqiya and Its Andalusis, 1200–1400* (Philadelphia: University of Pennsylvania Press, 2011).

[22] On the "Malikization" of the Zab region, see Allaoua Amara, "Entre le massif de l'Aurès et les oasis: apparition, évolution et disparition des communautés ibâḍites du Zāb (VIIIe–XIVe siècle)," *Revue des mondes musulmans et de la Méditerranée* 132 (2012): 115–35. See also al-Darjīnī's discussion of the Sufi shaykh in Touzeur: al-Darjīnī, *Kitāb al-ṭabaqāt*, 516. On these last three major figures of Maghribi Sufism, see Abū Madyan, *The Way of Abū Madyan: Doctrinal and Poetic Works of Abū Madyan Shuʿayb ibn al-Ḥusayn al-Anṣārī (c. 509/1115–16–594/1198)*, ed. V. Cornell (Cambridge: Islamic Texts Society, 1996); Alexander D. Knysh, *Ibn ʿArabi in the Later Islamic Tradition: The Making of a Polemical Image in Medieval Islam* (Albany: State University of New York Press, 1999); Mohamed Mackeen, "The Rise of al-Shādhilī (d. 656/1256)," *Journal of the American Oriental Society* 91 (1971): 479–80.

These factors help explain the regional focus of the later chapters of the *Kitab al-tabaqat*, but what about the absence of Jerba and the Jebel Nafusa? After all, al-Darjini wrote the work while on Jerba. Perhaps he chose not to include these regions because he knew of the efforts by one or more of his contemporaries to compose a work addressing the lives of recent generations of scholars in those places. For example, al-Darjini's contemporary Muqrin b. Muhammad al-Baghturi (d. early thirteenth century) was writing a prosopography of scholars from the Jebel Nafusa around the same time. This explanation remains unconvincing, since al-Darjini clearly drew from other written and oral sources of his near contemporaries. In addition, as a resident of Jerba he would have had plenty of potential sources for writing about the scholars of the island and the Jebel Nafusa.[23]

Political and religious events in the west could explain both the focus on a region where Ibadi communities were under threat of disappearance in the twelfth and thirteenth centuries and the absence of anecdotes from two of the areas that remained Ibadi strongholds in al-Darjini's lifetime: Jerba and the Jebel Nafusa. While the *Kitab al-tabaqat* may not explicitly express the fear of its predecessors that the Ibadis were facing the threat of extinction, it was responding to the actualization of those fears as Ibadi communities disappeared from southern Ifriqiya.

REFINING THE WRITTEN NETWORK

These different indications of a move toward the formalization of the Ibadi tradition likewise play out in the written network itself. I now turn to an analysis of the revised and augmented written network of the *Kitab al-tabaqat* to show what it can reveal about the author, his subjects, and the context in which he composed the book.

Just as the *Siyar al-Wisyani* built upon the written network of the *Kitab al-sira* by adding new scholars from the early twelfth century, so too the *Kitab al-tabaqat* expands the network to include scholars and personalities from the late twelfth and early thirteenth centuries. In addition, al-Darjini restructures the network into the defined chronological model of the *tabaqa*, an increment of fifty years. This had the effect of connecting scholars from similar periods—regardless of their geographic separation—who might previously not have been associated with one another. Such a structure allows for the visualization of two different forms of the same

[23] al-BaghṬūrī, *Siyar mashāyikh nafūsa*.

network. The first depicts instances of personal interaction similar to those in the previous two chapters. The second visualizes the network according to al-Darjini's chronological restructuring of it into fifty-year periods.

If the first volume of al-Darjini's work amounted to little more than a revised version of the *Kitab al-sira*, the network graph of both versions of that part of the text would look very similar. Upon comparison, however, the visualizations of the two texts show significant differences (Figure 4.1 and Figure 4.2).

The two network maps demonstrate some of the ways in which al-Darjini restructured the written network of the *Kitab al-sira*. The five scholars with the highest degrees remain large in al-Darjini's work. However, several other nodes also now appear larger. The explanation lies in al-Darjini's choice to limit the number of anecdotes found in the *Kitab al-sira*. That is, the first part of the *Kitab al-tabaqat* did not expand the written network, but rather simplified and contracted it by limiting the number of individuals in the network and omitting anecdotes from the entries of even prominent individuals. For example, the principal node in the *Kitab al-sira*, Abu ʿAbdallah Muhammad b. Bakr, went from a degree of 21 connections to 15 in the *Kitab al-tabaqat*. Table 4.1 and Table 4.2 summarize the contents of both maps.

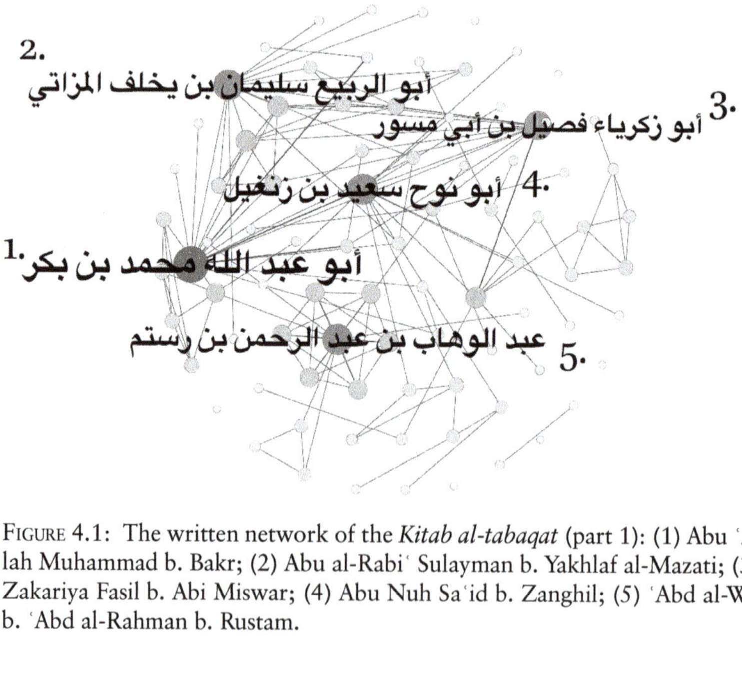

FIGURE 4.1: The written network of the *Kitab al-tabaqat* (part 1): (1) Abu ʿAbdallah Muhammad b. Bakr; (2) Abu al-Rabiʿ Sulayman b. Yakhlaf al-Mazati; (3) Abu Zakariya Fasil b. Abi Miswar; (4) Abu Nuh Saʿid b. Zanghil; (5) ʿAbd al-Wahhab b. ʿAbd al-Rahman b. Rustam.

Table 4.1 Network Summary of the *Kitab al-Sira*

Kitab al-sira **(part 1): network summary**	
Total number of nodes	94
Total number of edges	129
Degree range	1–21
Average degree	2.702
Average path length	4.854
Network diameter	11

Table 4.2 Network Summary of the *Kitab al-Tabaqat*

Kitab al-tabaqat **(part 1): network summary**	
Total number of nodes	87
Total number of edges	147
Degree range	1–15
Average degree	3.057
Average path length	3.239
Network diameter	7

Figure 4.2: Network map of the *Kitab al-sira* (part 1): (1) Abu ʿAbdallah Muhammad b. Bakr; (2) ʿAbd al-Wahhab b. ʿAbd al-Rahman b. Rustam; (3) Abu Nuh Saʿid b. Zanghil; (4) Abu al-Rabiʿ Sulayman b. Yakhlaf al-Mazati; (5) Abu Zakariya Fasil b. Abi Miswar.

While the total number of nodes decreased slightly in the *Kitab al-tabaqat*, the number of edges between those nodes increased from 129 to 147. By creating more edges among a smaller number of scholars, the

Kitab al-tabaqat brought the individuals in the written network closer together. In addition, the degree range decreased from 21 to 15, meaning that al-Darjini chose to omit some previous connections among scholars. These two features of the *Kitab al-tabaqat* also had the effect of decreasing the average path length (the average number of links separating two nodes) between any pair of individuals. While the average degree remained under two links, the path length decreased from 4.854 to 3.239. Between any two individual scholars in the written network, an average distance of around three people separates them. This is remarkable considering the chronological span (eighth–eleventh centuries) of this part of the text. Finally, these three features meant that the entire network diameter (the greatest path between any two nodes) decreased significantly from 11 to 7. Al-Darjini's addition of new edges but subtraction of nodes resulted in a tightly knit and clearly defined written network of scholars from the Rustamid period to the eleventh century.

The second part of the *Kitab al-tabaqat* lends itself to a different approach to the written network due to al-Darjini's decision to arrange the scholars of that network into chronological divisions of fifty years (*tabaqat*). Some of the scholars in this section appeared in the first part of the book, and in those instances al-Darjini chose simply to refer the reader to that earlier section. Al-Darjini includes only scant information on the first few centuries, and as a result only in the eleventh century does the number of scholars increase substantially. The distribution of scholars in this section appears in Figure 4.3.

The ninth and tenth *tabaqas*, corresponding to the mid-eleventh to mid-twelfth centuries, are far better represented in the *Kitab al-tabaqat*. These two or three generations of scholars lived in the period following the fall of the Rustamids and the beginnings of the development of the

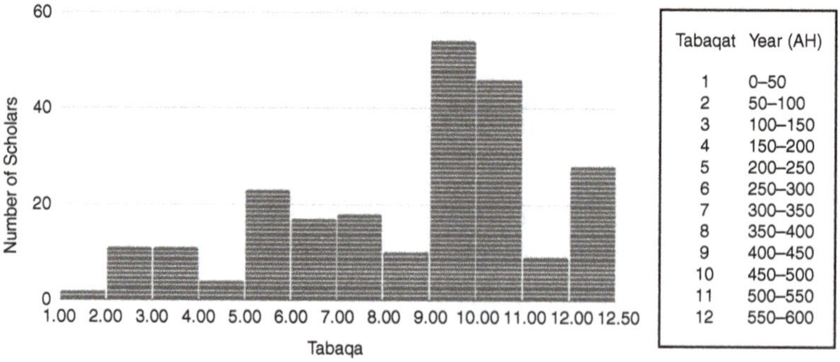

FIGURE 4.3: Temporal distribution of scholars in part 2 of the *Kitab al-tabaqat*.

ʿ*azzaba* system. This period corresponds to the genesis and growth of the Ibadi prosopographical tradition. The scholars of these generations, representing about 42 percent of the second part of the *Kitab al-tabaqat*, were the students of the generation of Abu ʿAbdallah Muhammad b. Bakr and his contemporaries (Figure 4.4).

The most prominent figures of these generations are in some ways the most surprising. After Abu ʿAbdallah Muhammad b. Bakr (no. 1), the scholar with the highest degree is Abu Muhammad Maksin b. al-Khayr (no. 2). He is a well-known figure in Ibadi *siyar* texts and among the most famous of Abu ʿAbdallah's students. Significantly, however, he left no written works behind, and appears mainly as a transmitter of traditions (*rawi*) in later sources. Abu al-Rabiʿ Sulayman al-Mazati (no. 3), who consistently appears as a well-connected node in all previous graphs, holds the second-highest degree. His importance stems not from his literary output but rather from his connections to the two generations of the mid-eleventh and mid-twelfth centuries and his role as the principal oral source for large portions of both the *Kitab al-sira* and the *Siyar*

FIGURE 4.4: Network map of the ninth and tenth *tabaqa*s (400–500 AH/eleventh and twelfth centuries CE): (1) Abu ʿAbdallah Muhammad b. Bakr; (2) Abu Muhammad Maksin b. al-Khayr; (3) Abu al-Rabiʿ Sulayman b. Yakhlaf al-Mazati; (4) Abu ʿImran Musa b. Zakariya al-Mazati al-Dimmari.

al-Wisyani.[24] Abu ʿImran Musa b. Zakariya al-Dummari (no. 4), although known as one of the authors of the *Diwan al-ʿazzaba* legal compendium, likewise left no other written work behind.

By striking contrast, the eleventh and twelfth *tabaqa*s (mid-twelfth–mid-thirteenth centuries) represent less than 16 percent of the sum of scholars in the *Kitab al-tabaqat* (Figure 4.5). Although some of the most famous authors of written works of *siyar*, theology, and law lived in this period, their representation and role in al-Darjini's work is marginal.[25] Indeed, the scholar with the highest degree in this part of the written network is not an otherwise famous Ibadi author but rather Yakhlaf b. Yakhlaf al-Tamijari (no. 1), al-Darjini's ancestor. By extension, al-Darjini himself (no. 2) also appears in the network. Abu Yaʿqub Yusuf b. Ibrahim

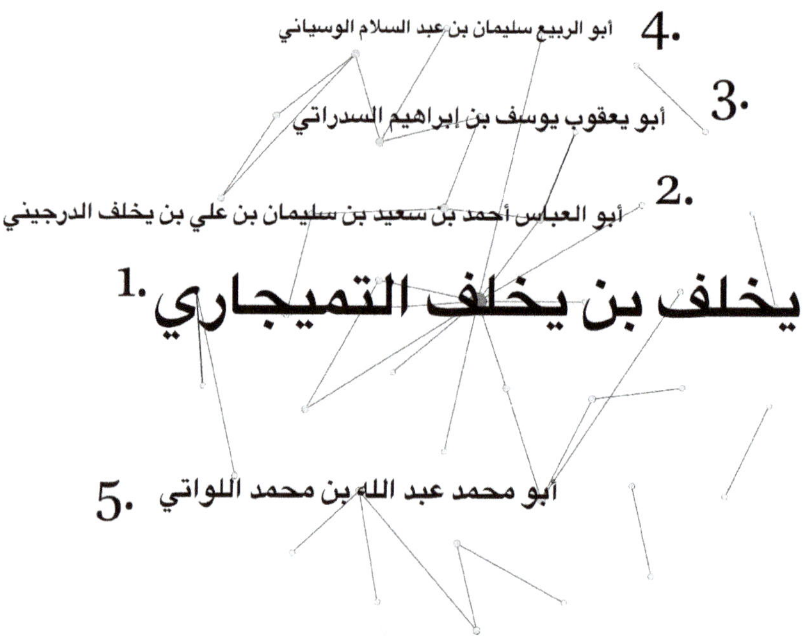

FIGURE 4.5: Network map of the eleventh and twelfth *tabaqa*s (mid-twelfth–thirteenth centuries) in the *Kitab al-tabaqat* (vol. 2): (1) Yakhlaf b. Yakhlaf al-Tamijari; (2) Abu al-ʿAbbas Ahmad b. Saʿid al-Darjini; (3) Abu Yaʿqub Yusuf b. Ibrahim al-Sadrati; (4) Abu al-Rabiʿ Sulayman b. ʿAbd al-Salam al-Wisyani; (5) Abu Muhammad ʿAbdallah b. Muhammad al-Lawwati.

[24] There are several works attributed to Abū al-Rabīʿ Sulaymān al-Mazātī, on which see Custers, *al-Ibāḍiyya* (2016), vol. II, 314–18.

[25] For example, see discussion of the foundational works of Ibadi creed and theology from this period in Cuperly, *Introduction à l'étude de l'ibāḍisme*, 47–167.

al-Sadrati [or al-Warjalani] (no. 3), despite his marginal role in the network, authored no fewer than twelve works, including two of the most influential and widely copied works of medieval Ibadi law in the Maghrib: the *Kitab al-ʿadl wa-ʾl-insaf* and the *Kitab al-dalil wa-ʾl-burhan*. In addition, he wrote a commentary on the Qur'an and compiled the *Musnad* of the eastern Ibadi Imam al-Rabiʿ b. Habib, the principal Ibadi collection of hadith traditions. Similarly, Abu al-Rabiʿ Sulayman al-Wisyani (no. 4) and his main source, Abu Muhammad al-Lawwati (no. 5), appear only on the fringes of this part of the network despite al-Darjini's heavy reliance on the *Siyar al-Wisyani* tradition attributed to those scholars. Already noted as one of al-Darjini's sources and author of the work that served as the model for the *Kitab al-tabaqat*, Abu ʿAmmar ʿAbd al-Kafi likewise appears as a minor node.

The marginal representation of the mid-twelfth and thirteenth centuries reflects the rapidly changing political and religious landscapes in the region. Indeed, the written network of the *Kitab al-tabaqat* depicts the numerical marginalization of Ibadi communities in the twelfth and thirteenth centuries as they found themselves caught in the middle of different political forces—the Almohads, the Banu Ghaniya, the Arabic-speaking tribes, and even the Ayyubids—vying for power in different regions. In part as result of this, both al-Darjini in Jerba and his contemporary al-Baghturi in the Jebel Nafusa produced works focused heavily on specific regions. The regional and temporal foci of the *Kitab al-tabaqat* reflect the fracturing of the Ibadi archipelago.

But if the lived reality of Ibadi communities was strained by changes to the political and religious landscape of Northern Africa in this period, the same cannot be said of the Ibadi written tradition into which the *Kitab al-tabaqat* situated itself. Indeed, it may be in part the fact that the twelfth and thirteenth centuries were a key period of Ibadi madhhabization that contributes to the marginal position of scholars in the written network this period. Rather than emphasizing either their own connections or those of their contemporaries, Ibadi authors such as al-Darjini and his predecessors had concerned themselves first and foremost with the formalization of the tradition. Al-Darjini's predecessor and inspiration for the *Kitab al-tabaqat*, the same Abu ʿAmmar ʿAbd al-Kafi with whom this chapter began, had similarly devoted himself to classification and commentaries. Abu ʿAmmar's contemporary Abu Yaʿqub Yusuf al-Sadrati did the same for Ibadi hadith in his *Kitab al-tartib* and Ibadi theological and legal traditions in his *Kitab al-dalil wa-ʾl-burhan*. As the Ibadi tradition crystalized (or "*madhab*-ized") in al-Darjini's lifetime, there was a steady shift toward formalization and classification that insured the long-term maintenance of Ibadi Islam in the Maghrib.

CONCLUSION

The composition of al-Darjini's *Kitab al-tabaqat* in the thirteenth century marked the formalization of the tradition of Ibadi prosopography begun in the eleventh century and continued in the twelfth. Whereas its two major predecessors, the *Kitab al-sira* and the *Siyar al-Wisyani*, represented the merging of separate collections of anecdotes and stories about Ibadi scholars from throughout the Maghrib, the *Kitab al-tabaqat* offered something at once new and familiar. While familiar in the sense that many of the same stories, characters, and anecdotes had appeared in the works of his predecessors, al-Darjini's book marked a departure from the previous tradition in that it formalized the chronology of the anecdotes, the language in which they were presented, and the structure of the community whose principal actors they described: the *ʿazzaba*.

Two important changes in the Ibadi landscape of the Maghrib account for composition of the *Kitab al-tabaqat*. The twelfth and thirteenth centuries witnessed growth in the production and circulation of manuscript books on paper. This translated to larger collections of written knowledge becoming available to scholars such as al-Darjini or other Ibadis who studied not only in Ibadi centers of learning but also in more cosmopolitan settings like Tunis. Al-Darjini's work reflects both the material and the ideological impact of this growth in book production in its reliance on written works by both Ibadi and non-Ibadi authors. In addition, this use of written works separates the *Kitab al-tabaqat* from its predecessors, and marks a decisive change in the history of Maghribi Ibadi communities.

The remarkable changes to the political and religious landscapes of the Maghrib during the twelfth and thirteenth centuries also laid the groundwork for the appearance of a work like the *Kitab al-tabaqat*, and they go a long way in explaining the regional foci of the book's second half. The final fall of Sedrata, the flight of Ibadi communities to the oases of the Sahara, and the growing impact of Sunni Islam (including Sufism) in the Zab and the Jarid all contributed to the numerical and geographical decline of Ibadis. If al-Darjini chose to write about scholars of these areas, he was likely attempting to preserve the memory of some of the greatest scholars of his recent past and to chronicle the history of Ibadi communities of those regions where Ibadism was well on its way to extinction by his own lifetime.

It is to the first of these transformations—the growing availability of paper and the development of an Ibadi manuscript culture—that I turn in the next chapter. I refocus attention on the importance of this precious commodity and companion of the Ibadi scholars who used it, because paper and book culture only increased in importance in the centuries after al-Darjini. As such, they demand attention and go a long way in explaining the changes to the Ibadi prosopographical tradition in the Middle Period and beyond.

5

Paper and People in Northern Africa

***

Abu Ishaq Ibrahim b. Yusuf al-Sadrati (d. 1203), son of the compiler of the primary collection of Ibadi hadith and author of some of the most important Ibadi texts of the Middle Period, was dedicated to book culture. Unlike his father, Abu Ishaq took more to making books than to writing them. For seven years he remained cloistered in his home. Whenever someone would come to visit him, al-Darjini's thirteenth-century account relates, "he would find [Abu Ishaq] either copying, studying, collating, fashioning reed pens, cooking ink, or binding a book. He did not turn away from this art for anything except to carry out a religious obligation."[1]

This story about Abu Ishaq merits attention because it is one of the few explicit descriptions of bookbinding and manuscript production in the Ibadi prosopographical tradition. But even if the production of books does not show up as a frequent theme in these texts, the previous chapters have demonstrated that each of the prosopographies takes for granted the presence and importance of paper and books in the Maghrib during the Middle Period. How did Ibadis obtain that paper? In which broader commercial networks did Ibadis operate that afforded them access to these materials? As a way of offering possible answers to those questions, this chapter surveys the history of paper and manuscript production in the world of medieval Northern Africa in which Ibadis lived. In the second half of the chapter I draw evidence from the manuscript copies of the Ibadi prosopographies to shed light on the place of Ibadis in the larger culture of paper in the central and eastern Maghrib from the early modern period up through the twentieth century.

[1] al-Darjīnī, *Kitāb al-ṭabaqāt*, 492.

PAPER IN MEDIEVAL NORTHERN AFRICA

The clear majority of extant manuscript copies of the Ibadi prosopographies were copied on supports dating to the sixteenth century or later.[2] Yet the compilers of these works and the scholars whose lives they describe were active between the eleventh and sixteenth centuries—and Ibadis in the Maghrib were no doubt writing things down long before the sixteenth century. This raises the question of how Ibadis might have obtained the paper on which to copy their texts in the period prior to the sixteenth century. The answer to this question lies in the much broader history of paper production and distribution in Northern Africa and the Mediterranean world.

In the period prior to the ninth and tenth centuries the chief writing materials in Northern Africa had been those made from either a plant native to the Nile Valley, papyrus, or a writing surface made from the skin of goats or sheep, parchment. In the eastern half of Northern Africa and in western Asia, especially in Egypt, papyrus had served for millennia as the writing surface of choice. Moreover, the climate of the Egyptian desert insured the long-term preservation of texts written on papyrus. The climate to the west of Egypt was generally less amenable to their preservation. More importantly, however, the Northern African littoral was home to many sheep and goats, which contributed to the widespread use of parchment as a writing surface even long after the introduction in the eighth century of its cheaper rival, paper.[3]

Knowledge of paper production, introduced from China to the eastern Islamic lands in the eighth century, spread rapidly from central into western Asia in the ninth and tenth centuries. Although it probably took a bit longer to reach the Maghrib, by the eleventh century the Zirid prince Ibn Badis (d. 1062)—a contemporary of Abu Zakariya al-Warjalani—had composed a treatise on the production of paper and the preparation of inks and related materials.[4] The most explicit reference to and evidence

[2] Based on my survey of 112 extant copies of the texts of prosopographical corpus, 97 of the manuscripts were on supports dating from the sixteenth century onward. The dating of these supports came from either paratextual evidence (e.g. colophons and ownership statements) or approximate dating based on watermark evidence.

[3] Jonathan Bloom, *Paper before Print: The History and Impact of Paper in the Islamic World* (New Haven: Yale University Press, 2001), 85.

[4] Abū al-Qāsim b. Bādīs, *Kitāb ʿumdat al-kuttāb wa-ʿuddat dhawī al-albāb* (Alexandria: Dār al-Wafāʾ li-Dunyā, 2013). A partial translation was published in Martin Levey, *Mediaeval Arabic Bookmaking, and Its Relation to Early Chemistry and Pharmacology* (Philadelphia: American Philosophical Society, 1962).

for the production and trade in paper in the eastern Maghrib comes from the extant manuscripts associated with the Jewish communities of the eastern Mediterranean, centered on the community in Fustat in Egypt. A large collection of manuscripts dating primarily to the Fatimid and Ayyubid eras (tenth–thirteenth centuries) were discovered in the Ben Ezra Synagogue in Cairo in the late nineteenth century. Known as the Cairo Genizah, these manuscripts have since their discovery illuminated the history not only of Mediterranean Jewish communities in this period but also the world of Mediterranean and Indian Ocean trade networks more broadly.[5]

References to paper and related materials in the Genizah were meticulously compiled by Shelomo Goitein, demonstrating the widespread trade in and distribution of paper and leather in the region. In the eleventh and twelfth centuries, for example, paper mills were found throughout Fustat and that type of paper, known as *talhi*, competed with the much finer quality Damascene paper known as *shikara*. Goitein noted that this type of paper was exported westward to Ifriqiya. But book-related materials also moved in the opposite direction. Other documents from the Genizah describe how leather book covers were pre-fabricated in the Maghrib for export eastward, due again to the large number of sheep and goats that helped fuel the leather industry throughout Northern Africa west of Egypt.[6]

By the twelfth and thirteenth centuries two other cities had joined Fustat as centers of paper production and trade in the Islamic west: Fez (in what is today Morocco) and Jatíva (in Spain). Well-known accounts of Fez in the thirteenth century suggest that the city was home to the surely exaggerated number of over four hundred paper-making shops. What Fez had that was sorely lacking in many other parts of Northern Africa—including southern Ifriqiya and the pre-Sahara where most Ibadis lived—was the most important natural resource to produce paper: water. Another city in the western Maghrib, Sabta, also appears to have had a

[5] Most famously, the multi-volume pioneering study of the Genizah documents by Shelomo D. Goitein, *A Mediterranean Society: The Jewish Communities of the Arab World as Portrayed in the Documents of the Cairo Geniza*, 6 vols. (Berkeley: University of California Press, 1967–93). On the history of the collection see Stefan Clive Reif and Shulamit Reif, eds., *The Cambridge Genizah Collections: Their Contents and Significance* (Cambridge: Cambridge University Press, 2002). An ever-growing bibliography of studies using documents from the Cairo Genizah is available online through the Taylor–Schechter Genizah Research Unit Cambridge University: www.lib.cam.ac.uk/collections/departments/taylor-schechter-genizah-research-unit.

[6] Goitein, *A Mediterranean Society*, vol. I: *Economic Foundations* (1999), 81 (Damascene and Egyptian paper), 112 (bindings).

booming trade in paper by the fourteenth century. As cities near the sea on both its northern and southern coasts, both Jatíva and Sabta connected the paper trade in the western Maghrib with markets and producers in the central and eastern Mediterranean. That none of the extant copies of Ibadi prosopographies were written on papers of identifiably northwestern Maghribi or Iberian origin may suggest that two different spheres of paper trading operated during the later Middle Period: one in the western Maghrib and Iberian Peninsula; and another encompassing the central and eastern Maghrib, including the Sahara.[7]

Many of the texts composed and compiled in the central and eastern Maghrib up to the fourteenth century would have been written on paper either produced farther to the west or, more likely, imported via port cities such as Tunis and Tripoli and urban centers from Egypt or farther afield from the east. Given the small number of extant copies of Ibadi prosopographies from prior to the sixteenth century, whether Ibadis were writing their texts on paper from the west or the east of their settlements throughout central and eastern Northern Africa must rely on inference rather than direct evidence until someone carries out more thorough research on manuscripts from this earlier period. But Ibadi scholars were writing plenty in the Middle Period, and it can hardly be a coincidence that the twelfth and thirteenth centuries—the beginning of a period of increasing availability of paper in Northern Africa—were those during which some of the most important works of Ibadi legal and religious literature were compiled. After all, in the anecdote mentioned at the opening of this chapter Abu Ishaq Ibrahim was busying away at his copying and binding in the Saharan city of Sedrata in the late twelfth century. Moreover, given their active participation in Saharan, Northern African, and Mediterranean trade since the eighth century, Ibadis would have been capable of obtaining paper from the same centers of production as their contemporaries elsewhere in the region, regardless of distance.

But by the late fourteenth century the centers of paper production in the Mediterranean were shifting. The development of improved papermaking techniques in the Italian Peninsula in the thirteenth and fourteenth centuries combined with the growing importance of Italian merchants from city-states such as Genoa, Venice, and Pisa led to the introduction

[7] Halima Ferhat, "Le livre instrument de savoir et objet de commerce dans le Maghreb médiéval," *Hespéris-Tamuda* 32 (1994): 53–62, esp. 53, 60; Leor Halevi, "Christian Impurity versus Economic Necessity: A Fifteenth-Century Fatwa on European Paper," *Speculum* 83, no. 4 (2008): 917–45, esp. 917–19 and references.

of Italian-made papers to Northern Africa. One Italian innovation from the thirteenth century altered not only the nature of the paper trade in the Mediterranean but also the ability of historians many centuries later to understand that trade: the watermark.[8]

Watermarks were the culmination of several important changes to the process of paper production. In both eastern and western Islamic lands during the early medieval period, wooden paper molds framed a grid pattern made of organic materials (such as fibers or horse hair). On inserting the mold into a large vat of pulp made from rags or similar materials, the pulp would cling to the frame. Once the water had drained, the resulting sheet of pulp remaining on the mold would be removed, pressed, and dried. The deterioration and flimsiness of these various organic components sometimes meant an uneven distribution of pulp or other materials, and the resulting quality of the paper was often thick and opaque. Italian producers exchanged the frame of organic materials for a grid pattern made of metal (first iron and then bronze), which proved much more durable. Likewise, marks in the shapes of letters, animals, or other objects specific to each paper maker could be fixed onto the metal grid, and these marks would appear clearly when the paper was held up in the light.

These "watermarks" associated with particular makers helped assure buyers of the quality of the product they were buying.[9] But as a famous legal opinion (*fatwa*) from the city of Tlimsan in the fifteenth century demonstrates, the watermarks carried by European paper could cause controversy when they included Christian symbols such as crosses or paschal lambs.[10] This helps explain why the leading merchants of paper in the Mediterranean, the Venetians, began selling a watermarked paper that became synonymous with Northern and Western African Islamic manuscripts: the *tre lune* or "three moons" (known as *waraq hilali* in Arabic) watermark from at least the fifteenth century onward.[11]

[8] Richard L. Hills, "Early Italian Papermaking: A Crucial Technical Revolution," in *Produzione e Commercio Della Carta e Del Libro Secc. XIII–XVIII*, ed. Simonetta Cavaciocchi (Florence: Le Monnier, 1992), 73–97. For a description of the utility of watermarks in providing dates for manuscripts, see Charles-Moïse Briquet, *De la valeur des filigranes du papier comme moyen de déterminer l'âge et la provenance de documents non datés* (Geneva: Impr. Romet, 1892); "Evidence for Dates of Marks," in Edward Heawood, *Watermarks Mainly of the 17th and 18th Centuries* (Hilversum: Paper Publications Society, 1950), 29–40.

[9] Hills, "Early Italian Papermaking," 88–91.

[10] Halevi, "Christian Impurity."

[11] On the *tre lune* watermark see Asparuch Velkov, *Les filigranes dans les documents ottomans: trois croissants* (Sofia: Éd. "Texte – Trayanov," 1983).

IBADIS AND PAPER IN THE LATE MEDIEVAL AND EARLY MODERN PERIODS

Watermarks are one of the clearest signs that papers produced on the northern shores of the Mediterranean (especially the Italian Peninsula) came to dominate the paper trade in Northern and Western Africa from the fifteenth century onward if not earlier. In addition to the fifteenth-century *fatwa* on European paper mentioned above, another well-known example is the fourteenth-century correspondence between the courts at Tunis and Aragon, written on paper bearing European watermarks.[12] Similarly, the watermarks carried by the earliest extant copies of the Ibadi prosopographies demonstrate the importance of Italian-made papers in Ibadi communities. In addition, these same manuscripts point to the growing importance of two sites of Ibadi intellectual activity from the sixteenth century onward: the valley of the Mzab and the city of Cairo (see Chapter 8). But while watermark evidence suggests a provenance for many of the extant copies of the Ibadi prosopographies from the sixteenth to the twentieth centuries, the question remains: how did these papers arrive in Ibadi communities on in Jerba, the mountains of Jebel Nafusa, or the oases of the Mzab valley?

The obvious answer is through trade with European merchants, although the details of when and where this trade took place are less apparent. Terence Walz has demonstrated that in the eighteenth and nineteenth centuries, Italian and to a lesser extent French merchants sold paper in Egypt, and that pilgrims would often purchase these papers on their way to or from Mecca on pilgrimage. Likewise, Walz shows how Saharan caravans then moved those Europeans papers across the great desert westward to the Bilad al-Sudan (the "Land of the Blacks"), which is to say towns and cities of the southern Sahara, the Sahel, and West Africa.[13]

Ibadi merchants and scholars in late medieval and early modern Northern Africa would have relied on a similar combination of urban commerce and caravan trading to obtain paper. Like their contemporaries,

[12] Oriol Valls i Subirà, *Paper and Watermarks in Catalonia* (Amsterdam: Paper Publication Society, 1970), 11–12.

[13] Walz also notes the ubiquity of this watermark in Western Sudanic and Egyptian manuscripts. He also notes that from the mid-eighteenth century French mills also began producing *tre lune* paper: Terence Walz, "The Paper Trade of Egypt and the Sudan in the Eighteenth and Nineteenth Centuries and Its Re-Export to the Bilād as-Sūdān," *Trans-Saharan Book Trade: Manuscript Culture, Arabic Literacy and Intellectual History in Muslim Africa*, ed. Graziano Krätli and Ghislaine Lydon (Leiden; Boston: Brill, 2011), 73–107, at 83.

Ibadis no doubt also purchased European papers from Egypt—especially after the seventeenth century, when Maghribi Ibadis operated a trading agency and school in Cairo (see Chapter 8). But even in earlier centuries Ibadis would have joined their Muslim coreligionists in the journey eastward to Mecca, passing through the Jebel Nafusa and crossing the Libyan coast to Alexandria. Alternatively, pilgrims could take sea passage along the coastal cities and towns of the Northern African littoral which connected, among other places, the Ibadi island of Jerba to the cities of Tripoli and Alexandria via coastal "cabotage" trade.[14] Regardless of how they arrived, Ibadis would have had multiple opportunities to engage in trade for European papers, whether directly with European merchants or local resellers in the coastal cities of Northern Africa and the Iberian Peninsula. For example, the itineraries of two Venetian merchant ships in the mid-fifteenth century include stops in Syracuse, Valencia, Majorca, Tripoli, Tunis, Bougie, Algiers, and Oran.[15]

The Ibadis in Jerba during the Middle Period could also have purchased paper directly from the Venetians, who since the fourteenth century had been regularly stopping at the island to trade for textiles.[16] But it was more likely through Jerba's neighbor some 300 kilometres to the east, Tripoli, that much of the European watermarked paper arrived in the Maghrib and made its way to places such as the Jebel Nafusa, Jerba, and southwest into the Mzab valley. European merchant and traveler accounts from the eighteenth and nineteenth centuries provide some of the clearest evidence that paper was among the goods being moved inland from Tripoli. Many of these accounts testify to the continuing importance of Cairo as a center for the trade in and distribution of paper throughout Northern Africa, as studied in detail by Walz. But he points out that in the seventeenth century a major shift took place in Saharan trade, with the ascendance of Tripoli in regional trade.[17] Trade between Tripoli and its regional neighbors both within and across the Sahara was connected to Ottoman attempts to maintain influence in Northern Africa and the

[14] Cabotage trade as a defining feature of Mediterranean history is a constant theme of Peregrine Horden and Nicholas Purcell, *The Corrupting Sea: A Study of Mediterranean History* (Oxford; Malden, MA: Blackwell, 2000). On pilgrims specifically, see pp. 445–46.

[15] Bernard Doumerc, *Venise et l'émirat hafside de Tunis (1231–1535)* (Paris; Montreal: L'Harmattan, 1999), 245, 249.

[16] Bernard Doumerc, "Les relations commerciales entre Djerba et la République de Venise à la fin du Moyen-Âge," in *Actes du Colloque sur l'histoire de Jerba* (Tunis: Institut national d'archéologie et d'art, 1982), 36–45.

[17] Walz, "The Paper Trade of Egypt and the Sudan," 98.

Sahara, a process that continued well into the nineteenth century when, as part of its broader set of political reforms, the Ottoman Empire competed with other European powers in their own "Scramble for Africa."[18]

Already from the seventeenth century, among the most important destinations for trade to and from Tripoli was the region of the Fezzan (in what is today southern Libya and northern Chad), where Ibadis had a long-established presence. At the end of the seventeenth century there was already a well-established trade route connecting Tripoli, Fezzan, Xao, and Bornu.[19] From Tripoli merchants carried coral, cloth, and "papier de Venise" to the Fezzan.[20] In the first decade of the eighteenth century the French consul to Libya, Claude Lemaire, noted relations between the Kingdom of Tripoli and the Sudan. The majority of goods, including paper, moving in and out of Tripoli, much to the consternation of the French observers, were of Italian provenance. When paper, especially the *tre lune* variety, is mentioned explicitly in nineteenth-century accounts, it is often connected to Venice. But the Venetians were not the only Italians producing or trading in *tre lune* paper; Genoese and Livornese papers bearing the mark were also traded in Tripoli and Benghazi, and from there to the "interior of Africa."[21]

As Walz notes in relation to Egypt and the Sudan, *tre lune* became a generic name for imported papers in Egypt, which, alongside the production of similar marks by a variety of Italian and French mills, make

[18] On the Ottoman and their early efforts to establish political and economic ties in the Sahara, see "Ottoman Libya, the Eastern Sahara, and the Central African Kingdoms," in Mostafa Minawi, *The Ottoman Scramble for Africa: Empire and Diplomacy in the Sahara and the Hijaz* (Stanford: Stanford University Press, 2016), 1–23. On nineteenth-century reforms in Ottoman African provinces see Lisa Anderson, "Nineteenth-Century Reform in Ottoman Libya," *International Journal of Middle East Studies* 16, no. 3 (1984): 325–48.

[19] Paul Masson, *Histoire des établissements et du commerce français dans l'Afrique barbaresque (1560–1793) (Algérie, Tunisie, Tripolitaine, Maroc)* (Paris: Hachette, 1903), 177–78. Walz, "The Paper Trade of Egypt and the Sudan," 98.

[20] "Des observations que le sieur Claude Lemaire, consul de France, au Royaume de Tripoly, a fait en voiagent le long de la coste de Derne et du golf de la Sidre, en 1705 et 1706, et sur diverces relations qu'il a eu du Soudan, qui signiffie pais de nègre," in Henri Auguste Omant, ed., *Missions archéologiques françaises en Orient aux XVIIe et XVIIIe siècles: documents publiés par H. Omont* (Paris: Imprimerie Nationale, 1902), 1037; for the reference to Venetian paper in the trade between Tripoli and Fezzan, see 1048.

[21] Jakob Gräberg di Hemsö, "Prospetto del commercio di Tripoli d'Affrica e della sue relazioni con quello dell' Italia. Articolo 1," in *Antologia* 27 (Florence: Gabinetto scientifico e letterario di G. P. Vieusseux, 1827), 90. According to Walz, Genoese and Tuscan *tre lune* papers were considered inferior in the Egyptian marketplace: Walz, "The Paper Trade of Egypt and the Sudan," 88.

identifying the provenance or date of a particular manuscript difficult. The periodization of alternating French and Italian dominance in the Cairene paper market likely does not apply to the areas within the commercial orbit of Ibadi communities west of Egypt. With Tripoli as the main port of entry for European papers into the eastern Maghrib and northern Sahara, Ibadis would most likely have been using Italian rather than French or other European papers from the seventeenth to nineteenth centuries.[22]

Alongside European narratives, extant manuscript copies of the Ibadi prosopographies themselves suggest European—and especially Italian—provenance for paper in the Mzab valley. Many of the papers upon which the *siyar* are written bear watermarks of European provenance. Although evidence for the period prior to 1600 still requires much more research, most extant copies of the prosopographies dating to before the seventeenth century carry Italian watermarks. The *tre lune* is among the most ubiquitous marks in manuscript copies of the *siyar* dating to the seventeenth to nineteenth centuries.[23] Even from the nineteenth all the way up to the start of the twentieth century, significant numbers of Ibadi manuscripts transcribed in the Mzab, Jerba, and Cairo carry Italian watermarks.[24]

The advent of manufactured, less-expensive machine-made paper at the beginning of the nineteenth century certainly impacted the trade in

[22] Although demonstrating the connection will require further research, another possible port of entry for papers used by Ibadis would have been the city of Tunis. While Italian merchants had been trading in Tunis for centuries, by this point the French would also have been supplying some of the paper, as they had been in Morocco since the seventeenth century. Specific mention of paper being traded in early eighteenth-century Tunis appears in accounts of Libyan caravans from Ghadames arriving in the city twice a year—and that paper would also have been Italian. See Masson, *Histoire des établissements*, 318, 320.

[23] In a survey of the 112 copies of the prosopographies, the *tre lune* mark appeared in 44 different papers.

[24] Examples from the prosopographical corpus include: BNT A-MSS-03606 [*tre lune* and "A.G.F. FABRIANO" watermarks, mid-nineteenth century]; Makt. al-Istiqāma, MS 35 (*al-khizāna al-ūlā*) [*tre lune* watermark, dated 24 Jumādā al-thāniya 1303/30 March 1886]; Makt. Irwān, MS 70 ["Three Crescents with Faces" watermark, nineteenth century]; Makt. al-Istiqāma, MS 67 (*al-khizāna al-ūlā*) [*tre lune* and bird with letters watermarks, dated 2 Rabīʿ al-thānī 1229/24 March 1814]. For additional examples, see "Ibāḍī Manuscript Production and Circulation from the Late Sixteenth to the Early Twentieth Centuries," in Paul M. Love, "Writing a Network, Constructing a Tradition: The Ibadi Prosopographical Corpus in Medieval Northern Africa (11th–16th C.)" (Ph.D. thesis, University of Michigan, 2016), 211–27.
Paul M. Love, "Ibāḍī Manuscripts in the Bibliothèque Nationale de Tunisie: Descriptions, Watermarks, and Implications," *Journal of Islamic Manuscripts* 7 (2016): 1–35.

paper in Northern Africa, and the Ibadi manuscript tradition reflects some of the changes that accompanied it. Extant Ibadi texts from the Mzab valley, Jerba, and the Jebel Nafusa were transcribed on machine-made paper. These manuscripts, dating from the mid-nineteenth century onward, overlap with the use of handmade, watermarked paper for several decades. This serves as a reminder that machine-made paper, like the printed book later, did not immediately transform the manuscript tradition in the Maghrib. Instead, a period of transition followed its introduction, in which machine-made papers slowly replaced handmade laid papers. Moreover, machine-made paper appeared first in France in the nineteenth century, during which time Northern African Ibadis were primarily using Italian-made paper. The advent of French colonialism in the late nineteenth century would doubtless have introduced Ibadis in Algeria and Tunisia to machine-made paper of French origin.[25]

Even inexpensive graph or ruled papers carried Ibadi texts well into the twentieth century. For example, the latest (dated) manuscript copy of the Ibadi prosopographies is a copy of the *Siyar al-Wisyani* transcribed in June 1973 on ruled notebook paper.[26] These less-expensive alternatives did not immediately replace hand-made Italian papers, however, as the latter continued to be used for Ibadi manuscripts into the first decades of the twentieth century.[27]

[25] On the changes in materials and technology used to make paper, see Dard Hunter, *Papermaking: The History and Technique of an Ancient Craft* (New York: Dover Publications, 1943), 374–99. Machine-made paper had the advantage of being cheaper and faster to produce. Even machine-made paper could and often did carry watermarks, however (on which see Hunter, *Papermaking*, 400–27). These included embossed marks, like that found on a copy of al-Barrādī's *Kitāb al-jawāhir* (a "BATH" watermark written under a crown) (e.g. f.85 of Makt. Irwān, MS 80, early to mid-nineteenth century). A copy of a book entitled *Sharḥ ʿalā al-urjūza fī l-tawḥīd* by Qāsim b. Sulaymān al-Shammākhī (d. thirteenth/nineteenth century) in the Bibliothèque nationale de Tunisie bears the same mark. On this manuscript and watermark see Love, "Ibāḍī Manuscripts in the Bibliothèque Nationale de Tunisie," 23–25.

[26] Makt. Irwān, MS *ṣād* 23, "Siyar mashāyikh al-maghrib," dated June 1973; in the same library and also on notebook paper, MS *mīm ṣāḍ* 10, a copy of the *Kitāb al-sīra*, carries the date 11 Dhū al-qaʿda 1374/15 March 1965; a copy of the *Siyar al-Baghṭūrī* was also transcribed in 1974 by Maḥmūd b. Sālim b. Yaʿqūb (d. 2009): al-Baghṭūrī, *Siyar mashāyikh nafūsa*, 18–19. This particular manuscript is interesting not only for its late date but also because it does not appear from the digital facsimile to be copied on notebook paper.

[27] For example, a handsomely bound copy of the *Siyar al-Wisyānī* written on paper bearing a "three moons with faces" watermark was transcribed in 1924: Makt. Āl Yaddar, MS 45, "Siyar al-mashāyikh." Another manuscript, a copy of the *Kitāb al-sīra* dated 10 Ṣafar 1345/19 August 1926, carries a European watermark of unidentified origin: Ivan Franko National University of Lviv, MS 1054 II, "Kitāb al-sīra wa-akhbār al-aʾimma," e.g. f.154.

CONCLUSION

This brief survey of the distribution of paper among Ibadis in the Maghrib suggests that Ibadi written scholarly culture operated within a much larger world of Mediterranean and Saharan trade in paper from the medieval period onward. Even the earliest manuscript examples of the Ibadi prosopographies indicate the key importance of Italian papers in the central and eastern Maghrib, to the exclusion of what was probably a separate commercial circuit of paper in the far northwestern corner of the continent. Mirroring the rise to dominance of European papers in the late medieval period, through trade with distribution centers such as Tripoli and Cairo, Ibadi communities in Jerba and the Jebel Nafusa had regular access to Italian and other European papers from the fifteenth century forward.

Watermark evidence and European traveler and merchant accounts suggest that the next few centuries saw the persistent ubiquity of Italian papers from the towns of the Mzab to the city of Cairo, acquired through a variety of distribution networks linking the port cities of the Maghrib, especially Tripoli. Italian papers appear as the dominant source of the paper trade in extant copies of the Ibadi prosopographies. This remained the case all the way up into the first decades of the twentieth century, when handmade Italian papers (probably produced at the end of the nineteenth century) were used for books like those bound with fine leather covers in the Mzab valley. But paper and manuscript culture persisted well into the first half of the twentieth century, although lower-quality machine-made and mass-produced papers of either European (primarily French) or (in Egypt) local origin gradually replaced the Italian products.

What emerges from this cursory look at history of the paper trade in the central and eastern Maghrib is a long-term centrality of paper as both a regional commodity and a tool of production and communication for Ibadi intellectual culture. Moreover, it demonstrates that Ibadi scholars belonged to a much larger culture of paper and manuscripts in the Mediterranean and Sahara. I will return later (Chapter 9) to theme of Ibadi manuscript culture in later centuries to explore how Ibadis used this paper to help maintain the written network.

In the next chapter, however, I return to the prosopographical tradition as it existed in the fourteenth century, by which time paper had already become a ubiquitous commodity in northern Africa. This increased availability of paper would translate to the ability of Ibadi scholars to access books by both eastern Ibadis and non-Ibadi Muslims. Just as Ibadis participated in the broader Mediterranean and Saharan trade in paper, so too would they come into conversation with the larger world of other Muslim communities in Northern African and western Asia.

6

Retroactive Networking

***

Born in the Jebel Dummar in the mid-fourteenth century, Abu al-Qasim al-Barradi trained with some of the most renowned scholars of his day in both Jerba and the Jebel Nafusa. Theologian and jurist, bibliophile and traveler, he left behind epistles, commentaries, and legal opinions on a wide variety of subjects. His life, career, and writings are emblematic of the culmination of the Ibadi prosopographical tradition and typify the final steps in the formalization of the Ibadi *madhhab* in late fourteenth-century Northern Africa.

Although al-Barradi's own contribution to the Ibadi prosopographical corpus, the *Kitab al-jawahir*, follows in the tradition of prosopography, it also employs a very different approach to achieving that tradition's aims. Unlike its predecessors, the *Kitab al-jawahir* does not offer a collective history of the Ibadis in Northern Africa comprising anecdotes and stories about its scholars and pious exemplars. Instead, al-Barradi sought to universalize the history of the Ibadi community, establishing Ibadi intellectual and religious history as *the* narrative history of Islam and linking the earliest generations of Muslims in the east to the Maghribi Ibadi communities of later centuries. In order to do so, the *Kitab al-jawahir* starts at the period of Islamic history that al-Darjini so carefully avoided: the beginning.

The *Kitab al-jawahir* highlights two important features of the Ibadi prosopographical tradition in the fourteenth century. The first regards the way in which the tradition aimed to construct a "retroactive" component to the written network in which Maghribi Ibadis joined *ex post facto* a long tradition of Islamic learning stretching back to the Prophet Muhammad and leading up to the Rustamids. This retroactive network established the early Islamic credentials of the Ibadi communities in the

Maghrib, connecting them to a much broader history of Islam in the face of the changing religious landscape of the region in the fourteenth century.

The second feature of the prosopographical tradition in this period grew out of the first. In order to situate Ibadis in the much broader tradition of Islam, al-Barradi required many more written works than had been the case for any of his predecessors. Rather than bringing the work up to date by discussing the scholars of the late thirteenth and fourteenth centuries, the manuscript tradition of the *Kitab al-jawahir* followed the account of the Rustamid era with a list of Ibadi books extant in the fourteenth century. The widespread circulation of paper in the region discussed in the previous chapter meant that there were more books around to read, and more materials to make them. Al-Barradi's book list, in a much longer version, also circulated independently of the *Kitab al-jawahir*. The list's inclusion as a part of the *Kitab al-jawahir* speaks to the ever-increasing importance of written works to the Ibadi tradition and provides a glimpse into the manuscript libraries of the fourteenth century—including evidence for the circulation of eastern Ibadi works in the Maghrib. The *Kitab al-jawahir* marks a culmination of the gradual process of expanding the written network of the Ibadi tradition in the Maghrib, connecting it to the east through both narrative and material means.

PURPOSE AND AIMS OF THE *KITAB AL-JAWAHIR*

Al-Barradi wastes little time on introductions. Following in the prosopographical tradition, he opens his work by noting what he has seen of his predecessors' works and how that provided the impetus for his own:

> I found that the *Kitab al-tabaqat* went astray from its requestor and its objective, like a sweet watering hole that lacks both animals and water. But since it contains many strange accounts and wondrous virtues of the most upright and pious predecessors, it has become like the centerpiece of a necklace and more trusted than distinguished sermons ... I occupied myself with it since I learned of its existence but I did not find [a manuscript of it] save a copy that makes the eye sore and makes the heart come into error and fog. This [continued] until God provided [me with] another copy [that was] a bit clearer than the first. So I flipped through its pages and breathed in its odors and found it as people speak of it, containing what souls desire and eyes delight in, except that he neglected to mention the first generation [of Muslims] and failed to mention what was reliable. Instead, he included many obscure things and left out particulars entirely. He clung to tradents, relating from

those who were distant from him and claiming that their renown made it possible to dispense with evidence [for the veracity of their accounts].[1]

This introductory passage lays out in full how and why al-Barradi had taken a good look at the work of al-Darjini and found it sorely lacking. Indeed, the full title of the book, *The Book of Choice Pearls in Completing What the Kitab al-tabaqat Neglected* (*Kitab al-jawahir al-muntaqat fi itmam ma akhalla bihi Kitab al-tabaqat*), expresses that exact sentiment. Especially egregious in al-Barradi's eyes had been al-Darjini's failure to include the lives of the Prophet Muhammad and his Companions. As al-Darjini's critic, but also as a loyal coreligionist, al-Barradi suggests that the historical context in which the former wrote the *Kitab al-tabaqat* helps excuse this oversight:

Through the eye of discernment, a certain thing became clear to me about Shaykh Abu al-ʿAbbas Ahmad b. Saʿid—may God be pleased with him—that excused him [from his exclusion of the first generation of Muslims]. My faculties aided me regarding some of his [al-Darjini's] circumstances until his secret became clear to me: that he was amid the dissenters, [who were] spiteful and critical, and his wariness of the evil of the envious and united contemporaries. For this reason, he neglected—and God knows best—to mention the discord [of the community] and he passed over those tribulations.

So then, al-Darjini had been living amid a powerful group of dissenters (*mukhalifin*), who prevented him from writing freely about the earliest generations. Al-Barradi does not specify whether he means Nukkaris or non-Ibadis, but in any case he makes it clear here that he believed that circumstances had prevented al-Darjini from writing about the Prophet and the early history of Islam.[2]

After explaining what al-Darjini did not write, al-Barradi turns to the story of why his predecessor wrote the *Kitab al-tabaqat*. A visitor had come to Jerba from Oman and brought with him a request from the Ibadis back home to compile a book containing the accounts of the pious Ibadi forbears of the Maghrib:

One of the *ʿazzaba* told me the reason for Abu al-ʿAbbas' composition of this book. When al-Hajj ʿAysa b. Zakariya arrived in the Maghrib from Oman with the books he had brought ... among the things his brothers [in Oman] told him they desired of him was that he [say], "Compile for us a book containing the accounts of our earliest predecessors and the virtues of our pious forbearers among the

[1] Abū al-Qāsim b. Ibrāhīm al-Barrādī, *al-Jawāhir al-muntaqāt fī itmām mā akhalla bihi Kitāb al-ṭabaqāt* (Cairo: al-Maṭbaʿa al-Bārūniyya, 1884), 3.

[2] al-Barrādī, *al-Jawāhir*, 3–4.

people of the Maghrib." ... And so the *'azzaba* and jurists of Jerba of that time deliberated ... and they initially thought of the book of Shaykh Abu Zakariya Yahya b. Abi Bakr [al-Warjalani] but found it missing some detail and falling short of the full extent of learning, together with the terms of the Berber tongue [that] appeared in troubling places and the insufficiency of his attention to the rules of Arabic, with solecisms having entered into his expressions. So they decided to commission the writing of a book that would include the stories of the Rustamid [Imamate] and the virtues of the pious forebears as had been requested of them. They saw no person [better] for this composition that Abu al-'Abbas.

Al-Barradi thus explains that it had been the *'azzaba* who requested the book. The passage is interesting because it demonstrates the historical importance of the *Kitab al-sira* up to al-Darjini's lifetime. Moreover, it is telling that the *'azzaba* deemed the book problematic because of the terms in Berber that "appeared in troubling places and the insufficiency of his attention to the rules of Arabic." So the *'azzaba* decided to commission a new book and saw no person better for the task than Abu al-'Abbas al-Darjini. "God knows," added al-Barradi, "if the book made it to Oman or not!"[3]

This story suggests a provenance for Ibadi books from the east in the Maghrib, some of which al-Darjini himself had used in writing his work. Oddly, the account also states quite clearly why the author of the *Kitab al-tabaqat* did not go back further than the Rustamids in any detail: that was not what he was commissioned to do. In any case, al-Barradi remained dissatisfied, and set out to fill in the gap left by the *Kitab al-tabaqat*. While the title of the *Kitab al-jawahir* suggests that it is a complement to its predecessor, the work departs significantly from all previous works of Ibadi prosopography. Rather than attempting to present the lives of the earliest generations of Muslims in anecdotes or individual biographies organized by chronology, geographic region, or *tabaqat*, the *Kitab al-jawahir* offers what by the fourteenth century had become a standard history of early Islam—with the uniquely Maghribi Ibadi feature of having this history culminate in the Rustamid dynasty of the eighth century.

In addition to completing it, al-Barradi's work also aimed at critiquing the *Kitab al-tabaqat* and subjecting it to thorough analysis. In his study of the *Kitab al-jawahir*, Roberto Rubinacci points to what al-Barradi saw as the four basic problems of the *Kitab al-tabaqat*: (1) al-Darjini neglected to mention the accounts of the earliest generations of Muslims; (2) he left gaps in the accounts that he did provide; (3) generalizations and lack of detail; (4) reliance upon questionable sources. In other words, al-Barradi criticizes al-Darjini for not having written an entirely different kind of

[3] al-Barrādī, *al-Jawāhir*, 13.

book. The later writer, looking back on his coreligionist of the thirteenth century, was unable to understand why al-Darjini had not composed a history of Islam that would conform to the standards and serve the interests of Ibadi communities in the fourteenth century. The use of unreliable or questionable traditions and sources, the lack of detail, and similar critiques that he offered came from al-Barradi's background as a jurist and theologian. Nowhere in the work is this more apparent than in the first few pages, where al-Barradi quotes the opening passages of al-Darjini's work phrase by phrase, offering a commentary of word choices and Qur'anic quotations. Indeed, these opening paragraphs, along with the third and final section of the work, which offers a theological discussion of death, exemplifies al-Barradi's background as a theologian.[4]

THE *KITAB AL-JAWAHIR* AND THE MAGHRIB OF THE FOURTEENTH CENTURY

Al-Barradi wrote his book in a time of great transformation in the Maghrib. By the time he composed the *Kitab al-jawahir* in the fourteenth century, the Ibadi communities of Ifriqiya lived in a religious and political landscape that was much different from that in al-Darjini's lifetime. The author of the *Kitab al-tabaqat* had already noted the destruction of Sedrata, the growing expansion of Sunni Islam in the traditional Ibadi centers in the Jarid and the Jebel Dummar, and attacks on the communities that still remained in those areas. Al-Barradi's Maghrib had changed. By the fourteenth century the Almohads had fractured into numerous different principalities, and Ibadis had already lost their traditional strongholds in Ifriqiya. Much of southern Ifriqiya had embraced both Arabic and Sunnism in one form or another, thanks in part to the Banu Ghaniya and Arabic-speaking tribes having taken control of the region, as well as the spread of Sufism.[5]

[4] On al-Barrādī's critique of the *Kitāb al-ṭabaqāt*, see Rubinacci, "Il 'Kitāb al-Jawāhir' di al-Barrādī," esp. 98. For the corresponding pages in the lithograph edition of the *Kitāb al-jawāhir*, on the topic of death, see al-Barrādī, *al-Jawāhir*, 221–39. Al-Barrādī's written legacy, especially in theological and juridical opinions, is considerable: Custers, *al-Ibāḍiyya* (2016), vol. II, 72–77.

[5] On the transition to the Hafsid era in Ifriqiya, see Maribel Fierro, "The Almohads and the Ḥafṣids," in *The New Cambridge History of Islam, vol. II: The Western Islamic World: Eleventh to Eighteenth Centuries*, ed. Maribel Fierro (Cambridge: Cambridge University Press, 2010), 66–105. See also the detailed account in "The End of the Banū Ghāniya and the Transition to Hafsid Rule in Ifrīqiyā," in Baadj, *Saladin, the Almohads and the Banū Ghāniya*, 167–73.

Meanwhile, Ibadis were driven further into the geographic pockets of the Ibadi archipelago, now concentrated in Jerba and the Jebel Nafusa, with smaller communities scattered in the Sahara. Throughout the late thirteenth century the old strongholds of Ibadism in the Zab and Jarid had been theaters in the struggle for power between the late Almohad and early Hafsid leaders, remnants of the Banu Ghaniya, and the various Arabic- and Berber-speaking tribes with whom these two allied or fought. After a failed attempt to conquer the island of Jerba by the (later) Hafsid emir Ibn al-Lihyani (r. 1311–17), the island did eventually come under Hafsid control. Either at the end of al-Barradi's lifetime or shortly thereafter, even the island of Jerba would see efforts by the Hafsid prince Abu Faris to suppress Ibadi Islam on the island and convert its inhabitants to Sunni Islam.[6] This slow but steady process continued well into the early modern period as Ibadis gradually became a minority there. It deserves note that the first non-Ibadi book referenced in the *Kitab al-jawahir* was by the Sunni theologian and philosopher Abu Hamid Muhammad al-Ghazali (d. 1111). Strikingly symbolic of these new Sunni incursians, the Hafsid period also witnessed the reconstruction of a Roman-era bridge connecting Jerba to the mainland.[7]

In addition to the spread of Sunni Islam in southern Ifriqiya and the political dominance of different kinds of non-Ibadi powers throughout the region, Ibadis faced strong competition from the influence of Sufism in the region. Indeed, Maliki Sunnism and Sufism had long operated as complementary forces in the Maghrib farther to the west.[8] Asceticism, mystical practices, and saint veneration had long enjoyed popularity in the Maghrib, and some likely predated Islam itself. But the late thirteenth and fourteenth centuries brought even more momentum to the popularity of Sufism. Like the Ibadi tradition, Sufi communities of the Maghrib had grown increasingly formalized. The appearance of key Sufi figures such as Ibn al-ʿArabi and Abu al-Hasan al-Shadhili in this period (and, more importantly, their legacy in the form of followers during al-Barradi's lifetime) helped catapult the popularity of Sufism in town and country. The

6 An account was given in al-Tijānī's (d. fourteenth century) *Riḥla*: Abū Muḥammad ʿAbdallāh b. Muḥammad b. Aḥmad al-Tijānī, *Riḥlat al-Tijānī* (Tunis: al-Dār al-ʿArabiyya li-ʾl-Kitāb, 1981), beginning on p. 121; On further attempts to convert the island's inhabitants at the end of al-Barrādī's lifetime, see Brunschvig, *La Berbérie Orientale*, 215.

7 For the *Iḥyā ʿulūm al-dīn* passage, see al-Barrādī, *al-Jawāhir*, 9. On the bridge linking Jerba to the mainland, see Virginie Prevost, "La chaussée d'al-Qanṭara, pont entre Djerba et le continent," *Lettres Orientales* 11 (2006): 165–88.

8 Vincent J. Cornell, *Realm of the Saint: Power and Authority in Moroccan Sufism* (Austin: University of Texas Press, 1998).

formalization of Sufi brotherhoods (*tariqas*) and their patronage by Sunni rulers such as the Marinids and the Hafsids in the fourteenth century helped insure the success and continued spread of their activities.[9]

The increasing marginalization of Ibadi communities in Ifriqiya and the necessity of engaging with Maliki Sunni and Sufi communities—even in the traditional stronghold of Jerba where al-Barradi wrote and taught—called for a history of the Ibadi tradition that could meet these challenges and legitimize their place in the broader Muslim community. The *Kitab al-tabaqat*, whose author had failed to offer such a narrative and had drawn from local traditions of (in al-Barradi's eyes) doubtful authenticity, simply would not suffice. Circumstances demanded that a new work be written, one that would legitimize the historical narrative of the Ibadi community by connecting it to the very beginning of Islam itself and following through to the establishment of Ibadis in Northern Africa.

MAKING IBADI HISTORY ISLAMIC HISTORY

By the fourteenth century the corpus of written Ibadi works had grown significantly. The previous two centuries had witnessed the composition of some of the most important works of theology, law, and even the establishment of a written Ibadi hadith tradition in the Maghrib in the form of Abu Yaʿqub Yusuf al-Sadrati's *Kitab al-tartib*. These ever-larger corpora of written sources furnished al-Barradi with the authority he needed to build his history of Islam. To a far greater extent than any of his predecessors, al-Barradi makes explicit reference to many written sources, both Ibadi and non-Ibadi. Significantly, he quotes both Northern African and Omani Ibadi sources, meaning that he had access to both.

Al-Barradi was more than aware of the various non-Ibadi written accounts of the key moments in the early history of Islam like the murder of Caliph ʿUthman and the Battle of Siffin. When drawing comparisons with these (often unnamed) non-Ibadi traditions, he also chose to tell his reader that he acquired the information from "the books of the people

[9] See "The Rise of the *Ṭarīqas*," in Alexander D. Knysh, *Islamic Mysticism: A Short History*. (Leiden: Brill, 2010), 172–79. Many practices normally thought of as characteristic of Sufism, such as saint veneration and pilgrimage to holy sites associated with them, are just as common in Ibadi communities as elsewhere in the Maghrib. For example, see Fatma Oussedik, "The Rise of the Baba Merzug: Diaspora, Ibadism, and Social Status in the Valley of the Mzab," in *Saharan Frontiers: Space and Mobility in Northwest Africa*, ed. James McDougall and Judith Scheele (Bloomington: Indiana University Press, 2012), 93–108; Aillet and Gilotte, "Sedrata: l'élaboration d'un lieu de mémoire."

of dissidence." Viewed as part of the prosopographical tradition into which al-Barradi explicitly placed it, the *Kitab al-jawahir* sought to do much more than present an Ibadi take on early Islamic history. The *Kitab al-jawahir* belongs to a widespread trend in medieval Islamic literature, in which chains of transmission or authority stretching back to earliest Muslims lent legitimacy to a different community. From jurists to hadith transmitters, Sufi shaykhs to Shiʿi Imams, pre-modern Muslim scholars followed remarkably similar strategies for authenticating their roots and legitimizing their communities.

At the same time, al-Barradi sought to do more than establish a chain of authority stretching back in time to the Prophet Muhammad. His work presents the establishment of the Ibadi community in Northern Africa as the culmination of the history of Islam. It is no coincidence that the narrative begins with the life of the Prophet Muhammad and ends with stories about the Rustamid Imams in Tahart. His prosopographical forebears had each augmented and maintained the written network of scholars and pious individuals in Northern Africa, slowly expanding the boundaries of community by bringing their accounts forward in time. Al-Barradi, on the other hand, sought to do just the opposite. The *Kitab al-jawahir* instead moved backward in time, retroactively linking the written network of Northern Africa to the earliest generations of Muslims. In doing so, al-Barradi crafted the history of the Ibadi community as the history of Islam itself.

AL-BARRADI'S BOOK LIST

The wide array of written sources, both Ibadi and otherwise, cited in the *Kitab al-jawahir* suggests greater access to manuscript works in the fourteenth century than had been available previously. Like so many of his coreligionists, al-Barradi did a lot of traveling in his early years as a student and teacher. Unlike those before him, however, he decided at some point to record the written works held in various libraries and mosques he had visited. The resulting list of books, which belongs to the same manuscript tradition as the *Kitab al-jawahir*, provides a glimpse into Ibadi manuscript libraries of the fourteenth century. In naming books from outside the Maghrib, the list also reinforces the connection between the Ibadi community of Northern Africa and their eastern counterparts.

The introduction to the *Kitab al-jawahir* does not mention this list of books. Since at least the sixteenth century, and likely before then, however, it belonged to the same manuscript tradition. In the extant manuscript tradition (and the nineteenth-century lithograph based on manuscripts), the list follows al-Barradi's narrative of Islamic history and precedes a short discussion of death. The list remains remarkably consistent across the manuscript tradition, with books appearing in the same order, and their titles contain only very minor differences in spelling. Most manuscripts provide a total of fifty-nine titles, including thirty-six from the Maghrib and twenty-three from the east. An alternative manuscript tradition, which circulated independently of the *Kitab al-jawahir*, includes many more titles, for a total of eighty-six.

This second tradition, according to the editor of its published edition, ʿAmmar Talibi, represents not a different recension but a distinct composition. In his view, al-Barradi composed the longer version of the list after the *Kitab al-jawahir*.[10] The independent circulation of the elongated version of the list serves as a reminder that boundaries of texts in the Ibadi manuscript were fluid and that the process of composing and copying a text was no less iterative than today. The elongated tradition, unlike its shorter equivalent, offers an introduction that explains how it came about:

> May the peace, mercy, and blessings of God be upon you my brother, including those students and brothers who surround you. I did not understand from the messenger your request for a list of compositions nor for the names of the authors, since I myself have not attained much more than a passing familiarity [with them] whereas you are much more aware of writings than I.[11]

At least in its elongated version, the text resulted from a request from a colleague for a list of books. Access to written works probably varied dramatically throughout the region, but al-Barradi through both his travels and extended time as a teacher on Jerba had access to a lot of manuscripts. The large number of written Ibadi sources from which al-Barradi drew in his *Kitab al-jawahir* certainly means an equally large number of manuscripts. The breakdown of the list by genre highlights the relative importance of different subjects in the manuscript tradition in the fourteenth century (Table 6.1).

[10] ʿAmmār Ṭālibī, *Ārāʾ al-khawārij al-kalāmiyya: al-mūjaz li-Abī ʿAmmār ʿAbd al-Kāfī al-Ibāḍī*, vol. II (Algiers: al-Sharika al-Waṭaniyya li-l-Nashr, 1978), 281–95. This is the same "elongated" tradition presented (in French translation) in the nineteenth-century printed edition: Adolphe Motylinski, "Bibliographie du Mzab: les livres de la secte abadhite," *Bulletin de Correspondance Africaine* 3 (1885): 15–72, at 6–20.

[11] Ṭālibī, *Ārāʾ al-khawārij al-kalāmiyya*, 82–83; Motylinski, "Bibliographie du Mzab," 6.

Table 6.1 al-Barradi Book List by Genre

al-Barradi book list (by genre)	
Prophetic traditions (*ḥadīth*)	3
Theology and doctrine (*kalām*, *ʿaqāʾid*)	21
Jurisprudence/law (*fiqh, furūʿ, uṣūl)*	27
Mixed theology and jurisprudence (*kalām wa-fiqh*)	4
History, prosopography (*siyar, sīra*)	9
Responsa, letters (*jawābāt, rasāʾil*)	5
Exegesis (*tafsīr*)	3
Morality/praxis (*akhlāq, sulūk, farāʾiḍ*, etc.)	5
Poetry	2
Unknown/unclear	7
TOTAL:	**86**
Total:	

Of course, these categories sometimes overlapped, and the books in question often included material that blur the lines between them. In general, however, the genre distribution points to some interesting features of Ibadi manuscript collections in the fourteenth century. The clear dominance (fifty-two, or 59.5 percent) of works on law, theology, and doctrine indicates the widespread use of these types of texts by Ibadi scholars. These constitute the staples of religious education, followed in importance by biographies and anecdotal traditions (*athar*) about pious forebears that make up the prosopographical tradition. The small number of works on Qur'an commentary or hadith traditions indicate the peripheral role these types of texts played in the medieval Northern African Ibadi tradition, even up to the fourteenth century. Unlike their Sunni contemporaries, for example, medieval Ibadis did not make systematic or extensive use of codified hadith in legal arguments.[12]

[12] The well-known work by al-Warjalānī entitled *al-Dalīl wa-ʾl-burhān* dealt with questions of both jurisprudence and theology; likewise, *responsa* literature—especially from the Rustamid Imams—dealt with a variety of topics. On the *responsa* of Aflaḥ b. ʿAbd al-Wahhāb, see Cyrille Aillet and Muḥammad Ḥasan, "The Legal Responsa Attributed to Aflaḥ b. ʿAbd Al-Wahhāb (208–58/823–72): A Preliminary Study," in *Ibadi Jurisprudence: Origins, Developments, and Cases*, ed. Barbara Michalak-Pikulska and Reinhard Eisener (Hildesheim: Georg Olms Verlag, 2015), 137–46. The observation regarding Ibadi use of codified hadith collections is John Wilkinson's, on which see Wilkinson, "Ibadi Hadith."

The list also reveals something about the Ibadi prosopographical tradition more specifically. First of all, al-Baradi lists a work entitled the *Kitab al-mashayikh*, which he attributes to Abu Zakariya al-Warjalani. This book, the first work of the Ibadi prosopographical corpus and known today as the *Kitab al-sira*, remained in circulation in a manuscript tradition independent of the *Kitab al-tabaqat*, which of course also appears in the book list. Al-Barradi noted, though, that he had only seen the second half of Abu Zakariya's work, meaning that by the fourteenth century the manuscript tradition of that book recognized two distinct parts. Conspicuously absent, however, are the collections of traditions known later as the *Siyar al-Wisyani* (twelfth century) and the book of *siyar* from the Jebel Nafusa attributed to al-Baghturi (thirteenth century). Indeed, aside from the *Kitab al-sira* and the *Kitab al-tabaqat*, the list does not contain any other identifiable works of prosopography.[13] That al-Barradi, who did quite a lot of traveling, saw only one copy of one half of the *Kitab al-sira* and two copies of the *Kitab al-tabaqat*, tempts the conclusion that prosopographical works occupied a marginal space in the Ibadi manuscript libraries of the fourteenth century, perhaps similar to the marginal importance of historical works in the broader medieval Islamic tradition.[14]

An alternative and equally compelling explanation for both this and the relatively small number of works in the list is that libraries, much like Ibadi manuscript libraries of the early modern period, were in the first place modest, private collections of books, copied, purchased, and sold among an elite class of scholars literate in Arabic. The anecdotes and communal history that the prosopographies carried would have been communicated to a much wider audience through student–teacher study circles (*halqa*s), often in oral form. Al-Barradi visited the private libraries of colleagues or teachers, but he would not have encountered any grand public libraries. The prosopographical tradition mentions no large Ibadi libraries except for scattered references to the Rustamid Maʿsuma Library in Tahart and the Qasr Wallam in the Jebel Nafusa—both of which had been destroyed centuries earlier. There were also no Ibadi madrasas, in the sense of the Sunni institutions of learning that enjoyed the patronage of Maghribi rulers from the eleventh century forward, which held collections of endowed books.[15]

13 A possible exception could be a work al-Barrādī mentioned entitled the *Kitāb al-Muʿallqāt*: Custers, *al-Ibāḍiyya* (2016), vol. II, 71–72.

14 For his comments on the copies of the *Kitāb al-sīra* and the *Kitāb al-ṭabaqāt*, see al-Barrādī, *al-Jawāhir*, 3–4.

15 The point regarding these two exceptionally large libraries was made by Amr Khalifa Ennami, "A Description of New Ibadi Manuscripts from North Africa," *Journal of Semitic*

Al-Barradi's book list also hints at some of the physical characteristics of the manuscripts themselves. In several cases, for example, he relates whether a work is in a single volume or multiple volumes (*sifr*, pl. *asfar*). He also distinguishes between different sections (*juz*ʾ, pl. *ajza*ʾ), which presumably refer to items sewn together and bound as single volumes. In a couple of instances he even refers to the poor physical condition of books. Similarly, in his introduction to the *Kitab al-jawahir* he notes that he had seen two copies of the *Kitab al-tabaqat* and that one of them was in exceptionally poor condition. When talking about another book in the list, he adds that the work was missing its first two folios. These descriptions deserve attention because they demonstrate that pests and time already challenged the preservation of manuscript libraries in the fourteenth century, which also helps account for the small number of Ibadi manuscripts dating to before the sixteenth century.[16]

The book list also refers to how manuscripts were copied and acquired. When he mentions an Omani work known as the *Kashf al-ghumma*, al-Barradi says that while in Mecca on pilgrimage he had tasked an Ibadi there with having a copy made for him:

> I entrusted one of our friends [i.e. Ibadis] from Mecca with the task of having [the book] copied. Someone who accepted [the task of copying] brought [the book so he could copy it] but he did not encounter anyone there who was aware of [my request]. The man carrying [the book] demanded his fee and did not find it, so he took the book from there and left. There is no strength except in God.

This anecdote is telling because it speaks not only to one of the ways in which manuscripts could be acquired (commissioning) but also to a key event in the exchange of oral and written knowledge between the eastern and western Ibadi communities: the hajj.[17]

The story of al-Barradi's meeting with Ibadis in Mecca speaks to a final goal achieved by the book list. While the prosopographical tradition before it remained a regional one, drawing and redrawing the boundaries

Studies 15, no. 1 (1970): 63–87, at 63–64. Konrad Hirschler has made similar observations on the modest size of libraries and their readership in the Mashriq: "Local and Endowed Libraries and their Readers" in Hirschler, *The Written Word in the Medieval Arabic Lands*, 124–63.

16 Discussion of the *Kitāb al-ṭabaqāt* manuscripts: al-Barrādī, *al-Jawāhir*, 3–4. On the missing pages in another manuscript see Ṭālibī, *Ārāʾ al-khawārij al-kalāmiyya*, 249.

17 Interestingly, this detail only appears in the elongated version of the text: Ṭālibī, *Ārāʾ al-khawārij al-kalāmiyya*, 287. More problematic, however, is that the book being copied in the anecdote, known as the *Kashf al-ghumma*, dates to the seventeenth century, and so it would seem that al-Barrādī is referring to a different work with a similar title. Many thanks to Adam Gaiser for pointing out this anachronism.

of community in the Maghrib, the *Kitab al-jawahir* expanded that written network backward in time and eastward in space to include the Prophet and the earliest generations of Muslims. In the same way, al-Barradi's book list presents texts from both the eastern and western Ibadi traditions, establishing the physical links between them in the form of manuscript books.

CONCLUSION

The *Kitab al-jawahir* ultimately contributed to the Ibadi prosopographical tradition in two important ways, both of which distinguish it from its predecessors. In the first place, al-Barradi's work broke with the tradition of using anecdotes of Ibadi scholars to build a written network of Ibadi communities in the Maghrib. Instead, he chose to link the prosopographical tradition of the eleventh to fourteenth centuries with the foundation and early development of Islam as a way of legitimizing the community and its place in the Maghrib of the fourteenth century, where Ibadis had come to represent an increasingly small minority. The *Kitab al-jawahir* began by situating itself in the prosopographical tradition with its critique of the *Kitab al-tabaqat*, rebuking its author for his failure to discuss the events of the earliest generations of Islam. Al-Barradi then presented the early history of Islam, bringing that story to its culmination in the eighth century with the establishment of the Ibadi Rustamid Imamate in Northern Africa. In doing so, al-Barradi linked the prosopographical tradition and the written network it described with the larger history of Islam.

The second distinguishing characteristic of the *Kitab al-jawahir* and its contribution to the Ibadi prosopographical tradition was the list it offered of works by both eastern and western Ibadi scholars. Both the short version in the *Kitab al-jawahir* and the long version that circulated independently point to certain features of Ibadi manuscript libraries in the Middle Period. The genres represented in the longer version of the list indicate the importance of theological, doctrinal, and legal works for Ibadi scholars. At the same time, the surprisingly small number of works overall—eighty-six titles representing the entire Ibadi corpus that al-Barradi could recall having seen or heard of—suggests that Ibadi manuscript collections would in the first place have been small, private collections rather than anything akin to royal libraries or endowed madrasa collections. To acquire or to read many of these works a student or scholar would have been obliged (like al-Barradi) to do a lot of traveling. This would have been the case especially for eastern Ibadi works, with the hajj in particular providing an important opportunity for both regional communities to exchange books.

Lastly, the book list also served the broader aim and purpose of the *Kitab al-jawahir*. Just as the bulk of the text aims at connecting the Ibadi communities of the Maghrib to the early history of Islam by beginning with the Prophet Muhammad and ending with the Rustamids, so too the book list links the eastern and western traditions by bringing together works from the early and medieval Ibadi communities of Oman with those of early and medieval Maghribi scholars.

7

The End of a Tradition

***

The period from the eleventh to the fourteenth centuries witnessed a gradual but steady numerical decline of the Ibadi community in Northern Africa. Largely in response to this process and the religious and political marginalization that accompanied it, each work in the Ibadi prosopographical tradition up to the fifteenth century sought to define the external and internal boundaries of the Ibadi community. These books did so by strengthening the ties among scholars of the past and present, preserving their memory for posterity through the formation of a written network. This moved toward formalization from the eleventh to the fourteenth centuries, culminating in the connection of the written network in Northern Africa to the broader history of Islam in al-Barradi's *Kitab al-jawahir.*

The final work of medieval Ibadi prosopography, the *Kitab al-siyar* by Abu al-ʿAbbas al-Shammakhi (d. 1522), brought the tradition of the Middle Period to a close. A grand compilation of anecdotes and biographies of Ibadi scholars from the origins of the community in the east up to nearly his own lifetime, al-Shammakhi's *Siyar* is by far the most comprehensive work of Ibadi prosopography. Like that of each of his forebears, al-Shammakhi's book reflects the historical context out of which it emerged. Likewise, the *Siyar* marked both the end of a tradition and the beginning of an era in which Ibadis would establish a new intellectual and geographic center: the Mzab valley in what is today Algeria.

The *Kitab al-siyar* functions as a lens through which to view the long-term written network of the Ibadi prosopographical tradition because it is the cumulative result of everything that came before it. Al-Shammakhi had far greater access to sources than any of his predecessors, and his comprehensiveness reflects the widespread reliance on written sources by the end of the Middle Period (eleventh–sixteenth centuries). He had access to the entire prosopographical corpus that preceded him as well as many non-Ibadi sources made available to him in Hafsid-era Ifriqiya. As a result, his work presents an impressive and comprehensive synthesis of the Ibadi prosopographical tradition that had developed over the previous four centuries while at the same time reflecting the political and religious landscape of the Maghrib in the late fifteenth and early sixteenth centuries.

Finally, al-Shammakhi's synthetic work marks a kind of plateau in the historical trajectory of the geography of Ibadi communities in the Maghrib reached by the fifteenth century. By the end of al-Shammakhi's life in 1522 the political, religious, and linguistic marginalization of the Ibadis in the Maghrib had largely reached its apogee. Ibadis were now concentrated in a small set of geographic pockets in the region that has remained constant down to the present. The numerical decline of Ibadis did continue into the early modern period, although mostly among the non-Wahbi communities on the island of Jerba. As such, the *Kitab al-siyar* signals the final iteration of the written network.[1]

AL-SHAMMAKHI'S *KITAB AL-SIYAR* IN CONTEXT

The opening lines of the *Kitab al-siyar* echo those of its predecessors—with one important and symbolic difference: a dedication.

An epistle arrived from someone interested in our matters, wanting to learn about our state of affairs and to gain knowledge of the accounts of our country where our brothers live, which our enemy struck with his insolence. [He also wanted to have] knowledge of our [states] of open adornment and concealment, manifestation, and secrecy, as well as of the virtues of the [Ibadis] and the genealogy of the early Imams, those earliest possessors of legacy and beneficence ... The epistle included the notion that they [the Imams] revivified the soul of the radiant and luminous *shari'a* and the [rising] of the sun of the pure and white faith; [that they] observed forbearance, drank of purity, and ruled the people with justice; [that they] became influential in the land and humiliated the people of tyranny and corruption [through the leadership of] the upright, God-fearing, and generous Imam,

1 The *Kitāb al-siyar* is generally more explicit than its predecessors about distinguishing Wahbis from other Ibadi communities. For example, in his entry on Abū Sākin ʿĀmir al-Shammākhī, he writes: "Every *Wahbī* in the Maghrib traces his knowledge ... back to him" (*Abū l-ʿAbbās Aḥmad b. Saʿīd al-Shammākhī, Kitāb al-siyar*, ed. Muḥammad Ḥasan [Beirut: Dār al-Gharb al-Islāmī, 2009], 789).

glorifier of the gallant ancestors, the distinguished and most honorable, the generous and intelligent, Abu ʿAbdallah Muhammad, that just prince whose nobility goes back to Qahtan, whether [from the people of] Himyar, Azd, or Hamdan!

I delighted in the shining of the light of their guidance on our hearts. [And I delighted in] their following the path of those of our pious forebears, their making apparent the method of the community of truth, and their illuminating with a testament to these sieves of truthfulness.[2]

Like those before him, al-Shammakhi noted here that a principal aim of his work was to preserve the memory of the community's forebears. Unlike his predecessors, however, al-Shammakhi explicitly dedicated this work to a prince (*amir*). The dedication to this prince, who from the tribes mentioned (Azd, Qahtan) would appear to be Omani but could also be a Maghribi ruler claiming eastern origins, distinguishes the framing of al-Shammakhi's work from those of his predecessors. Not only did the compiler dedicate his work to a ruler or patron, he also fashioned a prosopography that served as a comprehensive introduction to the Ibadi historical tradition for both Ibadis and non-Ibadis. Works dedicated to princes and rulers were commonplace in the medieval Maghrib just as they were in eastern Islamic lands. But Ibadis had often held either ambiguous or openly hostile positions toward the ruling powers in the Maghrib. This makes al-Shammakhi's choice of dedicating the *Kitab al-siyar* to a prince even more remarkable. Moreover, the dedication symbolizes the new place of Ibadis in the Maghrib of the late fifteenth century.[3]

The works of the prosopographical tradition before him had all addressed themselves to an exclusively Ibadi audience, often with a tone that warned of the community's portending doom as it suffered from external forces or internal divisions. By contrast, al-Shammakhi seems to address his work to interested contemporaries, be they Ibadis or otherwise. Likewise, he presents his list of Ibadi scholars neither as an explicit effort to preserve the endangered memory of the community,

2 al-Shammākhī, *Kitāb al-siyar*, 108.

3 None of the extant manuscript copies of the *Kitāb al-siyar* (of the twenty-six copies I have examined) expands on the name "Abū ʿAbdallāh Muḥammad." Given that al-Shammākhī spent significant time in Hafsid-era Tunis and moved in scholarly circles there—including meeting the *amīr* Abū ʿAmr ʿUthmān—it could refer to the Hafsid *amīr* of Tunis, Abū ʿAbdallāh Muḥammad (or Muḥammad IV, r. 1494–1526). At a conference held in December 2015 in Tunis on the subject of al-Shammākhī's *Kitāb al-siyar*, Aḥmad b. Saʿūd al-Sābī suggested that the compiler dedicated his work to an Omani prince from the late fifteenth/early sixteenth century, Abū ʿAbdallāh Muḥammad b. Ismāʿīl al-Quḍāʿī. In any case, the identity of the prince will likely remain a point of speculation.

as the *Kitab al-sira* or the *Siyar al-Wisyani* had done, nor as a guide for Ibadis in the east like the *Kitab al-tabaqat*, nor as an exposition of the Ibadi place in Islamic history like the *Kitab al-jawahir*. Instead, al-Shammakhi's work presents the Ibadis as one Muslim community among others. At times, he explicitly notes that the purpose of the text is not to extol the virtues and miracles of the members of the community, but instead writes that "the intention of this book is familiarization" with the scholars of the Ibadi community.[4] This shift in presentation speaks both to al-Shammakhi's background as a member of a scholarly Ibadi family educated in Hafsid-era Northern Africa and to the very different space occupied by Ibadis in the Maghrib more generally from the fifteenth century onward.

Abu al-ʿAbbas al-Shammakhi came from a long line of scholars in the Jebel Nafusa and Jebel Dummar areas. Following in the tradition of itinerant Ibadi students and scholars, he traveled often among the different Ibadi centers of learning in the Jebel Nafusa, Jebel Dummar, the island of Jerba, and—most importantly for shaping his own presentation of Ibadi history—the Hafsid capital, Tunis. Through various indications in the *Kitab al-siyar*, al-Shammakhi makes it clear that he spent a significant amount of time in Tunis. For example, he makes explicit reference to his teacher there, whom he calls al-Shaykh al-Baydamuri, as well as to his having met the Hafsid emir Abu ʿAmr ʿUthman (r. 1435–1488). This would support the idea that al-Shammakhi dedicated his work to the contemporary Hafsid prince Abu ʿAbdallah Muhammad (Muhammad IV, r. 1494–1526), one of several successors to Abu ʿAmr ʿUthman in the last troubled days of Hafsid rule at the beginning of the sixteenth century.[5]

Al-Shammakhi's introduction suggests that this prince had come to the aid of the Ibadis, which could refer to the defense of the island of Jerba by the Hafsids against one of many attacks by the Aragonese in the fifteenth century.[6] The *Kitab al-siyar* also reflects the author's familiarity with both the non-Ibadi scholarly circles of Hafsid Tunis and the Ibadi tradition. As a result, the work presents the Ibadis of Northern Africa as one Muslim community among many, participating in the diverse religious landscape of the Maghrib in the late Hafsid period.

4 al-Shammākhī, *Kitāb al-siyar*, 292.

5 On Shammākhī's biography, see Bābāʿammī, *Muʿjam aʿlām al-ibāḍiyya*, 45; al-Shammākhī, *Kitāb al-siyar*, 13–17.

6 Fierro, "The Almohads and the Ḥafṣids," 96.

AL-SHAMMAKHI AND BOOKS IN HAFSID IFRIQIYA

Al-Shammakhi's sojourn in Tunis afforded him access to many more manuscript sources than would have been available in the mountains of the Jebel Nafusa, southern Ifriqiya, or Jerba. His reliance upon and citations of the work of the Zirid courtier and historian al-Raqiq (d. eleventh century), the *Muruj al-dhahab* of al-Mas'udi (d. ninth century), the chronicle of Ibn Saghir (ninth century), and probably the *Ansab al-ashraf* of al-Baladhuri (ninth century) all indicate the degree to which a well-educated Ibadi scholar studying in Tunis would have been exposed to non-Ibadi sources. Hafsid-era Tunis, rich in both royal and private manuscript collections, offered students and scholars access to a large pool of sources.[7]

In addition, the fact that he belonged to an important Ibadi scholarly family meant that al-Shammakhi had access to a large number of written Ibadi works. The *Kitab al-siyar* makes frequent reference to written Ibadi sources that al-Shammakhi himself had seen and read (*ra'aytuhu*, etc.). Like al-Barradi before him, al-Shammakhi also notes how certain sources are divided into multiple small volumes or bound together in a single large volume. Several works described in the *Kitab al-siyar* are accompanied by a comment that a manuscript is in the hand of a specific copyist. For example, when talking about one Abu Zakariya Yahya b. Abi al-'Izz al-Shammakhi, he wrote:

> He both studied and taught and was a copyist of books. But knowledge never prevented him from copying nor did copying keep him from knowledge ... And I have seen many books in his hand including Qur'anic commentaries (*tafsirs*) and commentaries on the [books] *al-Da'a'im* and *al-Diya'* and other books, such that no library of the [Jebel] Nafusa lacks a manuscript in his hand.[8]

Here and elsewhere al-Shammakhi refers to the substantial collections of manuscript books held in the towns and villages of the Jebel Nafusa, including the names of well-known copyists. In two specific cases he also provides a hint of the fate of manuscript collections following the deaths of their owners. In one case he notes that a collection went directly to its owner's son following his death. This probably represents the most common trajectory of Ibadi manuscript collections in pre-modern Northern Africa. More significantly, however, al-Shammakhi provides the first example from the prosopographical tradition of a manuscript collection being transformed into an endowment (*habus*). This practice, long-since adopted in Sunni circles of the Maghrib, had not been widely practiced

[7] Brunschvig, *La Berbérie Orientale*, 367–68.
[8] al-Shammākhī, *Kitāb al-siyar*, 781–82.

within Ibadi communities: "And among them was Abu Musa ʿAysa b. ʿAysa al-Tirmsi ... He never married on account of his intense focus on knowledge ... and he endowed the books he left behind to the students and jurists of Nafusa."[9]

The endowed library, as Konrad Hirschler has argued, marks a seminal shift in the Middle Period away from royal and institutional libraries to private collections that made them accessible to a much larger readership. Similarly, the endowment of Ibadi manuscript collections in the Maghrib at the end of the Middle Period would have allowed for an unprecedented accumulation of and access to books for students and scholars. Even a century earlier these seekers of knowledge would have been obliged to travel around Ifriqiya to read them, just as al-Barradi had done. The early modern endowed and family or clan collections on Jerba and the Mzab valley that survive to the present day as the main repositories of Ibadi manuscripts demonstrate the long-term effects of the adoption of the practice of endowing libraries.[10]

THE MAGHRIB IN THE FIFTEENTH CENTURY

If the fourteenth century remains an especially hazy period of eastern Maghribi history, the fifteenth does not offer much of an improvement. While the Hafsid princes never succeeded in bringing large territories under their exclusive control, the two main Hafsid leaders of the fifteenth century, Abu Faris (r. 1394–1434) and Abu ʿAmr ʿUthman (r. 1435–88), did at least manage to bring their internecine conflicts to an end and establish diplomatic relations with the other major powers of the central and western Mediterranean. Negotiation and compromise with the various city-centered principalities of southern Ifriqiya and Tripolitania continued to be the norm, which allowed for some degree of stability in the south. On the coast, the fifteenth century witnessed constant diplomatic relations between the Hafsids and the various Italian city-states and with Provence. The Aragonese rulers of Iberia and the southern Italian Peninsula challenged Hafsid rule of the Ifriqiyan coast on several occasions, although by the end of the fifteenth century relations had normalized.[11] An important result of this Italian trade, in particular, was a further

[9] al-Shammākhī, *Kitāb al-siyar*, 781.

[10] "Local Endowed Libraries and their Readers," in Hirschler, *The Written Word in the Medieval Arabic Lands*, 124–63.

[11] On Hafsid foreign relations see Brunschvig, *La Berbérie Orientale*, 210; on relations with Genoa, Venice, Pisa, Elba, Aragon, and Provence: 217, 251–57; Rouighi, *The Making of*

influx of Italian-made paper, which would come to dominate Northern African markets for centuries—completely eclipsing any locally made paper or "Arab" paper from the east.[12]

Meanwhile, Ibadi communities continued to operate under the radar of these larger political and diplomatic relations. Perhaps most significantly, the small towns of the Mzab valley in the pre-desert of what is today Algeria began to emerge together as a new intellectual and geographic center for Maghribi Ibadi scholars in the fifteenth century. Geographically poised to take advantage of Saharan trade and just far enough away from the action of the littoral to avoid political upheavals taking place there, it was in the Mzab that Ibadi scholarship in the Maghrib would flourish for the next several centuries. Although the first settlement of Ateuf (ʿAtf) had been founded a few centuries earlier, the important centers of Benisguen, Malika, and Ghardaia emerged as hubs of intellectual activity from the sixteenth century forward, followed shortly thereafter by a Maghribi Ibadi diaspora community in Cairo (Chapter 8). Similarly, the mountainous regions of Jebel Dummar and Jebel Nafusa continued to produce important Ibadi scholars, exemplified by al-Shammakhi's own family and the various branches of the al-Baruni family.[13]

By contrast, the inhabitants of the island of Jerba continued to suffer due to the island's geostrategic importance in the central Mediterranean. After an unsuccessful invasion of the island in the early fourteenth century described in detail in the *Rihla* ('Journey') of the historian al-Tijani, the Hafsids managed to take control of Jerba in the early fifteenth century, only to be challenged by the Aragonese a few decades later. Despite regular invasions, even Jerba remained home to, and would continue to educate, new generations of Ibadi scholars for the next several centuries. Significantly, though, in part resulting from the efforts of the Hafsids in the fifteenth century until the end of the eighteenth, many of the island's Nukkari (locally referred to as Mistawi) Ibadis converted to Maliki Islam.

a Mediterranean Empire, 97–122; Fierro, "The Almohads and the Ḥafṣids," 89 fn. 64 and 65; Doumerc, *Venise et l'émirat hafside de Tunis*.

[12] "Revival in the Nineteenth Century," in Walz, "The Paper Trade of Egypt and the Sudan," 90–92.

[13] A full history of the late medieval Mzab valley has yet to be written. Samples of the rich sources available to historians there have been published in articles in the Ibāḍī manuscripts journal *El-Minhāj* over the past several years. In particular, see Yaḥyā Būrās, "al-Ḥayāt al-fikriyya bi-minṭaqat mizāb fi-l-qarnayn 9–10 [AH]/15–16 [CE]," *El-Minhāj: dawriyya ʿilmiyya mutakhaṣṣiṣa fī makhṭūṭāt al-ibāḍiyya wa-Wādī Mīzāb fī wathāʾiqihā al-arshīfiyya* 2 (2013): 96–131; Yūsuf Ibn Bakīr al-Ḥājj Saʿīd, *Tārīkh Banī Mzāb: dirāsa ijtimāʿiyya wa-iqtiṣādiyya wa-siyasiyya*, 3rd edition (Ghardaia: n.p., 2014).

THE WRITTEN NETWORK OF THE *KITAB AL-SIYAR*

Having reviewed the historical context that produced the *Kitab al-siyar*, we now turn to the long-term written network it created. This last iteration of the written network in the Middle Period brought together all previous books in the Ibadi prosopographical corpus, in addition to biographies and lists of scholars from a variety of other written sources.

Like each of the works in the Ibadi prosopographical tradition, the *Kitab al-siyar* drew from, refined, and expanded the written network that preceded it. In addition to the impressive compilation of the biographies of and anecdotes about Ibadi scholars who came before him, al-Shammakhi contributed valuable information on a handful of scholars from al-Barradi's generation up to the mid-fifteenth century. For example, he provided the biographies of his own family, al-Shammakhi, demonstrating their prominent place in the formation of a new generation of late medieval scholars. Ultimately, the *Kitab al-siyar* marked the end of the medieval written network, cumulatively formed and maintained over more than four centuries.

The network summary from the *Kitab al-siyar* reveals several interesting characteristics of the written network described by al-Shammakhi (Table 7.1). Aside from a significant increase in the number of nodes and edges compared with earlier works in the prosopographical tradition, the average degree of any given node is remarkably small. Al-Shammakhi's work includes far more nodes with only one edge (either a self-edge or a single connection to one other figure in the network) than its predecessors. That 312 or 36.66 percent of the nodes in the *Kitab al-siyar* have only a single link shows the cumulative power of bringing otherwise isolated figures from Ibadi history into the broader written network of the prosopographical tradition. In turn, this much larger number means that

TABLE 7.1 A Network Summary of the *Kitab al-Siyar*

al-Shammākhī's *Kitāb al-siyar*: network summary	
Total number of nodes	850
Total number of edges	1,184
Degree range	1–39
Average degree	2.786
Average path length	8.0408 ...
Network diameter	23

the average path length is around 8 (a significant increase from the 3–4 of previous works).

The explanation for this large number lies in al-Shammakhi's comprehensive approach in listing scholars and pious figures from the earliest generations to the fifteenth century. For example, he includes entire sections on pious individuals who have no obvious relationship to the broader community, often only including their nicknames.[14] Likewise, al-Shammakhi's use of sources such as Ibn Sallam's *Kitab badʾ al-islam* and al-Baghturi's *Siyar Nafusa* mean that much of his data amounts to lists of names, rather than anecdotes or full biographies which establish connections among scholars. As had been the case since the beginning of the tradition, the absence of connections in the text does not mean that they did not exist; however, the number of isolates in al-Shammakhi's version of the written network is remarkable. One of the major contributions of the *Kitab al-siyar* to the tradition was to bring these otherwise marginal figures into the written network.

Several filtering tools help reveal communities that are otherwise unidentifiable a priori through broad visualization or a close reading of the text. From the perspective of a network analysis of connections, the large number of isolates and nodes with only one connection distort the data significantly. An initial filter in the Gephi visualization program called "giant component" helps identify the largest group of interconnected nodes. Then, since 36.66 percent of the nodes in the unfiltered version of the network have only a single edge, a second filter shows only those nodes with two or more edges. Finally, a third filter removes the isolates.[15]

The filtered visualization results in more compact and more easily legible network (Table 7.2). Filtering out those nodes with only a single connection reveals several interesting features of the written network in the *Kitab al-siyar*. First of all, the network now includes only 45.36 percent of all the nodes but still represents 62.25 percent of all connections. This suggests that, as was the case with its predecessors, the *Kitab al-siyar* forms a scale-free, "small-world" network in which a small number of hubs account for most connections.

[14] For example, one section entitled "faṣl adhkuru fihi baʿḍa ahli l-karamāt" lists the stories of individuals such "the man who prayed to God for rain." See al-Shammākhī, *Kitāb al-siyar*, 724–29.

[15] The "giant component" can refer to more than one thing in network theory and analysis depending, *inter alia*, on whether or not a network graph is random. Here I am using it in a more general (what Mark Newman calls "sloppy") way to refer to "a large component that fills most of the network … while the rest of the network is divided into a large number of small components disconnected from the rest": Newman, *Networks*, 235.

TABLE 7.2 Network Summary of the *Kitab al-Siyar* after Applying Filters

al-Shammākhī's *Kitāb al-siyar*: network summary (with filters)	
Total number of nodes	385 (45.36% of total)
Total number of edges	737 (62.25% of total)
Degree range	2–39
Average degree	3.829
Average path length	7.4372 ...
Network diameter	21

The increase in average degree and decrease in average path length are expected results from the filters having removed those nodes with only a single connection and eliminated self-loops. Equally remarkably, the diameter of the network—even when those nodes with only one connection have been removed—remains quite large: 21, versus 23 of the unfiltered network. That the longest path between two scholars is 21 over nearly nine centuries may not be all that surprising, yet it is significant that the average path length is less than eight, consistent with other "small-world" experiments on real-world networks. This path length demonstrates how the *Kitab al-siyar* brings together scholars across great swaths of time and space, uniting them in a written network.

While the *Kitab al-siyar* does bring all nodes together by virtue of including them within the same network, it also creates communities of scholars. It lends itself to the use of an additional concept borrowed from network analysis, called modularity, for identifying communities. Modularity, meaning "the extent to which like is connected to like in a network," identifies common features and shared connections among nodes to identify communities.[16] The use of a modularity algorithm when analyzing all the nodes and edges described in the *Kitab al-siyar* makes it possible to identify communities of scholars within the written network. However, those peripheral nodes with only one connection or self-loop connections distort the clarity of the graph. Filtering those individuals with only one connection and employing the modularity algorithm in Gephi reveals a much more defined set of communities. The communities appearing in the filtered version (represented by similar shades) help narrow down and organize the connections among different scholars (Figure 7.2).[17]

[16] Newman, *Networks*, 224.

[17] The modularity algorithm in Gephi is based on Vincent D. Blondel et al., "Fast Unfolding of Communities in Large Networks," *Journal of Statistical Mechanics: Theory and Experiment* no. 10 (2008): 1–12.

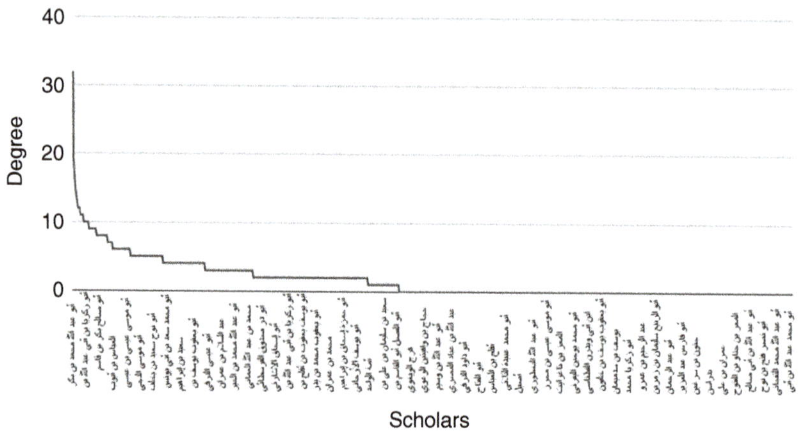

FIGURE 7.1: *Kitab al-siyar* degree distribution.

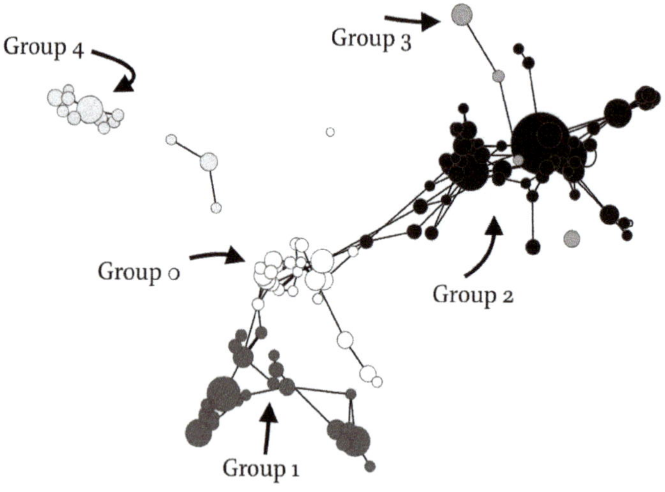

FIGURE 7.2: The *Kitab al-siyar* after applying the modularity algorithm in Gephi. Each shade represents a different group number.

Communities divide into five clusters. Although al-Shammakhi did not systematically organize his biographies and anecdotes into any chronological, geographical, or tribal organization, this version of the written network visualization reveals that these clusters of connections correspond broadly to both geographic and temporal divisions (Table 7.3).

TABLE 7.3 Group Numbers Showing the Results of the Modularity Algorithm on the *Kitab al-Siyar*, with Common Corresponding Places and Prominent *Nisbas*

Group number (color)	Number of nodes	Predominant geographic associations	Predominant chronological associations	Predominant *nisbas*
0	61	Jebel Nafūsa	tenth–eleventh centuries	al-Lālūtī; al-Nafūsī; al-Sharūsī; al-Tadimirtī; al-Baghṭūrī; al-Durfī
1	57	Tāhart; Jebel Nafūsa	eighth–tenth centuries	al-Fārisī (i.e. Rustamid dynasty); al-Maʿāfirī; al-Fursuṭāʾī; al-Wīghwī
2	150	Jerba; Jarīd; Dummar	eleventh–thirteenth centuries	al-Mazātī; al-Wisyānī; al-Lamāʾī; al-Yājrānī; al-Ya[h]rāsanī; al-Zawāghī
3	22	Warjālān; Sadrāta; Jarīd	eleventh–thirteenth centuries	al-Sadrātī; al-Tināwatī; al-Timījārī [al-Darjīnī]
4	48	Jebel Nafūsa	thirteenth–fifteenth centuries	al-Shammākhī; al-Jiṭānī; al-Bārūnī; al-Janāwanī; al-Nafūsī

TABLE 7.4 Rough Periodization of Maghribi Ibadi History with Corresponding Groups from the Network Map of the *Kitab al-Siyar*

Rustami period (eighth–tenth centuries)	Group 1
Transitional period (tenth–eleventh centuries)	Group 0
Formative ʿ*azzaba* period (eleventh–thirteenth centuries)	Groups 2 and 3
Established ʿ*azzaba* period (thirteenth–fifteenth centuries)	Group 4

These 338 nodes, representing roughly 40 percent of all nodes in the network, together form clusters broadly corresponding to the commonly accepted periodization of the Ibadi tradition in the Maghrib (Table 7.4).

Each of these periods also corresponds generally to a division of the prosopographical corpus itself, demonstrating the cumulative character of the *Kitab al-siyar*. If the degree range filter is removed, it becomes clear that these communities represent the principal divisions of the *Kitab al-siyar* (Figure 7.3). Without the filter, the graph depicts 623 nodes and 975 (82.35 percent) of all connections, and all communities remain clearly defined.

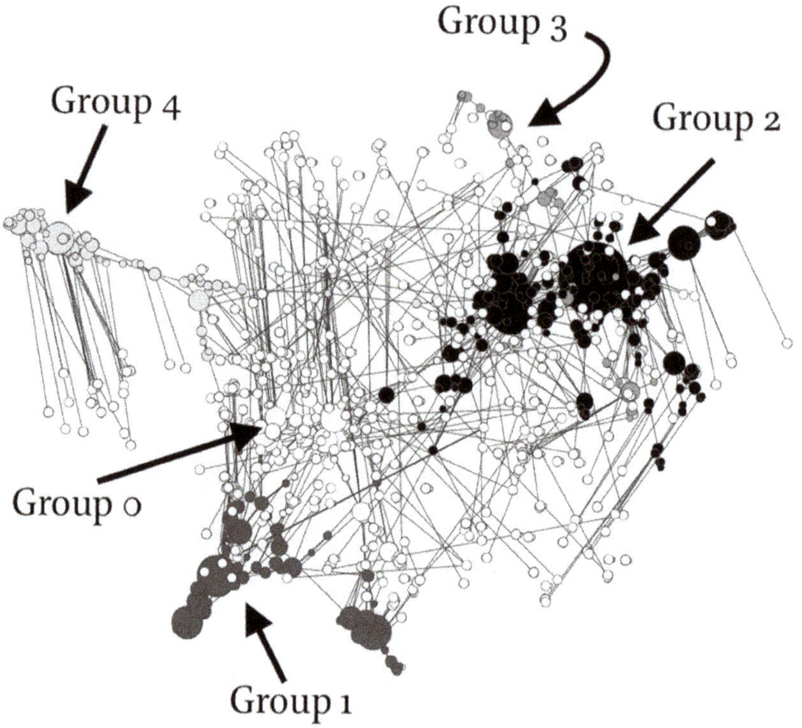

FIGURE 7.3: The *Kitab al-siyar* without a degree range filter (still using the "giant component" filter). Communities are still clearly defined, and the graph now shows 73.29 percent of all nodes and 85.35 percent of all edges.

CONCLUSION

In bringing together and presenting the biographies and anecdotes of Ibadi scholars from the beginnings of Islam to the fifteenth century, al-Shammakhi's work marked the cumulative result of four centuries of medieval Ibadi prosopography in the Maghrib. Of course, the *Kitab al-siyar* represents much more than a compilation of previous sources. Al-Shammakhi's choices of whom to include or to exclude, the prominence of his own family, the absence of Berber texts, and a variety of other features of the book's contents speak both to the compiler's lived context and to his authorial voice. Likewise, the *Kitab al-siyar* no doubt represents an important source for the history of Northern Africa well beyond the confines of Ibadi history. However, this chapter has situated the *Kitab al-siyar* in a long-term tradition of prosopography, each installment of which aimed at marking the boundaries of the Ibadi community and which together constructed and maintained the narrative of the Ibadi tradition in the Maghrib.[18]

As its dedication and introductory passages indicate, the *Kitab al-siyar*, unlike its predecessors, spoke to both an Ibadi and non-Ibadi audience. This reflects several differences between al-Shammakhi and his predecessors, as well broader changes to the political and religious landscape of the Maghrib from the eleventh to the fifteenth centuries. First of all, the work demonstrates the compiler's personal background and education in the diverse religious landscape of Hafsid Ifriqiya. Al-Shammakhi had access to a large number of Ibadi manuscripts thanks both to his family's distinguished scholarly past and to the increase in the number of written works available by his lifetime. Changes in manuscript-collection practices, including the endowment of collections, alongside the accumulation of written works more generally over the previous century or more meant that more manuscripts were available to read.

In addition, not only did al-Shammakhi study and read manuscripts in the established Ibadi centers of the Jebel Nafusa, Jerba, and Jebel Dummar, but he also spent a significant amount of time in the Hafsid capital, Tunis, interacting with both Ibadi and non-Ibadi scholars, reading their manuscripts and discussing their ideas. As a result, the *Kitab al-siyar* mirrors both al-Shammakhi's personal educational and scholarly journey and the religious milieu of the late fifteenth-century Maghrib in which Ibadis had in a way become participants rather than outsiders.

Since the eleventh century Ibadi communities had been struggling to maintain their place in an increasingly diverse political and religious landscape in Northern Africa. By the fifteenth century the cumulative prosopographical corpus had constructed the boundaries of the community and the history and place of Ibadis in the Maghrib. The *Kitab al-siyar* marks the end of that long-term process of building an Ibadi tradition. But the framing of al-Shammakhi's text and the life of its author also worked in concert with its content and structure to achieve this final presentation of the written network. Drawing from the toolbox of network analysis, including the use of modularity, this chapter has also demonstrated that the *Kitab al-siyar* forms clusters of scholars within the boundaries of the Ibadi community that mark both the geographic and

[18] For example, the only (partial) English translation of al-Shammākhī appears in a compilation of Arabic sources for the history of West Africa: J. F. P. Hopkins and Nehemia Levtzion, *Corpus of Early Arabic Sources for West African History* (Cambridge; New York: Cambridge University Press, 1981), 368–69.

chronological hubs of the Middle Period. The existence and identification of these hubs highlights the crucial importance of specific locations in loosely defined chronological periods to the formation of the written network. Likewise, the locations and periods represented by these clusters correspond to the contents of each of the previous works of the prosopographical tradition, which reflects a cumulative process of tradition building of five centuries.

8

Orbits

***

In mid-October 1679 Yusuf b. Ahmad al-Sadwikishi finished transcribing a copy of the *Kitab al-jawahir*. In the closing lines of the manuscript, he wrote:

> So ends, with praise to God, the *Jawahir al-muntaqat* ... The poorest and neediest of men, Yusuf b. Ahmad b. Muhammad b. Ahmad b. Abi al-Qasim al-Qasabi al-Sadwikshi by lineage, al-Jarbi by homeland, al-Ibadi by creed *(madhhab)* copied it in the middle of Ramadan of the [*hijri*] year 1090 in the Egyptian abodes *(al-diyar al-Misriyya)*. May God grant him and his parents forgiveness, *amin*.[1]

Like hundreds of other Ibadis between the sixteenth and twentieth centuries, Yusuf copied this manuscript while in Cairo. He had come to Egypt from the island of Jerba in what is today southern Tunisia to pursue his education. He sought to study under the scholars of the prestigious al-Azhar mosque and under the Ibadi shaykhs of a local trade agency and school known as the Wikalat al-Jamus. Founded in the early seventeenth century by an Ibadi trader from Jerba, for more than three centuries the agency provided Ibadi diasporas from across Northern Africa with services ranging from commercial transactions and subsidized education to marriage arrangements. In addition to being an Ibadi hub for trade and social services, the Wikalat al-Jamus also served as a school, and housed an impressive library. Students like Yusuf al-Sadwikshi often paid for their studies and living expenses by copying manuscripts in the Wikala. Ibadi scholars and students passing through Cairo would bring manuscripts with them, copies of which would be made and added to the library. Wealthy traders

[1] Makt. al-Quṭb, MS *thāʾ* 1, f.122.b.

commissioned specific works as endowments, which helped the library to grow over the centuries. Likewise, students and scholars at the Wikala made their own copies from those in the library, carrying the books with them on the journey back home.[2]

A student from Jerba, Yusuf copied the *Kitab al-jawahir* in Cairo; but today that manuscript is housed in a private library in the Mzab. The biography and journey of this and other Ibadi manuscripts points to a final and essential component of the long-term maintenance of the written network: movement. Both the manuscripts of the prosopographies and the students and scholars who used them were constantly on the move, traveling back and forth along circuits connecting different hubs of intellectual activity and manuscript production throughout Northern Africa. Just as the relationships among people in the prosopographical corpus created a written network, so too the constellation of connections among the manuscript copies of those works formed a complementary material network.

In this chapter I turn my attention to the orbits along which people and manuscripts moved and which played a key role in maintaining the Ibadi tradition long after the compilation of the final work of the medieval prosopographical corpus at the beginning of the sixteenth century. In using the term orbits, I refer to the often elliptical and overlapping intellectual and commercial circuits along which these and other Ibadi manuscripts moved. These chains of human and non-human actors connected hubs like the Wikalat al-Jamus, enabling the prosopographies to link Ibadis across time and space. Through manuscripts, Ibadi scholars and copyists continued to travel even long after their deaths. An author, compiler, or copyist more often than not found his way back to his point of origin in some textual vestige. Just as the written network of the prosopographies created and maintained the Ibadi tradition in the Maghrib, the orbits of the corpus in manuscript form sustained the connections among people and places that marked the boundaries of the community.[3] After tracing these orbits in the long term, I turn to some exemplary cases of scholars whose lives traversed these circuits in the nineteenth and twentieth centuries.

2 Aḥmad Muṣlaḥ, *al-Waqf al-jarbī fī Miṣr wa-dawruhu fī 'l-tanmiya al-iqtiṣādiyya wa-ʾl-ijtimāʿiyya wa-ʾl-thaqāfiyya min al-qarn al-ʿāshir ilā ʾl-qarn al-rābiʿ ʿashar al-hijrīyayn (Wikālat al-Jāmūs namūdhajan)* (Kuwait: al-Amāna al-ʿĀmma lil-Awqāf, 2012).

3 This particular use of the notion of "orbits" belongs to John Wansbrough, who developed it as a way of talking about diplomatic and commercial contact in the Mediterranean. See Wansbrough, *Lingua Franca in the Mediterranean*.

WAYSTATIONS ON THE PROSOPOGRAPHICAL ORBIT

Yusuf was not the only member of his family to make the journey from Jerba to Cairo. His father Ahmad had followed a similar path, studying at al-Azhar before returning to the island to teach. Yusuf's cousin Muhammad b. ʿUmar al-Sadwikshi (d. 1677) studied under his uncle Ahmad while in Jerba, and then he too traveled to study and, later, to teach at both the Wikalat al-Jamus and al-Azhar. Muhammad stayed in Cairo for twenty-eight years, copying and commenting on dozens of different Ibadi texts. His prolific commentaries on some of the major works of Ibadi law, theology, and hadith earned him the nickname "the commentator" (*al-muhashshi*). Many libraries in the Mzab valley and Jerba today house manuscripts in his hand or copies of his commentaries.[4]

These three locations—Cairo, Jerba, and the Mzab—along with the Jebel Nafusa in Libya, functioned as waystations on the orbital system along which Ibadi students, scholars, and their manuscripts moved from the sixteenth century onward. Scholarly families like Yusuf's traveled for education and commerce, maintaining regular links among these different hubs. Although Jerba and the Jebel Nafusa had long served as Ibadi intellectual centers, the Mzab and Cairo entered the larger orbit only after the sixteenth century.

Before that, Ibadi manuscript books would have followed slightly different orbits. Their principal circuits would have connected the Jebel Nafusa, the island of Jerba, the Jarid, the Jebel Dummar, Warjalan, and Sedrata, with occasional disruptions or tangents southward farther into the Sahara or eastward toward Egypt—especially for pilgrims on hajj. Each work in the prosopographical corpus pointed to this largely latitudinal movement of books, people, and ideas among the islands of the Ibadi archipelago. The cumulative prosopographical tradition also made possible the formation of a collective memory of the lines connecting different communities. Regardless of the time and space separating these regions and the Ibadis who inhabited them, the prosopographies brought them together into the same historical orbit.

But the prosopographical corpus, along with other written works by Ibadi authors in this period, also established links among these regions in a different way. The paper upon which they were written likewise created a tangible, material connection among communities. Letters among scholars from two regions were common, and the greater availability of paper meant that there were more of them. Both the contents of manuscripts

[4] Bābāʿammī, *Muʿjam aʿlām al-ibāḍiyya*, 389–90.

and the physical objects themselves connected one Ibadi community with another. The journey of a book by a Nafusi author that was copied by a Mzabi student while studying in Jerba, which then traveled back to the Mzab valley, created a series of connections among the different communities in those places. Furthermore, it merits emphasizing that the two mediums of communication—people and paper—followed the same paths and worked in tandem to create and maintain connections. Like the written network, the material network before the sixteenth century relied on interconnected hubs that linked a series of smaller, satellite communities throughout the region. Through these hubs even the smallest, most remote Ibadi communities maintained a connection to places like Tahart and the Jebel Nafusa in the Rustamid period (mid-eighth–early tenth centuries) and Jerba and Warjalan in the Middle Period (eleventh–sixteenth centuries).

With each dramatic change to the religious and political landscape of Northern Africa came a change to the trajectory of the material network. The collapse of Zirid power in the eleventh century, the arrival of the Almohads in the twelfth, the disappearance of Ibadi communities in the Jarid, and the destruction of Sedrata each required a redrawing of the paths connecting Ibadi communities. On the narrative level, the prosopographies brought together people and places even long after some had ceased to be home to Ibadi communities. But the ebb and flow of the demographic and political changes in the region also affected the material network—composed of books and letters that Ibadi scholars copied, recopied, and circulated along ever-changing routes—by forming geographic hubs of manuscript production. While these changes led to the formation of new Ibadi centers from the sixteenth century onward, they also spelled destruction for other, now lost, archives.

THE RISE TO PROMINENCE OF THE MZAB

When Jerban émigré Saʿid b. ʿAli al-Khayri (d. 1521) arrived in the city of Ghardaia at the end of the fifteenth century, the Mzab valley was just beginning its rise to prominence as a new hub of intellectual activity and manuscript production in Northern Africa. The decline of the pre-sixteenth-century centers of the Jarid, the Jebel Dummar, Sedrata, and Warjalan had severed the Mzab from the intellectual activity in the Ibadi strongholds on the island of Jerba and the Jebel Nafusa. In response, a delegation of students who had studied under Saʿid traveled from the

Mzab to Jerba, where they convinced him to return with them. Saʿid had a lot to offer the Mzab. He had studied in Jerba with some of the Ibadi luminaries of his lifetime, including Abu al-Najat Yunis b. Saʿid al-Taʿariti (d. sixteenth century) who had himself been a pupil of Abu al-Qasim al-Barradi's son ʿAbdallah (d. after 1431). Saʿid also counted among his teachers another famous scholar of the period named Abu l-Qasim Zakariya b. Aflah al-Sidghiyani (d. 1498).[5]

The transformation of the Mzab into the major regional hub for Ibadi intellectual activity and manuscript production owed much to its geographic position. Situated along routes connecting the Sahara, Western Africa, and the Mediterranean littoral, the towns of the Mzab were well poised to take advantage of Saharan trade. In addition to profiting from Saharan commerce, Ibadi traders and scholars of the Mzab would also have benefited from a specific trade good circulating in Northern Africa: Italian watermarked paper. As discussed in Chapter 5, the papers upon which the oldest manuscript copies of the Ibadi prosopographies were written, dating from the fourteenth to the sixteenth centuries, all suggest Italian provenance through their watermarks.[6] That scholars in the Mzab, Jerba, and the Jebel Nafusa were all writing on paper from Italy highlights how Ibadi communities in Northern Africa belonged to much larger commercial networks connecting the Sahara, the Maghribi littoral, and the Mediterranean.

Saʿid arrived in the Mzab at a time when commercial activity was enjoying a boom. And just as Abu ʿAbdallah Muhammad b. Bakr had established a link between Jerba and the mainland in the eleventh century, so too Saʿid linked the Ibadi tradition of the island with the Mzab valley in the sixteenth. Later known as ʿAmmi ("Uncle") Saʿid, he stayed in the Mzab for the rest of his life, training many important Ibadi scholars, copying numerous manuscripts, and founding a manuscript library in Ghardaia. Today, the ʿAmmi Saʿid Library remains a rich and fascinating archive. His life and career reflect the increasingly close relationship between Ibadi communities in Jerba and the Mzab valley, as well as marking the beginning of the latter's rise to prominence in the material

[5] On Saʿid b. ʿAli al-Khayri see Būrās, "al-Ḥayāt al-fikriyya."

[6] E.g. Makt. Āl Faḍl, MS dāl ghayn 015 (dated 5 Dhū al-qaʿda 883/29 January 1479); Makt. al-Quṭb, MS *thāʾ* 8 (dated 7 Ṣafr 758/28 January 1357); Makt. Bin Yaʿqūb, MS *qāf* 65 (late fifteenth century, based on watermark evidence); Makt. al-Bārūnī, MS 81 (sixteenth century, based on watermark evidence); Makt. Bābakr, MS 27 (sixteenth century, based on watermark evidence); Makt. al-Istiqāma, MS 118 (*al-khizāna al-ūlā*) (sixteenth century, based on watermark evidence).

network connecting these and other sites in the early modern and modern periods.[7]

A NEW HUB: THE WIKALAT AL-JAMUS IN CAIRO

Whereas the Mzab rose to prominence thanks to the activities of a Jerban scholar, the other new Ibadi hub of the post-sixteenth-century period owed its existence to a Jerban merchant named ʿAbd al-ʿAziz b. Mansur al-Bahhar. His decision to provide an endowment for the founding of a trade agency in the Tulun district of Cairo had a massive impact on the future of the Ibadi material network. First known as the Wikalat al-Bahhar after its founder, the Wikalat al-Jamus provided both spiritual and temporal support for Ibadi students, scholars, and traders in Cairo from its foundation in the early seventeenth century until the closing of its doors in the mid-twentieth.[8]

The agency and school carried different names over the centuries, but it remained a center for the copying of manuscripts from its beginning to its end. Regularly supported through endowments by wealthy Ibadi traders, students could spend anything from several weeks to several years at the Wikala. The volumes in its library's manuscript collection were copied and recopied, sometimes at the hands of multiple students, who transcribed texts in order to gain experience or else to finance their studies. The existence of this library, combined with the availability of writing materials and a supply of students-cum-copyists, meant that the Wikalat al-Jamus served at once as a site of production and a point of departure for manuscript books. Whether a scholar passing through to visit or to teach at the mosque of al-Azhar, a trader doing business in the city, or a pilgrim on his way to or from Mecca, any Ibadi who came through Cairo from the seventeenth century onward would have stopped at the Wikalat al-Jamus.[9]

The extant manuscript corpus of the Ibadi prosopographies reflects the rise in the practice of manuscript production in both Cairo and the Mzab valley alongside its traditional center in Jerba. The sixteenth to

[7] Ibrāhīm b. Bakīr Baḥḥāz, ed., *Fihris makhṭūṭāt khizānat Dār al-Talāmīdh (Irwān)* (Ghardaia: Muʾassasat al-Shaykh ʿAmmī Saʿīd, 2009).

[8] Muṣlaḥ, *al-Waqf al-jarbī fī Miṣr*, 59; Custers, *Ibāḍī Publishing Activities*, 39.

[9] A handwritten list of endowed books from the Wikālat al-Jāmūs was compiled by the late Jerbian historian Shaykh Sālim b. Yaʿqūb and translated in Martin H. Custers, "Catalog of Waqf-Books in Wikālat Al-Baḥḥār (Jāmūs)" (unpublished document received from author via e-mail on 12 January 2016).

the twentieth centuries represented an unprecedented period of copying and transmission of the prosopographical tradition. Manuscripts copied between the seventeenth and nineteenth centuries, an especially active period for intellectual activity at the Wikalat al-Jamus and in the Mzab valley, make up 61 of 112 extant copies of the prosopographies (Figure 8.1).

The modern-day (twenty-first-century) distribution of these manuscripts likewise points to the historical and contemporary importance of the Mzab and Jerba, in particular, as sites of preservation for the Ibadi manuscript tradition over the long term. Libraries in these two places hold 60 percent of the extant corpus.

The endowment process that allowed the libraries of the Mzab and the Wikalat al-Jamus to grow also left behind textual vestiges in the extant manuscripts themselves. An eighteenth-century copy of al-Shammakhi's *Kitab al-siyar*, for example, bears an endowment statement making explicit reference to the Wikala:

> Endowed by the authority of God, may He be exalted, for the students of knowledge who study in the Wikalat al-Jamus—not to be sold, bought, or pawned.[10]

Additional manuscript copies of the prosopographies and many other Ibadi manuscripts bearing endowment statements like this one have survived, testifying to the long-term impact of the Wikalat al-Jamus on Ibadi manuscript production from the seventeenth century onward. A list of the endowed books at the Wikala's library from the 1930s also

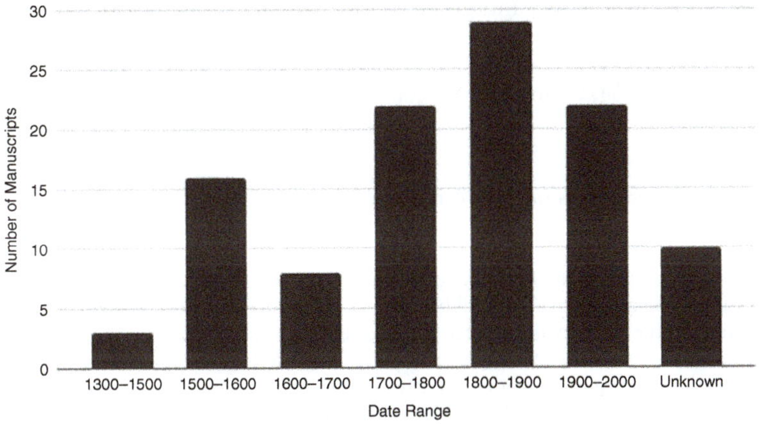

FIGURE 8.1: Temporal distribution of manuscript copies of the Ibadi prosopographies based on colophons, ownership statements, and watermark evidence.

[10] Makt. al-Khalīlī, MS 139, f.1.a.

survives, providing many of the names of the endowers and the dates of endowment. The dates are concentrated in the eighteenth and nineteenth centuries, during the most active period of the Wikala's existence and further emphasizing its role as a center for manuscript production. The list also includes many non-Ibadi works as well, suggesting that the horizons of knowledge for Ibadi students in Cairo extended well beyond the limits of their community.

As Ibadis passed through the Wikala they brought books with them, and they carried others copied from the library there with them with then left, expanding the orbit of the Ibadi material network to include not only the Mzab, Jerba, and the Jebel Nafusa but also Cairo as a central hub connecting Ibadis from Northern Africa to hitherto largely separate communities of the Hijaz and Oman. This new connection would have a big impact on the formation of a new, global sense of the Ibadi tradition from the nineteenth century onward.

THE ORBIT OF THE IBADI *SIYAR* IN COMPARATIVE CONTEXT

Comparing the manuscript tradition of some key Ibadi texts outside the prosopographical tradition provides some meaningful context for the orbital circuits proposed above. I base this comparison on a catalog-based survey of the following texts from libraries throughout Northern Africa and Oman, aimed at identifying both similarities and differences with the historical production and geo-temporal distribution of Ibadi prosopographical corpus:[11]

1. *Kitab al-tartib* (attr. to) Abu Yaʿqub Yusuf b. Ibrahim al-Warjalani (d. 1174/5)[12]

[11] The catalog survey draws from the entries in the al-Barrādī search engine developed by the Jamʿiyyat Abī Isḥāq in Ghardaia. This engine currently (2016) searches all collections cataloged by the Association and the Jamʿiyyat ʿAmmī Saʿīd, which includes most major manuscript libraries in the Mzab valley as well as the Bārūniyya Library in Jerba, the collection of Shaykh Aḥmad al-Khalīlī in Oman, and those manuscripts housed in the collections of the Ministry of National Heritage and Culture in Oman.

[12] This work, also known by the longer title *Kitāb al-tartīb fī ʾl-ṣaḥīḥ*, represents *the* principal collection of Prophetic hadith in Maghribi Ibadi communities. It is actually a revised and compiled version of several collections of Prophetic traditions, associated with *inter alia* the Baṣran-era Ibadi Imam al-Rabīʿ b. l-Ḥābīb, whose work *al-Musnad* or *al-Jāmiʿ al-ṣaḥīḥ* represents the primary collection of hadith in Omani Ibāḍī communities. The two works are connected in terms of their manuscript history, but *al-Jāmiʿ al-ṣaḥīḥ* is only a part of the *Kitāb al-tartīb*. The distribution of manuscript copies in libraries today reflects this long-term history, with the *Kitāb al-tartīb* found primarily in Maghribi libraries and

2. *Kitāb al-idah* (attr. to) Abu Sakin ʿAmir b. ʿAli al-Shammakhi (d. 1389)[13]
3. *Kitāb al-wadʿ* (attr. to) Abu Zakariya Yahya b. al-Khayr al-Janawani (d. eleventh century)[14]
4. *Kitāb al-ʿadl wa-ʾl-insaf* (attr. to) Abu Yaʿqub Yusuf b. Ibrahim al-Warjalani[15]
5. *Kitāb al-suʾalat* (attr. to) Abu ʿAmr ʿUthman b. Khalifa al-Sufi (d. twelfth century)[16]

These works dating from the eleventh to the thirteenth centuries, all of which have enjoyed long manuscript traditions, make up part of the "core curriculum" of pre-modern Northern African Ibadi education.[17] That is, they represent some of the texts that alongside the Qur'an would have served as the primary readings or objects of study for Maghribi Ibadi scholars-in-training. The large number of extant commentaries (*hashiya* or *sharh*) and abridgements or summaries (*mukhtasar*s) of these texts reinforces their popularity.[18]

the *Musnad* of Abū al-Rabīʿ found primarily in Omani libraries. Printed editions in the twentieth century did much to make the two spheres of Ibadi communities aware of one another. See *Kitāb al-tartīb* in Custers, *al-Ibāḍiyya* (2016), vol. II, 493. Cf. "Closed and Open Scholarship: Abū Yaʿqūb Yūsuf al-Wārjalānī," in Wilkinson, *Ibāḍism*, 430–37.

13 This work represents one of the principal compendiums of Ibadi *fiqh* from the Middle Period. On manuscript copies and printed editions see "Kitāb al-Īḍāḥ," in Custers, *al-Ibāḍiyya* (2016), vol. II, 406–11.

14 An important work in *furūʿ* from the Middle Period, on printed editions and commentaries see "K. al-Waḍʿ" in Custers, *al-Ibāḍiyya* (2016), vol. II, 249–52.

15 This is a work of Ibadi *uṣūl al-fiqh* in the Middle Period. On manuscript copies and print editions see "K. al-ʿAdl wa-ʾl-inṣāf fī maʿrifat ūṣūl al-fiqh wa-ʾl-ikhtilāf" in Custers, *al-Ibāḍiyya* (2016), vol. II, 488–90.

16 This work of *ʿaqīda* from the twelfth century enjoyed centuries of popularity in manuscript form. On extant copies see "K. al-Suʾālāt," in Martin H. Custers, *al-Ibāḍiyya: A Bibliography*, 3 vols. (Maastricht: Universitaire Pers, 2006), vol. II, 298.

17 In using the term "core curriculum," I have in mind something akin to the historic core curriculum analyzed by Bruce Hall and Charles Stewart for early modern West Africa. See Bruce S. Hall and Charles C. Stewart, "The Historic 'Core Curriculum' and the Book Market in Islamic West Africa," in *The Trans-Saharan Book Trade: Manuscript Culture, Arabic Literacy and Intellectual History in Muslim Africa* (Leiden; Boston: Brill, 2011), 109–74.

18 Each of the five works from the sample core curriculum has a long history of commentaries (*ḥawāshī* and *shurūḥ*). From Mzab libraries and the Bārūniyya Library in Jerba alone, the al-Barrādī search engine from Jamʿiyyat Abī Isḥāq in Ghardaia shows the following number of commentaries: *Kitāb al-tartīb* (10); *Kitāb al-ʿadl wa l-inṣāf* (9); *Kitāb al-waḍʿ* (9); *Kitāb al-īḍāḥ* (3); *Kitāb al-suʾālāt* (4). The Bin Yaʿqūb Library in Jerba also houses numerous *shurūḥ* and *ḥawāshī* on these and other core curriculum Ibadi texts. Examples from complete titles in the preliminary inventory: Makt. Bin Yaʿqūb, MS *sīn* 2, "Ḥāshiyya ʿalā sharḥ *al-ʿAdl*"; MS *sīn* 12, *Sharḥ mukhtaṣar al-ʿAdl wa sharḥuhu* [*sic*]; MS *kāf* 5,

The number of extant copies of these titles conforms generally to the extant Ibadi prosopographical corpus (Figures 8.2 and 8.3), suggesting that the prosopographical works and their historical trajectories and orbits of transmission represent broader trends. More specifically, however, these five works from the "core curriculum" reflect similar contours to the temporal distribution of Ibadi manuscript survival and production. As in the case of the prosopographies, far fewer manuscripts have survived from the fourteenth to sixteenth centuries than for later periods, although with a slightly larger number of extant copies from the late medieval period. Likewise, these comparisons also further emphasize the importance of the seventeenth to nineteenth centuries for the production of Ibadi manuscripts in Northern Africa (Figure 8.4). Consistent with the evidence from the Ibadi prosopographical corpus, this core period of the operation of the *Wikalat al-Jamus* witnessed the clear majority of transcriptions in the sample.

While the colophons of many of the manuscripts from this sample core curriculum do not mention their place of transcription, those that

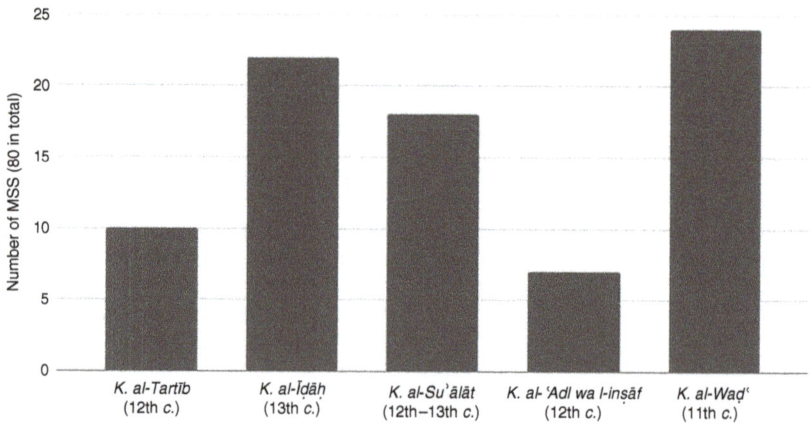

FIGURE 8.2: Sample of core curriculum texts. This corpus of eighty manuscripts comes from libraries across Northern Africa and two collections from Oman.

Ḥāshiyat Ibn Abī Sitta 'alā al-juz' al-thālith min Kitāb al-īḍāḥ; MS *kāf* 23, *Sharḥ 'Umar al-Tilātī 'alā mukhtaṣar al-Shammākhī [al-'Adl wa l-inṣāf]*. For a full inventory of the Bin Ya'qūb collection, see Paul M. Love Jr., "The Sālim Bin Ya'qūb Ibāḍī Manuscript Library in Jerba, Tunisia: A Preliminary Survey and Inventory," *Journal of Islamic Manuscripts* 8 (2017): 257–80.

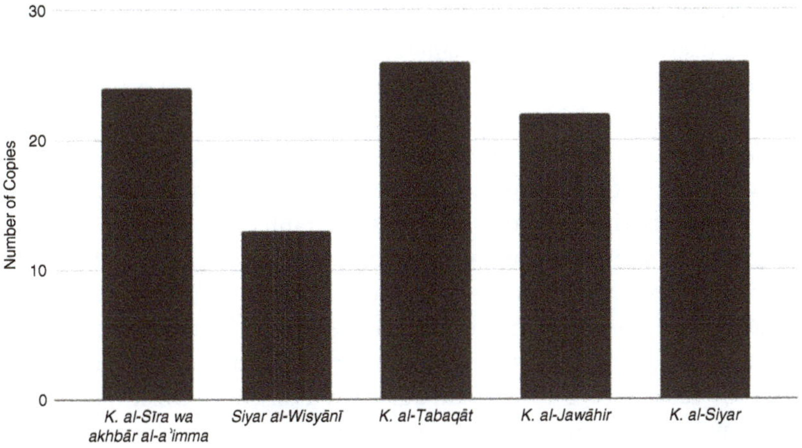

FIGURE 8.3: Graph showing the extant number of copies of each of the five main Ibadi prosopographical texts (totaling 112 copies).

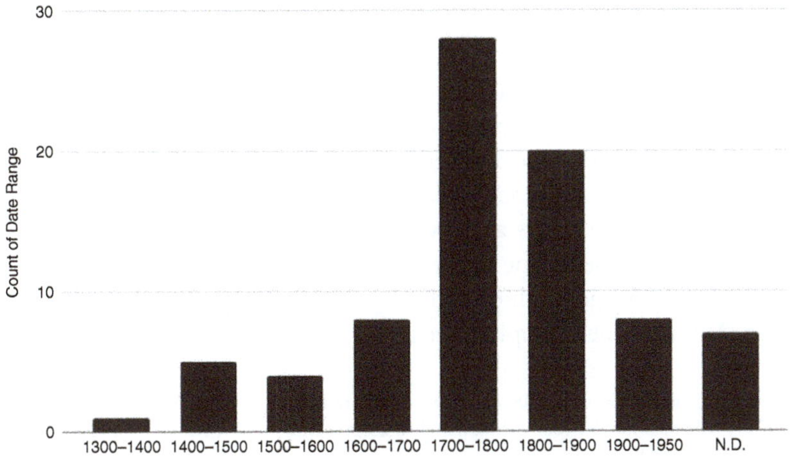

FIGURE 8.4: Temporal distribution of the sample core curriculum. Noteworthy are the spikes in manuscript production in the eighteenth and nineteenth centuries.

do consistently mention the Wikalat al-Jamus.[19] According to colophon and *waqf* statements, at least twelve manuscript copies from this sample

[19] In some cases colophons mention that the manuscript was transcribed in the Wikālat al-Jāmūs. In other cases the manuscript's location of transcription derives from a *waqf* statement, endowing the manuscript to the Wikāla. Yet other colophons note that the manuscript was copied in the "Egyptian abodes/houses" (*al-diyār al-Miṣriyya*), which sometimes refers to the Wikāla and its Ibāḍī school and residence in the Ṭūlūn district.

(15 percent of the total) were transcribed there.[20] Furthermore, the geographic distribution of these manuscripts in current archives reinforces the contours of the orbit of Ibadi manuscripts proposed above, since the majority come from either the Mzab valley or Jerba.

The two main sites represented in Northern Africa, the Mzab valley and the island of Jerba, belong to the late medieval and early modern orbit of manuscripts in which the prosopographies moved. Upon closer investigation, the somewhat surprising absence of Egypt and the large representation of Oman in this distribution actually support the centrality of the Wikalat al-Jamus in the orbit of Ibadi manuscripts from the late medieval period up to the twentieth century.[21] The majority of these texts from the sample core curriculum currently housed in Oman originated in the Wikalat al-Jamus. These manuscripts, originally belonging to the endowed library of the Wikala, were purchased in the twentieth century by Shaykh Ahmad al-Khalili.[22]

EXEMPLARY TRAJECTORIES

While in most cases the journeys of Ibadi manuscripts along this expanded orbit escape detailed description, a handful of individual cases exemplify the connections among the different hubs of Ibadi manuscript production and highlight the orbits along which the prosopographies and other texts moved. Three nineteenth- and twentieth-century Maghribi Ibadi scholars, all of whom spent time at the Wikalat al-Jamus, trace the trajectory of the Ibadi prosopographies and other Ibadi manuscripts in Northern Africa. Although the examples date to this later period, the orbits of these

[20] Makt. al-Shaykh Ḥammū, MS *ḥā' mīm* 49 (dated Sha'bān 1191/September–October 1777); MS *ḥā' mīm* 32 (dated Sha'bān 1304/April–May 1887); Makt. Āl Faḍl, MS *dāl 'āyn* 010 (dated Ramaḍān 1139/April–May 1727); Makt. al-Khalīlī, MS 46 (dated Jumādā al-ūlā 1214/October 1799); MS 49 (dated 3 Ramaḍān 1133/8 July 1721); MS 55 (dated 6 Rabī' al-thānī 1225/13 May 1810); MS 72 (dated Sha'bān 1198/June–July 1784); Makt. 'Ammī Sa'īd, MS *mīm* 18 (*al-khizāna al-'āmma*) (dated late Sha'bān 1166/mid–late June 1753); Makt. al-Istiqāma, MS *alif* 98 (dated 16 Rabī' al-awwal/27 April 1679); MS 60 (dated 3 Shawwāl 1304/25 June 1887); Makt. al-Ḥājj Ṣāliḥ La'alī, MS *mīm* 222 (dated 5 Rajab 1273/2 March 1857); Makt. Bābakr, MS *bābakr* 21 (dated Jumānā al-thānī 1141/ January 1729).

[21] Examples from the sample "core curriculum": Makt. al-Khalīlī, MS 46 (dated Jumādā al-ūlā 1214/October 1799); MS 49 (dated 3 Ramaḍān 1133/8 July 1721); MS 55 (dated 6 Rabī' al-thānī 1225/13 May 1810); MS 72 (dated Sha'bān 1198/June–July 1784). The only example from the prosopographical corpus is a copy of al-Shammākhī's *Kitāb al-siyar* (Makt. al-Khalīlī, MS 139 [n.d., eighteenth century?]).

[22] Muṣlaḥ, *al-Waqf al-jarbī fī Miṣr*, 124, fn.1.

individuals and their books had been traversed by Ibadi scholars since the sixteenth century, with the rise of the Mzab and Cairo as hubs of intellectual activity alongside Jerba and the Jebel Nafusa. The examples are especially instructive because the scholarly life of each figure also led to the establishment of at least one major manuscript collection that has survived to the present.

The first and earliest of the three was Sa'id b. 'Aysa al-Baruni (c.1865). Born in the Jebel Nafusa in what is today northwest Libya, Sa'id belonged to a scholarly family already well known by the time al-Shammakhi composed his *Kitab al-siyar*. Sa'id completed his primary education in the Jebel Nafusa before traveling to Cairo to study at the al-Azhar mosque. Like so many other Ibadi students before him, he took up residence in the Tulun district and later served as the director (*nazir*) of the Wikalat al-Jamus. After completing his studies he spent some twenty years in Cairo teaching at the Ibadi school of the Wikala and at al-Azhar. While in Egypt he took advantage of access to Ibadi and non-Ibadi manuscripts there. He began purchasing books and copying manuscripts in the Wikalat al-Jamus. Many of those manuscripts in his distinctive hand survive to the present.

Following his return to the Jebel Nafusa, Sa'id continued teaching and collecting manuscripts. Among others, he purchased an entire library belonging to his relative Musa b. 'Ali al-Baruni al-Nafusi. A fortuitous visit to Jerba led to an invitation to take up a teaching position at the famed Miswariyya mosque, the founding of which was attributed to Abu Miswar Yasja al-Yarasani in the early tenth century. The death of the mosque's imam and teacher, Sulayman al-Shammakhi, had left the mosque inactive, and so Sa'id accepted the position and relocated to Jerba in 1811. He spent the remainder of his life teaching at the Miswariyya and the Jami' al-Shaykh mosque in the nearby town of Houmet Souk.[23]

When Sa'id moved to Jerba he took with him his impressive collection of manuscript books. The library continued to grow, today comprising well over a thousand titles, a great many of which are non-Ibadi works. These manuscripts came from Egypt and the Jebel Nafusa, and their journey represents one of the basic circuits in the orbit of Ibadi scholars and manuscripts from the sixteenth century onward. Beginning in the Jebel Nafusa, Sa'id traveled to Cairo, where he spent a significant period of his life affiliated with the Wikalat al-Jamus. The manuscripts

[23] Sa'īd al-Bārūnī, ed., *Fihris makhṭūṭāt maktabat al-Bārūnī bi-Jarba* (Tunis: n.p., 1998), 3; Bābā'ammī, *Mu'jam a'lām al-ibāḍiyya*, 184; Muṣlaḥ, *al-Waqf al-jarbī fī Miṣr*, 63.

he collected there traveled back to Libya before continuing on to Jerba. These manuscripts, inherited by his children and grandchildren, are now housed at the Baruniyya Library in Jerba. The opening of a new facility for that library in 2016, financed in part by the Omani government, points to the convergence of the two hemispheres of the Ibadi world in the twentieth and twenty-first centuries. In recent decades the Baruniyya Library has served as a rich source of information for scholars and students from Jerba, the Mzab, Jebel Nafusa, Oman, and Europe.[24]

The library today holds seven copies of the Ibadi prosopographies, including three copies of the *Kitab al-jawahir*, a fragment of the *Siyar al-Wisyani*, two fragments of the *Kitab al-tabaqat*, and one copy of the *Kitab al-siyar*.[25] Multiple copies of the same work, especially fragmentary copies, became a standard feature of nineteenth- and twentieth-century Ibadi libraries. Notably, not a single copy of any of these prosopographies dates to the lifetime of the library's founder. With one exception from the eighteenth century, they all date to the late sixteenth and seventeenth centuries. These dates point again to the especially active period of manuscript production and scholarship throughout the early modern period at Wikalat al-Jamus and elsewhere. Watermark evidence from these manuscripts reinforces the continued popularity of Italian papers in both Tripolitania and Egypt, where Ibadi communities could purchase the papers directly from Italian and French merchants or through intermediaries. Moreover, the orbits of Ibadi scholars and traders overlapped in these places with circuits of Mediterranean trade. Once they had exchanged goods for paper, Ibadis then brought that paper along the well-defined routes connecting Ibadi communities in the Maghrib and Egypt. The orbital movement of the manuscripts of the Baruniyya Library and its founder, who traveled with his books from the Jebel Nafusa to Egypt and back before continuing on to Jerba, reflects a standard Ibadi circuit for the movement of people, ideas, and manuscripts in early modern Northern Africa.

[24] Paul M. Love, "Écouter le conte d'un manuscrit: penser avec une copie d'une chronique ibadite de la bibliothèque Barouni à Djerba," *Études et Documents Berbères* 35–36 (2016): 301–13.

[25] Makt. al-Barūnī, MSS 73 (dated Ramaḍān 1090/October 1680); MS 72 (n.d., watermark suggests seventeenth century); MS 82 (n.d., sixteenth century?); MS 69 (n.d., mid-seventeenth century?); MS 80 (dated Dhū al-ḥujja 1173/July–August 1760); MS 81 (n.d., "Bull head and cross" watermark suggests sixteenth century); MS 70 (n.d., seventeenth century?).

The second representative figure of the orbits along which Ibadi books and people traveled, Salim b. Yaʿqub (d. 1991), was born in the village of Ghizen on the island of Jerba. Unlike Saʿid al-Baruni, Salim did not come from an old and distinguished family of Ibadi scholars. After his primary education in Jerba, he took a long break from his studies to work as a merchant in the northern Tunisian town of Bizerte. He described himself as a terrible student, and it was only in his early twenties that he returned to his studies in Jerba. He then went on to study for five years at the Zaytuna mosque in Tunis before moving to Cairo in 1933 to attend courses at the al-Azhar mosque. While in Cairo he stayed at the Wikalat al-Jamus, where he devoted five years to studying and to the copying and collecting of Ibadi manuscripts. Salim counted among his most prominent teachers Abu Ishaq Ibrahim Atfayyish, the director of the Wikala and a prominent Algerian Ibadi journalist, editor, and political activist. Upon his return to Jerba in 1939, Salim brought with him hundreds of manuscript fragments collected or copied in Cairo, along with magazines, journals, and lithograph books from Egypt. These include a number of valuable texts copied in Shaykh Salim's own hand, gathered together in several notebooks. The collection, today held at the Bin Yaʿqub Library on Jerba, includes manuscripts from as early as the sixteenth century up through the twentieth.[26]

Unlike the Baruni Library or many of the manuscript collections in the Mzab valley, which often reflect generations of collecting passed on through a family, the Bin Yaʿqub Library resulted from the efforts of a single individual in the first half of the twentieth century. This also explains the somewhat fragmentary nature of the collection, which comprises hundreds of titles ranging from incomplete fragments of one page to several quires. The Ibadi prosopographies, in particular, are characteristic of the collection. The library holds at least fourteen copies of the prosopographies, including at least one copy of each. These range from a one-page fragment of the *Kitab al-siyar* to a complete bound copy of the second half of al-Darjini's *Kitab al-tabaqat* in Salim's own hand.[27]

[26] ʿAlī al-Būjadīdī, "*al-Shaykh Sālim b. Yaʿqūb: ḥayāt rajul wa-tajribat jīl*," *Majallat al-ḥayāt* 12 (2012): 170–82; Sālim b. Yaʿqūb, *Tārīkh jazīrat jarba wa ʿulamāʾihā* (Tunis: Cérès Éditions, 2009), 3; Bābāʿammī, *Muʿjam aʿlām al-ibāḍiyya*, 167–68.

[27] Makt. Bin Yaʿqūb, MS *sīn* 14, *Kitāb al-ṭabaqāt* (dated 11 Ramaḍān 1357/4 November 1938 in the hand of Sālim b. Yaʿqūb); MS qāf 43, *Kitāb al-jawāhir al-muntaqāt* and [first folio from] *Kitāb siyar al-Shammākhī*; MS qāf 101, *Kitāb al-siyar*; MS qāf 102, *min siyar al-Shammākhī*; MS qāf 103, *min siyar al-Shammākhī*; MS qāf 168, *Sīrat Ibn ʿAbd al-Sallām [al-Wisyānī?]*; MS qāf 208, *min Kitāb al-ṭabaqāt li ʾl-Darjīnī*; MS qāf 238, *al-Siyar li ʾl-Shammākhī*; MS qāf 239, *min Kitāb siyar Abī Zakarīyāʾ b. Bakr al-Wārjalānī*;

The Bin Ya'qub collection owes its existence to the orbits followed by its founder at the beginning of the twentieth century from Jerba to Tunis to Egypt. Like al-Baruni before him, Salim traveled from Jerba to Tunis and then on to the Ibadi trading and intellectual hub of the Wikalat al-Jamus in Cairo. He collected hundreds of manuscripts, which made the return journey with him to Jerba. In the case of al-Baruni and Bin Ya'qub, the Wikalat al-Jamus played a central role in the production and distribution of Ibadi manuscripts in the eastern Maghrib. Alongside the Wikala, the fourth regional hub within this orbit, the Mzab valley, remained integral to the creation and maintenance of larger manuscript collections. In fact, the Mzab eventually overtook its predecessors in terms of the number of manuscript collections. The third representative scholar, Salim's teacher Abu Ishaq Atfayyish (d. 1965), completes the orbit of Ibadi manuscripts by bringing in the Mzab valley. In addition, the history of the collection associated with him demonstrates the changes to the material network following the loss of one its principal geographic hubs in the twentieth century.

The importance of this third and final Ibadi scholar extends well beyond the network of manuscripts and the orbits of Ibadi books and scholars. Nephew and student of the famous Shaykh Amuhammad b. Yusuf Atfayyish (d. 1914)—known as the Qutb al-din ("pole of the religion")—Abu Ishaq Ibrahim Atfayyish was born in 1896 in Benisguen in Algeria. Whereas the lives and libraries of Sa'id al-Baruni and Salim b. Ya'qub traced the circuits connecting the Ibadis of Jerba and the Jebel Nafusa to the Wikalat al-Jamus in Egypt, the career of Abu Ishaq emphasizes the distinction attained by Ibadi scholars of the Mzab valley. In particular, his story highlights the unparalleled prominence of this region in the formation of large manuscript collections by the nineteenth and twentieth centuries. Following his primary education in the Mzab, Abu Ishaq continued his studies first in Algiers and then in Tunis, where he studied at the Zaytuna mosque under the two great Tunisian juridical figures, Muhammad Tahir b. 'Ashur (d. 1879) and 'Abd al-'Aziz Ja'ayyit (d. 1970). In Tunis he became associated with the newly founded Dustur political party, which along with his outspoken opposition to French

MS qāf 240, *min tārīkh Abī Zakarīyā' [al-Wārjalānī]*; MS qāf 241, *al-Ṭabaqāt*; MS qāf 242, *min Kitāb siyar al-Shammākhī*; MS qāf 243, *min Kitāb al-jawāhir li 'l-shaykh Qāsim al-Barrādī*; The fourteenth copy was of the *Kitāb al-jawāhir al-muntaqāt*, listed in Custers, *al-Ibāḍiyya* (2006), vol. II, 74.

colonialism earned him an exile in Egypt.[28] This final detail also points to the ways in which Abu Ishaq was representative of Maghribi Ibadis in the twentieth century, in that he was far from the only Algerian or Tunisian Ibadi scholar or journalist to be an outspoken critic of French colonialism. Colonial-era archives in Tunis demonstrate a sustained interested in Ibadis like Abu Ishaq by the French colonial state. For example, the archives hold dossiers that keep track of Ibadi and other Tunisian endowments in Egypt as well as a file on the relationship between Ibadis in Oman and those in Northern Africa.[29]

In Cairo, Abu Ishaq continued his work as an active participant in the anti-colonial conversation already current in Egypt. He wrote for journals and newspapers, in addition to founding and editing the widely distributed journal *al-Minhaj*.[30] He counted among his friends an impressive list of both Ibadi and non-Ibadi reformers. His Ibadi colleagues included Abu al-Yaqzan Ibrahim b. ʿAysa (d. 1973), who composed a supplement to al-Shammakhi's *Kitab al-siyar* in an effort to bring the prosopographical tradition up to date, as well as the famed opponent of Italian colonialism in Libya, international diplomat, intellectual, and reformer Sulayman al-Baruni (d. 1940). His non-Ibadi colleagues were no less distinguished, including Rashid Rida' (d. 1935), Sayyid Qutb (d. 1966), and Hasan al-Banna (d. 1949).[31]

Alongside his connections to the broader anti-colonial and reformist circles, Abu Ishaq also played an important role in the promotion and preservation of Ibadi manuscript culture. From the time of his arrival in Cairo, he served as the final director (*nazir*) of the Wikalat al-Jamus, where he also undertook the editing and printed publication of many Ibadi manuscript texts. In the 1950s the Egyptian government confiscated the endowments maintaining the Wikalat al-Jamus, and the institution closed its doors definitively. In the years leading up to its closure, the fate of the Wikala's library rested largely in Abu Ishaq's hands. He sent many of the manuscripts back home to the Mzab valley, especially to the library of his uncle in the town of Benisguen, the valuable collection

[28] Bābāʿammī, *Muʿjam aʿlām al-ibāḍiyya*, 24; Custers, *Ibāḍī Publishing Activities*, 42.
[29] See Archives Nationales de Tunisie: FPC / A / 0281 0006 1949–1950 and FPC / E / 0499 0001 1934–1954.
[30] Abū Isḥāq Ibrāhīm Iṭfayyish, ed., *al-Minhāj: majalla ʿilmiyya siyāsiyya ijtimāʿiyya niṣf shariyya* (Cairo, 1925–30).
[31] Muṣlaḥ, *al-Waqf al-jarbī fī Miṣr*, 103–07.

today known as the al-Qutb Library (Maktabat al-Qutb). He took other manuscripts with him to his residence in Cairo. A small collection also ended up in the Jebel Nafusa, although in recent years these manuscripts have been moved several time due to political instability in Libya. A number of manuscripts also found their way to the Dar al-Kutub Egyptian National Library, where Abu Ishaq served as the first director of the manuscripts division.[32]

Like Saʿid al-Baruni before him, Abu Ishaq Ibrahim Atfayyish's career followed the orbit that Ibadi students and scholars had been navigating for centuries. Born in the Mzab valley, which had risen to prominence in the fifteenth and sixteenth centuries, he then traveled to the great coastal cities of the Northern African littoral for education. Although not by choice, he then went to Cairo where the Maghribi Ibadi communities had operated a hub of intellectual and commercial activity in Wikalat al-Jamus since the early seventeenth century. In addition to following the traditional networks of other Ibadis, Abu Ishaq lived at a time when Ibadis were fast becoming a more tightly knit and decidedly trans-regional community, connected by circuits of people and books (both printed and manuscript) extending from Algeria to Zanzibar and Oman. In addition, Abu Ishaq's career represents an ongoing attempt since the late nineteenth century by Ibadis to guide academic and religious discourse surrounding their community, beginning with the publishing houses of Cairo all the way up to the present, in the form of academic conferences and publications.

The manuscripts of the Wikalat al-Jamus, like those of the Baruniyya and Bin Yaʿqub Libraries, followed a trajectory similar to that of Abu Ishaq himself. By the 1950s the Wikala housed manuscripts written in the hands of dozens of different Ibadis from throughout Northern Africa and elsewhere. These represented the material network connecting the people

[32] "Inhiyār al-waqf," in Muṣlaḥ, *al-Waqf al-jarbī fī Miṣr*, 187–88. Cf. discussion in Custers, *Ibāḍī Publishing Activities*, 43. On the manuscripts from the Wikālat al-Jāmūs in the Maktabat al-Quṭb in Benisguen, see "Kutub waradat min Miṣr al-Qāhira: Wikālat al-Jāmūs," in *Fihris makhṭūṭāt khizānat muʾallafāt al-shaykh al-ʿallāma Amuḥammad b. Yūsuf Aṭfayyish al-Yasjanī al-shahīr bi-l-quṭb* (Ghardaia: Maktabat al-Quṭb, 2013), 44–50. I base the note about the Libyan manuscripts on correspondence with Martin Custers, who kindly sent me an entry on Sālim b. Yaʿqūb from his second edition of his *al-Ibāḍīyya: A Bibliography* (at the time in advance of its publication) in which he writes: "On 7 Feb. 2007, on www.tawalt.com, a website designed by Muḥammad Umādī, it was announced that his organization had acquired 21 MSS from the former Wikālat al-Jāmūs, copied by Nafūsīs. These MSS were brought to the library of Tawalt in Paris, and, unfortunately, before I had the opportunity to go to Paris and have a look at them, they were transported to Morocco, where Umādī moved to" (personal correspondence with author, 7 August 2015).

and places of those regions together in one central hub. Following the dissolution of that hub, the manuscripts returned along the same orbits traversed by the copyists who produced them back to the Mzab valley, the Jebel Nafusa, and Jerba.

Finally, the journey of one last part of the manuscript collection from the Wikalat al-Jamus points to the expansion of the Ibadi material network in the twentieth and twenty-first centuries. Those manuscripts that Abu Ishaq brought to his home in Cairo remained in the possession of the Atfayyish family until purchased by the (now) Grand Mufti of Oman, al-Shaykh Ahmad al-Khalili. Like the Omani funding to support the new building for the Baruniyya Library, the acquisition of Ibadi manuscripts from Northern Africa by Omani Ibadis marks the beginning of a concerted effort by Ibadi communities worldwide at the end of the twentieth and beginning of the twenty-first centuries to create a shared past.

CONCLUSION

From the Middle Period through the twentieth century, the Ibadi prosopographies moved along orbits linking key sites of manuscript production and intellectual activity in Northern Africa. Manuscript books, along with the people who copied and used them, traveled these orbital circuits dotted with hubs of human and textual contact. These hubs did not remain static, however, changing throughout the Middle Period as Ibadi communities faced increasing challenges to their existence. Following the disappearance of Tahart in the tenth century and the loss of southern Ifriqiya in the following few centuries, Maghribi Ibadi communities concentrated in three principal geographic hubs from the fifteenth century onward: the Mzab valley, the island of Jerba, and the Jebel Nafusa. Just as the small number of Ibadi manuscripts from the centuries before this centralization reflect the loss of former hubs, so too does the large number preserved in the three hubs of the early modern period reflect the relative stability of the fifteenth to twentieth centuries.

Somewhat surprisingly, what was perhaps the most significant new hub of the material network—the Wikalat al-Jamus—lay outside the Maghrib. From its founding in the early seventeenth century to the closing of its doors in the mid-twentieth, the Wikala brought Ibadis from these different centers in the Maghrib together. In addition, it connected them with their coreligionists from Oman and elsewhere. The trajectories of Saʿid al-Baruni, Salim b. Yaʿqub, and Abu Ishaq Ibrahim Atfayyish show this significant expansion of the orbits of the prosopographies and other Ibadi texts, and exemplify the orbits of the Ibadi material network in Northern Africa.

On the narrative level, the prosopographies constructed links among generations of scholars across time and space to form a written network that overcame geographic or temporal distance to bring together the Ibadi community. Complementarily, the material network linked the different Ibadi centers of Northern Africa in a tangible way through the movement of manuscripts and the people who carried and used them. As the Ibadi prosopographies formed these written and material networks, adapting to changing circumstances but never ceasing in their orbit, they together constructed and maintained an Ibadi tradition in Northern Africa.

9

Ibadi Manuscript Culture

***

A rich manuscript culture among Ibadi scholars in the Maghrib undergirded the formation of the written network and the orbits along which these scholars and their books moved from the Middle Period all the way up to the mid-twentieth century. While a detailed study of Maghribi Ibadi manuscript culture over these centuries is beyond the scope of this book, in this final chapter I present an overview of some of the ways in which manuscript culture complemented the written network and contributed to the process of tradition building. Drawing examples from manuscript copies of the prosopographies, I divide the history of Ibadi manuscript culture in the Maghrib into three broad thematic periods: the earliest extant copies of the *siyar* dating to the late Middle Period (fourteenth–sixteenth centuries) context that created the corpus; the rise of the Mzab valley and the Wikalat al-Jamus in Cairo as centers for manuscript culture in the seventeenth to nineteenth centuries; and the relationship between manuscript culture and printing technology in the nineteenth and twentieth centuries.

IBADI MANUSCRIPT CULTURE IN THE MIDDLE PERIOD (FOURTEENTH–SIXTEENTH CENTURIES)

The earliest surviving copies of the prosopographies draw a picture of the world of the movement of these texts and their uses. In addition, the paratexts of these older copies of the prosopographies leave traces of the production and circulation of their exemplars, which disappeared centuries ago.

Of the nineteen copies of the prosopographies dating to the sixteenth century or earlier, only three likely date from before 1500.[1] The oldest extant copy of an Ibadi prosopography is of al-Darjini's *Kitab al-tabaqat*, dated 7 Safr 758 (28 January 1357). Fortunately, this oldest copy is also one of the most informative. The early date given in the colophon, corroborated by the watermarks of two circles under a cross and a bull, places the manuscript at less than a century from the lifetime of its compiler (al-Darjini, d. 1271/72).[2] It also dates the copy around the lifetime of al-Barradi (d. early fifteenth century), who in his *Kitab al-jawahir* noted that he had seen only two copies of al-Darjini's work.[3] Following the explicit, this copy of the *Kitab al-tabaqat* also bears a collation statement—embedded in the colophon and in the copyist's hand[4]—noting that it was both read aloud and collated (*ʿurida wa-qubila*) with an additional copy. Taken together, these physical and paratextual features of the manuscript carry several important implications.

First of all, this mid-fourteenth-century manuscript represents at once the oldest copy of the *Kitab al-tabaqat* and the oldest extant reference in the prosopographical corpus to its predecessor, the *Kitab al-sira*. The collation statement also speaks to the existence of an additional copy of the *Kitab al-tabaqat* with which this manuscript could be compared. Likewise, the collation statement tells us that Maghribi Ibadi scholars read works aloud (either to a scholar who had memorized the work or to another person who was comparing an additional copy) and collated the manuscripts. This practice of collation and one of the formulae that accompany it (*ʿurida wa-qubila*) were common practice in contemporary communities in fourteenth-century Egypt and Syria. While they may not have had formalized

[1] Makt. Āl Faḍl, MS dāl ghayn 015 (dated 5 Dhū al-qaʿda 883/29 January 1479); Makt. al-Quṭb, MS *thāʾ* 8 (dated 7 Ṣafr 758/28 January 1357); Makt. Bin Yaʿqūb, MS *qāf* 65 (dated late fifteenth century, based on watermark evidence).

[2] "Two circles and cross" watermark in Makt. al-Quṭb, MS *thāʾ* 8, f.97; this version of the watermark is commonly associated with thirteenth-century Italian mills. See Charles-Moïse Briquet, *Les filigranes: dictionnaire historique des marques du papier dès leur apparition vers 1282 jusqu'en 1600. A facisimile of the 1907 ed. with supplementary material contributed by a number of scholars*, 4 vols. (Amsterdam: Paper Publications Society, 1968), vol. I, 213–14. Cf. 3155–74 in the same volume. For the "bull" mark, see f.150. This mark is not as easily dated. Briquet did not offer any very close matches, but in his discussion of bull watermark he suggests this variation of the "fat bull" ("boeuf gras") is of Italian provenance (See "Boeuf simple ou taureau," vol. II, 195–96). The only "fat bull" marks in Briquet (2767–70), however, date primarily to the early fifteenth century.

[3] al-Barrādī, *al-Jawāhir*, 3.

[4] The collation statement inside the colophon, for example, suggests that it was not added at a later stage. Collation statements appear regularly in other copies of the Ibadi prosopographies, but in hands other than those of the copyists and without any indication of *when* they were made.

audition statements like their Ayyubid and Mamluk contemporaries, this early copy of the *Kitab al-tabaqat* bearing a standardized formula for collation suggests that late medieval Ibadi scholars followed the conventions of manuscript practices current elsewhere both in the Maghrib and throughout the central Islamic lands.[5] This, in turn, connects Ibadi manuscript practices to the broader Arabic manuscript tradition of the late medieval period.

Finally, although the Maghribi script of this copy suggests that it was transcribed in Northern Africa, the collation statement unfortunately does not indicate in which region.[6] Nevertheless, the manuscript's "two circles under a cross" watermarks, which are primarily associated with fourteenth-century Italian paper mills, point to the use of Italian papers in Maghribi Ibadi communities as early as the 1350s. Regardless of where in the Maghrib it was transcribed, this manuscript provides a documented example of the broader trend toward the use of Italian watermarked papers in the Maghrib in the late medieval centuries (Chapter 5). Another of the pre-1500 manuscripts of the prosopographies, another copy of the *Kitab al-tabaqat* from the Bin Yaʿqub library in Jerba, also bears a watermark associated primarily with Italian mills.[7] This manuscript, which would likely have come to Jerba from either Tripolitania or Egypt, helps further reinforce the importance of Italian papers to late medieval Ibadi communities in Northern Africa.

The remaining sixteen copies of the Ibadi prosopographies (representing eleven different volumes) that likely date prior to 1600 expand the details of Ibadi manuscript practices and further refine the picture of the paper trade in this period presented in Chapter 5 above.[8] First of all,

[5] On which see Konrad Hirschler, "Reading Certificates (*samāʿāt*) as a Prosopographical Source: Cultural and Social Practices of an Elite Family in Zangid and Ayyubi Damascus," in *Manuscript Notes as Documentary Sources*, ed. Andreas Görke and Konrad Hirschler (Beirut: Orient-Institut, 2012), 73–92.

[6] Maghribi script often helps locate a place of transcription within the region, but scholars and students moved around a lot so it is certainly no guarantee of the copyist's origin. In addition, "Maghribi" scripts continue to escape classification. See discussion and references in "Maghribi and African Scripts," in Adam Gacek, *Arabic Manuscripts: A Vademecum for Readers* (Leiden; Boston: Brill, 2009), 223.

[7] Makt. Bin Yaʿqūb, MS *qāf* 65. The watermark is of a crown with a cross above it. In general, this motif is widespread in terms of both time and space. This specific version of the watermark, however, Briquet associated with fifteenth-century Italian mills. Cf. nos. 4645 and 4546 in Briquet, *Les filigranes*, vol. II. See also no. 987 (dated 1473) in Heawood, *Watermarks*.

[8] Makt. al-Ḥājj Saʿīd, MS *dāl ghayn* 23; Makt. al-Istiqāma, MSS 118 and 120 (*al-khizāna al-ūlā*), MS *alif* 99 (*al-khizāna al-thāniya*); Makt. Bābakr, MS 27; Makt. al-Ḥājj Ṣāliḥ Laʿalī, MS *mīm* 186; Makt. ʿAmmī Saʿīd, MS *mīm* 63 (*al-khizāna al-ʿāmma*); Makt. al-Bārūnī, MSS 81 and 82; Dār al-Kutub (Egypt), MS *ḥāʾ* 10418; Ivan Franko, MS 1055 I [photograph].

the geographic distribution of transcriptions deserves consideration. All but two copies were probably transcribed during the mid-to-late fifteenth century in the Mzab valley in Algeria. The remaining two, a fragment of the *Kitab al-tabaqat* and a copy of the *Kitab al-jawahir*, which can only be dated to the sixteenth century by using watermark evidence, are currently found in the Baruniyya Library in Jerba.[9] Assuming that they are like most manuscripts from that collection (Chapter 8), they would have come to Jerba in the nineteenth century from Libya or, less likely, from Egypt.

In addition to demonstrating the growing importance of the Mzab valley, these sixteenth-century copies of the prosopographies also carry watermarks that taken together point to the continuing dominance of Italian papers in the central and eastern Maghrib. The version of the "Pilgrim (Pèlerin)" watermark found on the paper of five copies (in three volumes) is associated with mid-to-late sixteenth-century Lombardy and Genoa.[10] The *tre lune* watermark, the provenance of which normally escapes identification, fortunately appears in a volume carrying a second support bearing a watermark of a ten-petal flower associated with mills in sixteenth-century Lombardy.[11] The marks of a Greek cross in an oval, the anchor, a curved letter "M," and a specific version of the famous "bull's head" with a cross above it are all likewise associated with sixteenth-century Italian mills. The provenance of other marks, such as the hand/glove with a flower or star or a single letter "P" are far more ambiguous.[12]

The paratexts of these manuscript copies of the prosopographies also shed light on the world of late medieval Ibadi manuscript culture. One

[9] Makt. al-Bārūnī, MSS 81 and 82.

[10] Briquet, *Les filigranes*, vol. II, 415.

[11] The well-known catalog of *tre lune* watermarks by A. Velkov does provide some guidance, but the only real way to date this mark roughly is with a clear and specific countermark. Walz notes the ubiquity of the *tre lune* mark in Northern and Western Africa in his article on the paper trade of Egypt and the Sudan: Walz, "The Paper Trade of Egypt and the Sudan." This specific mark comes from Makt. Bābakr, MS 27, f.37 (and "twins" on f.9 and 10); See also "Fleur à 10 pétales," in Briquet, *Les filigranes*, vol. II, 375. For similar marks see nos. 6617–27 in the same volume.

[12] "Greek cross" watermark in Makt. al-Istiqāma, MS 118 (*al-khizāna al-ūlā*), f.112. Briquet argued that, in general, the Greek cross was primarily of Italian provenance. The Italian origin of this version of the mark is supported by the "Pilgrim" mark appearing in the same text on f.2. See "Croix grecque," in Briquet, *Les filigranes*, vol. II, 315; "letter M" watermark in Makt. ʿAmmī Saʿīd, MS *mīm* 63 (*al-khizāna al-ʿāmma*), f.91; cf. no. 8401 in Briquet, *Les filigranes*, vol. III; "bull's head" watermark in Makt. al-Bārūnī, MS 81, f.14 and 15. See "II. Tête de bœuf à yeux," in Briquet, *Les filigranes*, vol. IV; cf. no. 14.523 in the same volume; "star" watermark in Makt. al-Istiqāma, MS *alif* 99 (*al-khizāna al-thāniya*), f.34 and 37; "letter P" watermark Makt. al-Ḥājj Ṣāliḥ Laʿalī, MS *mīm* 186, f.30. Cf. no. 8493, 8494, and 8499 in Briquet, *Les filigranes*, vol. III.

especially detailed colophon from a copy of the *Kitab al-sira*, dated 4 Dhu al-Qaʿada 982 (15 February 1575), provides a number of fascinating details relating to the prosopographies and manuscript production:

> So ends what was found in the exemplar. Praise be to God, Lord of the two worlds ... Transcribed by a servant, lowly before a majestic Lord and seeking from Him His forgiveness and His contentment, Abu ʿAbdallah Muhammad son of the jurist Yusuf b. Saʿid [transcribing it] by himself and for himself and for whomsoever God should desire after him seeking the revivification of knowledge and desiring to achieve it. And I beseech God for His aid and support. The transcription was completed between the *zuhr* and *ʿasr* [prayers] on [the day of] *al-Arbiʿaʾ* when four days had elapsed from God's month *Dhu al-Qaʿda* 982 [Tuesday, 15 February 1575]. May God forgive the copyist, the reader, and the listener and whomsoever follows His path. I beseech God that a brother in God may correct whatever errors he may find [in the manuscript] because we copied it at a time of mental preoccupation and the only thing that induced me to transcribe it was [the book's] rarity in Warjalan.[13]

The first striking feature of this colophon is that the copyist asks God for the forgiveness of three different people: the copyist (*al-katib*), the reciter (*al-qariʾ*), and the listener (*al-mustamiʿ*). This short invocation emphasizes that the subsequent uses of this manuscript would have involved someone reading it aloud before an audience. As discussed in earlier chapters, the prosopographies themselves described the oral collation of texts and the recitation of texts before an audience of students—at times with the assistance of a translator—and hearing, reciting, and memorizing the *siyar* was a central component of any student's education. A reciter (and his listeners) could also have been present at the time of copying. The copying of texts, however, did not always need to be a public affair. Another copyist transcribing the *Siyar al-Wisyani* in the Mzab a few decades earlier had noted that he was carrying out his own transcription based on another copy riddled with errors, which would mean he was copying it from a written version rather than an audition.[14]

The copyist of the colophon quoted above also makes a remarkable indication regarding both his reason for making the copy and his mood when he transcribed the text. He warns the reader to be on the lookout for errors and asks him to correct them, noting that he made the copy during "a time of mental preoccupation (*zaman ishtighal al-bal*)" and

[13] Makt. al-Istiqāma, MS 118 (*al-khizāna al-ūlā*), f.70.a.

[14] The text reads: "ghayr annī nasakhtuhu min nuskha fīhā mā fīhā min al-taṣḥīf ...": Makt. al-Ḥājj Ṣāliḥ Laʿalī, MS *mīm* 186, f.97.a (dated 23 Shaʿbān 956/15 September 1549).

that he only did it because of the rarity of the *Kitab al-sira* in Warjalan. Although the copyist does not mention where he made the transcription (likely in the Mzab valley), this statement indicates that he resided in Warjalan and that copies of the work were unusual there in the late sixteenth century.

According to a later colophon in the volume, the copyist continued to transcribe despite his personal preoccupations. This second text following that of the *Kitab al-sira* in the same manuscript volume represents the third of three sections associated with the *Kitab al-jawahir* manuscript tradition entitled "On the subject of death (*fi dhikr al-mawt*)."[15] The significance of this short text lies in the copyist's choice to transcribe it alone, rather than transcribing the entirety of the *Kitab al-jawahir*. Regardless of whether he copied the text from an exemplar containing only this section or simply decided to copy only this final chapter, the inclusion of this section points to the independent circulation of portions of the Ibadi prosopographies. The tendency of historians to view manuscript copies like these as "incomplete" ignores the widespread tradition of circulating portions of these texts and combining sections of them within a single bound volume. This volume, for example, also contains *responsa* from two different Ibadi scholars, whose texts—thanks to their juxtaposition alongside the *siyar*—carry physical and symbolic connections with the earlier generations of scholars described in the prosopography.[16]

An ownership statement located just below the colophon of the *Kitab al-sira* in this same manuscript also contains the earliest example in the prosopographical manuscript corpus of a loan statement:

> Property of Muhammad, son of the jurist Yusuf b. Saʿid al-Warjalani. Not to be sold or gifted. Whoever finds [it] in his possession, [should note that] it is a loan [and should be] returned[17]

Loan statements like this one, common in later centuries in the Mzab valley, emphasize that manuscript copies of the prosopographies moved around locally among different Ibadi scholars and students. A final feature of this colophon is an additional paratext added in the left-hand margin in a different hand:

15 Makt. al-Istiqāma, MS 118 (*al-khizāna al-ūlā*), f.77.b (dated 5 Dhū al-qaʿda 982/16 February 1575).

16 "Jawāb ʿan asʾilat al-Shaykh Aḥmad b. Saʿīd al-Timāsīnī" (f.77.b–f.81.a) and "Jawāb fī nikāḥ al-rajul mazniyatahu" (f.81.b), respectively.

17 Makt. al-Istiqāma, MS 118, f.70.a.

So ends the first part of the account of the Shaykh ... Abu Zakariya Yahya b. Abi Bakr b. Muhammad W[akzin?] al-Yajrani al-Warjalani. May God be pleased with him, forgive him, sanctify his spirit [etc.].[18]

This marginal note, which a collator or reader added after the original transcription of the main body of the text, to my knowledge represents the only known instance in which the name of the attributed author of the *Kitab al-sira* appears in full, including both his father's and grandfather's name and the additional *nisba*, al-Yajrani. This paratext also notes that the colophon marks the end of the first of two parts of the *Kitab al-sira*, which by the fourteenth century circulated independently of one another and which al-Barradi regarded as two distinct texts.[19]

Another manuscript, a copy of al-Darjini's *Kitab al-tabaqat* currently housed in the Dar al-Kutub in Cairo, likewise points to the uses of the prosopographies and other Ibadi manuscripts in everyday life.[20] The colophon of this manuscript carries the date of late Jumada al-awwal [*sic*] 996 (April 1588).[21] Although the copyist does not identify himself outright, an ownership statement appears within the colophon and in the copyist's hand, noting that the manuscript belongs to one Yahya b. ʿAbd al-Rahman. The manuscript also contains several other texts. The variety of these texts, all but one of which are in the same copyist's hand, reveals something about the use of manuscripts like this one:

(1) *Kitab al-tabaqat*
(2) *Responsa* of [Abu] Mahdi ʿAysā b. Ismaʿil to dissenters (*mukhalifin*)
(3) A Letter to the Ibadis [of the Maghrib] from the people of Oman
(4) A response to a question from the jurist Ismaʿil, written by the aforementioned ʿAysa
(5) A letter sent by the Shaykh [Abu Mahdi] ʿAysa [b. Ismaʿil] to the Ibadis of Warjalan
(6) An announcement of the birth of the son of the manuscript's owner
(7) A fragment from *Surat al-baqara*

This variety of contents almost all in a single hand and designated for a single owner, the otherwise unknown Yahya b. ʿAbd al-Rahman, serves as a reminder that manuscript books like the prosopographies need not have

[18] Makt. al-Istiqāma, MS 118, f.70.a.
[19] See discussion of Barrādī's book list in Chapter 6.
[20] Dār al-Kutub, MS *ḥāʾ* 10418 [microfilm].
[21] Dār al-Kutub, MS *ḥāʾ* 10418, p. 217 in microfilm.

been bound alone or copied in their entirety.[22] A student or scholar may have (and often did) compiled a bound volume on the basis of his priorities and interests, without necessarily considering whether the contents of the volume had any relationship with one another.[23] Furthermore, while paper was no doubt a ubiquitous commodity in Northern Africa by the sixteenth century (Chapter 5), this does not mean that it was cheap for students or scholars. In the absence of royal patronage and scriptoria, the production of the majority of Ibadi manuscripts produced in the late medieval and early modern periods would have been self-financed—meaning that in most cases every page of a quire was used.[24] The choice to bind (or have bound) various texts into the same volume was likely an economic one before anything else.

Nevertheless, the specific choice of having this copy of the *Kitab al-tabaqat* bound alongside that of the Mzabi scholar Shaykh ʿAysa b. Ismaʿil again speaks to important changes taking place in the Ibadi communities of the fifteenth and sixteenth centuries. The life and scholarly activity of ʿAysa b. Ismaʿil—a student of ʿAmmi Saʿid in the Mzab—are part of the transformation of the Mzab valley into a hub in the Ibadi network from the end of the Middle Period onward. This copy of the *Kitab al-tabaqat*, dating to around the lifetime of ʿAysa b. Ismaʿil, speaks to his importance already in the sixteenth century. The second set of his *responsa* (presumably from the Mzab) included alongside a letter from Oman also reinforces the importance of paper for establishing connections between different Ibadi communities, whether a day's journey to Warjalan or thousands of kilometers away in Oman.[25]

On the micro level, the addition of the birth announcement of the manuscript owner's son to the contents of the *Kitab al-tabaqat* also provides a glimpse into the role of a manuscript in recording important moments in its owner's life:

Praise be to God alone! The blessed boy, ʿAbd al-Rahman, son of our uncle Yahya b. ʿAbd al-Rahman b. Yahya b. Musa b. Afdal b. Muhammad, was born on the …

22 The final text in the volume, a fragment from *Sūrat al-Baqara* (pp. 229–31 in microfilm), is not in the same hand.

23 Modern examples of this are found in the private library of Sālim b. Yaʿqūb. The majority of bound volumes there were *majmūʿ*s, often made up of texts bearing no relationship in terms of author, time, genre, or theme.

24 See, however, the discussion of the Wikālat al-Jāmūs below.

25 The historical relationship between pre-Modern Ibāḍī communities in Oman with those of Northern Africa still requires much research. For an overview of the evidence see Djaabiri, *ʿAlāqāt ʿUmān bi-shimāl Ifrīqiyā*.

fifth of God's month Shawwal [in] the year 997[AH]. O God, make him blessed with long life, a preserver of Your Book, and a follower of the Sunna of Your prophet.[26]

Snippets of family histories and genealogies, often included in the margins or extra folios of a manuscript, serve as reminders that, like other Arabic texts, Ibadi books did not exist in isolation but also bore close ties to their owners' lives.[27] Likewise, the addition of the birth announcement less than a year after the completion of the transcription of the *Kitab al-tabaqat* and other texts in the volume emphasizes that manuscript books speak to the multilayered histories and diachronic existence of their different users.

Overall, these copies of the prosopographies provide a window into manuscript culture in Maghribi Ibadi communities and the broader transformations to the Ibadi intellectual network of the fifteenth and sixteenth centuries of the Middle Period. The watermarks of these manuscripts serve as witnesses to the initial movement of paper from Italy to Ibadi settlements such as Jerba, Jebel Nafusa, Warjalan, and the Mzab in the late fifteenth and early sixteenth centuries. The specific paths by which these papers found their way to these places remain unclear. Nevertheless, watermark evidence drawn from these manuscripts emphasizes the integration of these communities into broader networks of trade within the Mediterranean region, and especially their ties with merchants of the Italian Peninsula.

On the local level, the paratexts of these early copies from the corpus of *siyar* manuscripts also reveal late medieval Ibadi manuscript practices. Unlike their late Mamluk or early Ottoman contemporaries, Ibadi communities had no chanceries, no court artisans, and probably no large local book markets (if for no other reason than because, except for Sedrata in the early Middle Period, the largest Ibadi communities were no larger than small towns). Manuscript production in the villages and towns of the Mzab, Jerba, or Jebel Nafusa operated under far more modest and less formalized practices than, say, late medieval Cairo or Damascus. Nevertheless, the fact that students and scholars transcribed and collated these manuscripts according to the practices of their time, including standardized collation formulae, signals that Ibadi manuscript practice operated within a much larger late medieval Arabic manuscript tradition. In addition to formalized practices, the paratexts speak to their

[26] Dār al-Kutub, MS Ḥā' 10418, f.227.a [folio number from microfilm].
[27] See "History of Manuscripts," in Gacek, *Arabic Manuscripts*, 126–28.

important role as witnesses and testaments to the everyday lives of the scholars and students, who transcribed, recited, listened to, learned from, and owned them.

Finally, the circulation of these works as well as the variety of titles bound together with the prosopographies suggests an ongoing exchange of knowledge and goods, both by people and by the books themselves, among the different hubs of the Ibadi network in Northern Africa. The growing centrality of the Mzab valley alongside the older hub of Jerba marks an important development in the history of Ibadi manuscript culture; from the sixteenth century onward, it was the Mzab that would begin producing and preserving the largest collections of Ibadi manuscripts in Northern Africa.

IBADI MANUSCRIPT PRODUCTION AND CIRCULATION FROM THE LATE SIXTEENTH TO THE NINETEENTH CENTURIES: THE WIKALAT AL-JAMUS

As noted in Chapter 8, the Mzab did not stand alone as a center for manuscript production. The early seventeenth century witnessed the establishment of the Wikalat al-Jamus in Cairo, which served alongside the Mzab as an important hub for Ibadi manuscript culture. Although Jerbans and Ibadis more generally had been doing business and traveling through Cairo before the seventeenth century, the foundation of the Wikalat al-Jamus provided both spiritual and temporal support for Ibadis.[28] The Wikala carried several different names over the three centuries of its existence, but it remained a center for the copying of manuscripts from its beginning to its end.[29]

The extant manuscript corpus of the Wikalat al-Jamus, produced over the course of its more than three centuries of operation, has left an especially rich collection of details regarding manuscript practice and usage among Ibadi communities in Northern Africa. Copies of the Ibadi prosopographies from the period of the Wikala's activity, many of which originated there, reflect its importance as a center for manuscript production and provide detailed information on Ibadi manuscript culture in the early modern period. Of the fifty-nine copies of the prosopographies dating from the beginning of the seventeenth to the end of the nineteenth

[28] André Raymond, "Tunisiens et Maghrébins au Caire au dix-huitième siècle," *Les cahiers de Tunisie* 7, no. 26–27 (1959): 335–71.

[29] "Tijārat al-naskh," in Muṣlaḥ, *al-Waqf al-jarbī fī Miṣr*, 121–23.

centuries, eight appear to have been transcribed in the Wikalat al-Jamus. The earliest of these, a copy of the *Kitab al-tabaqat* written in Maghribi script with a colophon dating it to Jumada al-ula 996 (April 1588),[30] is bound together with a table of contents (*fihris*) compiled later and written in *naskh* script. While perhaps not the case with this specific example, the combination of different hands and scripts in many other manuscripts produced at the Wikalat al-Jamus often resulted from several students having transcribed the same manuscript.[31] The mixture of Maghribi and Mashriqi scripts reflects a heterogeneous student and scholarly community as well as the influence of Maghribi students living and studying in Cairo. The colophon of this manuscript also makes it clear that someone (likely a student) copied the manuscript for its new owner.[32]

As noted in Chapter 8, Maghribi Ibadi communities had adopted the practice of endowing collections of books, evidenced by the manuscripts from the Wikalat al-Jamus library bearing endowment statements.[33] As had been the case previously in the Mzab valley and in the Jebel Nafusa, the adoption of the *waqf* by the Ibadi community at the Wikala allowed for the accumulation of a substantial library. Students and scholars passing through could then have copied these manuscripts and brought them home. An eighteenth-century copy of the *Kitab al-siyar* bears a *waqf* statement making explicit reference to its having been housed in the Wikala:

> Endowed by the authority of God, may He be exalted, for the seekers of knowledge who study in the Wikalat al-Jamus—not to be sold, bought, or pawned.[34]

This practice remained in place all the way up to the twentieth century, when in 1938 the Jerban historian Salim b. Yaʿqub (discussed in Chapter 8) made a copy of al-Darjini's *Kitab al-tabaqat* at the Wikala, the colophon of which reads:

> So ends the second part of the *Kitab al-tabaqat* ... I copied this part from another copy in riddled with errors written by Ibrahim b. Sulayman al-Shammakhi (may

[30] Dār al-Kutub, MS *ḥā*ʾ 10418, f.217 [microfilm].

[31] The shelfmark and description of the manuscript notes that it came from the Taymūriyya collection, belonging to Aḥmad Taymūr (d. 1930). In his description of this collection, Amīn Fuʾād Sayyid noted that Taymūr often added a handwritten *fihris* to manuscripts in his possession, which would suggest that the table of contents at the beginning of the present manuscript copy of al-Darjīnī's *Kitāb al-ṭabaqāt* is in his hand rather than that of a student at the Wikālat al-Jāmūs. See Amīn Fuʾād Sayyid, *Dār al-Kutub al-Miṣriyya: tārīkhuhā wa-taṭawwuruhā* (Cairo: Maktabat al-Dār al-ʿArabiyya lil-Kitāb, 1996), 74–75.

[32] See discussion in Muṣlaḥ, *al-Waqf al-jarbī fī Miṣr*, 120–22.

[33] "Part 3: Index of names of Waqf givers and copyists," in Custers, "Catalog of Waqf-Books."

[34] Makt. al-Khalīlī, MS 139, first folio in digital facsimile [f.1.b?]).

God have mercy upon him). He completed it on Monday at the beginning of [the month of] al-Rabi' al-thani of the year 1302 h[ijri]. I am the weak slave, hopeful for Almighty God's forgiveness, Salim b. al-Hajj Muhammad b. Ya'qub al-Jarbi. I completed the copying [of this manuscript] on the day of al-Khamis, at dawn on of the 11th of Ramadan 1357 in Cairo, Egypt. After staying in Cairo for five and a half years, I returned with [the manuscript] to Jerba on 20 Dhu al-qa'da 135[8]/1939.[35]

These two examples, along with an additional copy of the *Siyar al-Wisyani* dated 1942 that appears to bear a *waqf* statement from the Wikalat al-Jamus, are indicative of the long-term maintenance of the library there and the continued practice of endowing books in the collection.[36]

Alongside paratexts, many bindings of extant copies of the Ibadi prosopographies dating to the period of the Wikala's operation in Cairo reflect trends in the binding of Arabic manuscripts in the Ottoman era. For example, full leather bindings bearing embossed mandorla (pendant) and border designs are characteristic of the bound prosopographies dating from the seventeenth to nineteenth centuries. That these bindings were produced in a variety of geographic locations over this period speaks to the widespread use of similar binding decorations by Ibadi communities across the Maghrib. Some of the most characteristic Ottoman-style bindings come from libraries connected to Tripoli, Jerba, and Egypt.[37] By

[35] Makt. Bin Ya'qūb, MS *sīn* 14, f.119.a.

[36] Dār al-Kutub, MS *ḥā'* 9112, *Kitāb siyar al-Wisyānī* (dated 1781–82), f.1 [microfilm]. Aḥmad Muṣlaḥ gives a list of thirty-six endowed book and the names of their endowers based on a *fihris* of the manuscripts once held in the Wikālat al-Jāmūs currently housed in the library of Shaykh Aḥmad al-Khalīlī, the Mufti of Oman. Somewhat surprisingly, none of the prosopographies appear in that table—including the example from that very library cited above: Muṣlaḥ, *al-Waqf al-jarbī fī Miṣr*, 228–29.

[37] E.g. Makt. al-Bārūnī, MS 73, *Kitāb al-jawāhir* (dated 1091/1680); Makt. al-Bārūnī, MS 72, *Kitāb al-jawāhir* (seventeenth century); Makt. al-Bārūnī, MS 70, *Kitāb al-siyar* (mid-seventeenth century); Makt. al-Quṭb, MS *thā'* 1, *Kitāb al-jawāhir* (dated 1090/1679); Makt. al-Ḥājj Sa'īd, MS 38, *Kitāb al-jawāhir* (dated 1153/1740); Makt. al-Istiqāma, MS 84 (*al-khizāna al-ūlā*), *Kitāb al-jawāhir* (dated 1192/1778); Makt. 'Ammī Sa'īd, MS *mīm* 18, *Kitāb al-siyar* (dated 1163/1750); Makt. al-Istiqāma, MS 130/*alif*, *Kitāb al-siyar* (early eighteenth century); Makt. al-Ḥājj Sa'īd, MS 26, *Kitāb al-ṭabaqāt* (dated 1180/1767); L'Orientale, MS ARA 30, *Kitab al-siyar* (dated 1187/1773). Pendant designs of course long predate the Ottoman era, but the pendant/mandorla floral designs embossed on the bindings of those manuscripts listed appear much closer to Ottoman bindings than, say, the crisp, geometric designs of Mamlūk bindings. For contrasting images of different designs, as well as a preliminary typology, see François Déroche, Annie Berthier, and M. I Waley, *Islamic Codicology: An Introduction to the Study of Manuscripts in Arabic Script* (London: al-Furqān, 2006), 290–310.

contrast, those manuscripts from libraries in the Mzab valley have slightly different features. For example, many have simple leather binding covers without embossing, or show signs of specific types of repairs such as the mixing of various colors of leather or the reinforcement of joints by weaving thick, wide, thread through the boards or flap.

In terms of structure, those prosopographies that are still bound (or rebound) share characteristics with the broader, long-term pre-modern Arabic Islamic bookbinding tradition as it relates to average quire makeups (most quinions and quaternions), number of sewing stations (typically two), primary endbands sewn directly to the top and bottom of the text-block, and spine covers with flanges attached directly to the text-block.[38] Overall, manuscript copies of the Ibadi prosopographies from across Northern Africa reflect larger trends in early modern Arabic-Islamic bookbinding while in some cases still speaking local practices and preferences.

A final feature deserving emphasis is the number of manuscript copies of the *siyar* from this period (Table 9.1). The survival of large corpora of manuscripts from the early modern period doubtless derives in part from their being much newer than their medieval predecessors. At the same time, the commercial and scholarly activity among Ibadi communities in Cairo and throughout Northern Africa—especially the Wikalat al-Jamus and the cities of the Mzab valley—also played an important role in producing these manuscripts.

Table 9.1 Early Modern (Seventeenth–Nineteenth-Century) Copies of the Ibadi Prosopographies

Period	Number of MSS	Dates given in MSS
1600–1700	8	1651–52; 1652; 1679; 1680; 1698
1700–1800	22	1703–04; 1707; 1719; 1720; 1736; 1740; 1750; 1753; 1761; 1765; 1766; 1767; 1773 (x2); 1774; 1775; 1778 (x2); 1781–82(?); 1790
1800–1900	31	1803; 1814; 1828–29

[38] However, see Karin Scheper, *The Technique of Islamic Bookbinding: Methods, Materials and Regional Varieties* (Leiden; Boston: Brill, 2015), 263. Due to the ubiquity of this feature, the pre-nineteenth-century bindings in the Ibadi prosopographical corpus support Scheper's recent argument that "case-binding" is entirely inappropriate for *most* Arabic-Islamic bindings: see "A Problematic Term: Case-Binding," 107–13.

LATE NINETEENTH- TO MID-TWENTIETH-CENTURY IBADI MANUSCRIPT CULTURE

By the mid-to-late nineteenth century, the Ibadi communities of Northern and Eastern Africa, as well as those of Oman, entered what many historians regard as a period of "renaissance" (*nahda*) in which Ibadi scholars transmitted and composed works for their local communities as well as for much larger regional, or even global, Muslim audiences.[39] This period coincided with several important historical developments, including the introduction of the printing press, the broader Arab *nahda*, and the beginnings of opposition to European colonial rule in Africa and western Asia. All these transformations affected Ibadi communities in the Maghrib, and have enjoyed the recent attention of historians.[40] One of their less commonly considered impacts, however, has been their effect on the Ibadi manuscript tradition during this period.

Martin Custers' study of Ibadi printing activities from the late nineteenth through the mid-twentieth centuries demonstrates the long-term overlap between Ibadi manuscript production and printing in Algeria, Tunisia, Egypt, and Zanzibar. The Ibadi prosopographical corpus also reflects this overlap (Table 9.2).[41]

TABLE 9.2 Nineteenth- and Twentieth-Century Dated Copies of the Ibadi Prosopographies

Period	Number of MSS	Dates given in MSS
1800–1900	31	1803; 1814; 1828–29; 1866 (x2); 1873; 1880; 1865; 1885; 1886; 1897
1900–1965	19	1920; 1923; 1924 (x3); 1926; 1931(?); 1938; 1942; 1950–56; 1950–57; 1965; 1973

[39] The sixth in a series of conferences focused on the *naḥda* era and its proceedings are set to appear in the publication in the future: "Ibadi History: The Nahda Period," Institute of Oriental Manuscripts, Russian Academy of Sciences (St. Petersburg, 1–3 June 2015).

[40] Ibāḍī Islam in the nineteenth century has been the focus of studies by Valerie Hoffman and Amal Ghazal, both of whom deal with multiple regions. See, e.g., Amal N. Ghazal, *Islamic Reform and Arab Nationalism: Expanding the Crescent from the Mediterranean to the Indian Ocean (1880s–1930s)* (London; New York: Routledge, 2010); Amal N. Ghazal, "The Other Frontiers of Arab Nationalism: Ibadis, Berbers, and the Arabist–Salafi Press in the Interwar Period," *International Journal of Middle East Studies* 42, no. 1 (2010): 105–22; Valerie J. Hoffman, "The Articulation of Ibāḍī Identity in Modern Oman and Zanzibar," *The Muslim World* 94, no. 2 (2004): 201–16; Hoffman, *The Essentials of Ibāḍī Islam*.

[41] Custers, *Ibāḍī Publishing Activities*.

Before the last two decades of the nineteenth century many manuscript copies of the all the Ibadi prosopographies continued to be produced. By 1885 both al-Shammakhi's *Kitab al-siyar* and al-Barradi's *Kitab al-jawahir* became available in printed editions in Egypt, Algeria, and Tunisia. There was a remarkable decline in the production of those two works after that date.[42] Only one copy of the *Kitab al-jawahir* dates to the twentieth century, and to my knowledge not a single copy of the *Kitab al-siyar* was made after its print date.[43] This speaks to the reach of the Ibadi printing houses, centered in places like Constantine and Cairo but with distribution networks connecting them to locations across Northern and Eastern Africa as well as Oman. By contrast, the remaining three works from the corpus, which did not appear in print until the twentieth century, continued to be copied (Table 9.3).

The Mzab valley continued alongside the Wikalat al-Jamus as a center for the production of Ibadi manuscripts in the late nineteenth and early twentieth centuries. In addition to manuscripts commissioned in the Mzab by European orientalists in this period, manuscript copies of the Ibadi prosopographies transcribed by Mzabis for local use also reflect some interesting features of contemporary Ibadi manuscript culture.[44]

TABLE 9.3 Copies of the Ibadi Prosopographies from the Twentieth Century According to Title

Uniform title	Number of MSS transcribed in twentieth century	Dates given in MSS
Kitab al-sira wa-akhbar al-a'imma	10	1924 (x2); 1926; 1950–06; 1965
Kitab Siyar al-Wisyani	5	1920; 1924; 1973
Kitab al-tabaqat	3	1923; 1938; 1950–07

[42] Abū al-ʿAbbās Aḥmad b. Saʿīd al-Shammākhī, *Kitāb al-siyar* (Cairo: al-Maṭbaʿa al-Bārūniyya, 1883); al-Barrādī, *al-Jawāhir*.

[43] In the catalog, the manuscript appears under the title "Sygn. Depozyt 1.2 Fragment anonimowego ibadyckiego traktatu historyczno-biograficznego." The first page of the photocopy of the manuscript, however, correctly identifies the work as "Fragment rekopisu ibadyckiego/moze K. al-Ǧawāhir al-Barradiego?" Library of the Institute of Oriental Studies, Jagiellonian Library (Kraków). The manuscript came to Lviv in the early twentieth century from Algeria, where it was copied at the request of Zygmunt Smogorzewski, giving it a *terminus ante quem* of 1931.

[44] On orientalists commissioning Ibadi manuscripts, see Love, "The Colonial Pasts of Medieval Texts."

In terms of binding structures, local preference for or variation of one feature appears again and again: the unsewn text-block. Manuscripts of the prosopographical corpus alone include eighteen examples of unsewn text-blocks.[45] Two of these examples date to before the nineteenth century, with the first dating to the sixteenth century in the Mzab and the second (dated 1090/1679) having been transcribed in the Wikalat al-Jamus by the Jerban copyist Ahmad b. Muhammad b. Ahmad b. Abi l-Qasim al-Sadwikishi. The remaining sixteen copies appear to date to the nineteenth and twentieth centuries. Finally, most of these unsewn text-blocks were transcribed and remain housed in the Mzab valley today.

Codicologists have offered several explanations for this practice within the broader Arabic manuscript tradition. In the case of the Ibadi prosopographies the choice not to have a text-block sewn can be attributed to regional practice and Ibadi manuscript culture in the Mzab valley. Karin Scheper has noted in her study of Islamic manuscripts at the University of Leiden Library (UBL) that Northern and Western African bookbinding practices sometimes differed from broader trends in the Arabic-Islamic bookbinding tradition—including "Berber" bindings from Northern Africa that were often "stabbed" bindings.[46] Nevertheless, the same study points out that unsewn text-blocks have been identified in a number of different collections worldwide, although only a handful in the UBL collection can be localized to Egypt.[47] There, Scheper suggests that booksellers dealt in unsewn quires for economical and practical reasons. Finally, she noted that unsewn blocks, with a handful of exceptions, appear to be a trend of the nineteenth and early twentieth centuries.[48]

The Ibadi prosopographies written on unsewn quires conform remarkably well to Scheper's suggestions, although only one of the copies can

[45] Makt. Irwān, MS 70 [two texts in different hands] (late nineteenth century); Makt. al-Istiqāma, MS 67 (*al-khizāna al-ūlā*) (dated 1229/1814); Makt. al-Ḥājj Ṣāliḥ Laʿalī, MS *dāl ghayn* 001 (late nineteenth/early twentieth century); Makt. Āl Yaddar, MS 45 (dated 1343/1924); Makt. al-Istiqāma, MS 120 (*al-khizāna al-ūlā*) (sixteenth century); Makt. al-Ḥājj Ṣāliḥ Laʿalī, MS *mīm* 032 (dated 1297/1880); Makt. Āl Yaddar, MS 79 (dated Tripoli 1283/1866); Makt. al-Ḥājj Ṣāliḥ Laʿalī, MS *mīm* 035 (nineteenth century); Makt. al-Shaykh Ḥammū, MS *ḥāʾ dāl ghayn* 98 (late eighteenth/early nineteenth century); Makt. Irwān, MS 68 (dated 1283/1866); Makt. al-Quṭb, MS *thāʾ* 2 (dated 1310/1897); Makt. Āl Yaddar, MS 45 (dated 1343/1924); Makt. al-Quṭb, MS *thāʾ* 1 (dated Egypt 1090/1679); Ivan Franko, MS 1085 II (nineteenth century); Ivan Franko, MS 1088 II–II.4 (nineteenth century); Makt. Bin Yaʿqūb, *qāf* 97 (n.d.); Makt. Bin Yaʿqūb *qāf* 113 (n.d.).

[46] Scheper, *The Technique of Islamic Bookbinding*, 263.

[47] See "Unsewn Manuscripts with Wrapper Bindings," in Scheper, *The Technique of Islamic Bookbinding*, 91–93.

[48] Scheper, *The Technique of Islamic Bookbinding*, 281.

be traced to Egypt, and it belonged to the library of the Wikalat al-Jamus. Many of the other copies from the Mzab valley also belong to library collections from the nineteenth and twentieth centuries and so, in terms of period, the Ibadi prosopographies certainly support Scheper's suggestion that the unsewn text-block reflects a trend in the nineteenth and early twentieth centuries.[49] Although much more work would need to be done on other unsewn text-blocks in the Mzab, those manuscript examples from the Ibadi *siyar* suggest that in the nineteenth and twentieth centuries there was a preference among Ibadi scholars and in Ibadi libraries of the Mzab valley for unsewn text-blocks for popular works like the *siyar* texts.[50]

More specifically, this preference in Ibadi communities stemmed from a need for the circulation of texts among students or scholars who used manuscripts from private (or, in the case of the Wikalat al-Jamus, semi-public) library collections. That is, just as in contemporary Egyptian practice, the practice of leaving text-blocks unsewn allowed Ibadi students and scholars to circulate individual quires among themselves for study or copying. For the nineteenth century, this explanation amounts to much more than conjecture given that dozens of examples of loan statements for individual quires have been identified and documented in the Mzab valley by Ibadi historians.[51]

In terms of materials, the extant prosopographies also reflect a transition from the use of hand-made papers in the early-to-mid-nineteenth century toward the growing use of machine-made and even notebook paper by the twentieth. This is first and foremost an economic phenomenon connected to the growing availability of cheaper machine-made papers (Chapter 5). Nevertheless, watermark evidence suggests that up

[49] In addition to Scheper's examples and the Ibadi manuscripts noted here, during a recent (2015) inventory of part of the Jaʿayyiṭ family library in Tunis, I identified many texts written on unsewn text-blocks dating to the mid-nineteenth century. The results of that survey are currently in preparation for publication.

[50] An interesting local variation occurred in early twentieth-century Jerba, where the historian Sālim b. Yaʿqūb had many manuscripts that he had brought from the Wikālat al-Jāmūs quarter bound in leather and cloth. See Love, "The Sālim Bin Yaʿqūb Ibāḍī Manuscript Library."

[51] Loan statements represent only one part of the exhaustive, multi-authored study of the autograph manuscripts of Amuḥammad b. Yūsuf Aṭfayyish (d. 1914) in Benisguen in Algeria: *Fihris makhṭūṭāt khizānat muʾallafāt al-shaykh al-ʿallāma Amuḥammad b. Yūsuf Aṭfayyish al-Yasjanī al-shahīr bi-ʾl-quṭb*. An example within the corpus is a nineteenth-century binding made of printed French texts glued together as pasteboards. On the interior of the top board is a note from the binder, who had copied the original statement of loan that was on the interior of the original board (Makt. al-Quṭb, MS *thāʾ* 8).

until the end of the nineteenth and even the beginning of the twentieth century, Ibadi scholars still preferred to transcribe new manuscripts on Italian paper. A similar, largely unsurprising change occurs in writing materials, with the growing use of manufactured ink pens in copies from the twentieth century. One exception is a copy of the *Siyar al-Wisyani*, transcribed in the Mzab during the 1920s, elegantly bound in full leather and copied on hand-made, watermarked Italian paper.[52] Overall, however, the prosopographical manuscript corpus suggests a movement toward cheaper materials from the late nineteenth and early twentieth centuries onward.

A final aspect of Ibadi manuscript culture in this period deserves mention. Although historians are accustomed to drawing a distinction between manuscript and printed materials, a typical feature of many nineteenth-century libraries in Northern and Eastern Africa was the existence of what might be called "hybrid" works, containing both printed and handwritten sections—and Ibadi libraries are no exception. As many readers continue to do today, Ibadi scholars who purchased lithograph or, later, typeset editions of the *siyar* and other texts would often make extensive marginal notes by hand, in the style of a traditional manuscript *hashiya*. Likewise, it is common to find a handwritten table of contents either glued to or even sewn into a printed volume. Furthermore, handwritten statements of ownership, sale, purchase, or loan remained standard features of early printed editions of Ibadi texts. Many scholars also owned *both* manuscript and lithographed or typeset editions of the same texts.

In short, the Ibadi manuscript tradition did not come to an abrupt halt at the end of the nineteenth century. Instead, Ibadis throughout Northern Africa continued to transcribe manuscripts well into the twentieth century, although on increasingly cheaper materials. Likewise, the owners and users of printed Ibadi texts like the prosopographies did not suddenly cease to be part of the manuscript culture that preceded printing. On the contrary, the manuscript tradition fused with the new technology of printing and the users of those texts interacted with them in much the same way as their predecessors had done with manuscript books throughout the early modern period.

[52] Makt. Āl Yaddar, MS 45, *Kitāb siyar al-Wisyānī* (dated Benisguen, 1343/1924). Two other examples of this same elegant style of binding from the Mzab were brought to Lvov by Zygmunt Smogorsewski: Ivan Franko, MS 993 II, *Kitāb al-dalīl wa-ʾl-burhān* (mid-to-late nineteenth century) and MS 991 II, *Kitāb al-nīl* (dated 1287/1874).

CONCLUSION

This chapter has identified three major phases in the Ibadi manuscript tradition based on the extant manuscript copies of the prosopographical corpus. While the conclusions presented here await corroboration based on more extensive surveys of a variety of texts, a few points can be offered regarding Ibadi manuscript culture from the late fourteenth through the mid-twentieth centuries.

From the earliest examples onward, the corpus suggests that Ibadis conformed to practices that were widespread elsewhere, such as collation and audition, though in a far less formal fashion than their late medieval Muslim contemporaries in Northern Africa or western Asia. Also by the end of the Middle Period, as al-Shammakhi had already noted in the fifteenth century, Ibadis had adopted the practice of endowing books for posterity. This allowed for the formation of libraries housing much larger collections than had been the case in earlier periods.

Moving forward in time, the Wikalat al-Jamus and the Mzab valley emerge as important centers for manuscript production in the early modern period (seventeenth–nineteenth centuries). The Wikalat al-Jamus, in particular, served as a hub for the production of manuscripts, and this endowed collection provided students and scholars with dozens of titles for study and copy. The manuscripts produced at the Wikala were often a group effort, with two or more students working on the same manuscript. Scholars passing through Cairo could commission manuscripts either for their own personal use or with the aim of gifting them as endowments in the Wikala's library. Bindings of the prosopographies dating to the early modern period, whether from Egypt or elsewhere, demonstrate that Ibadis largely conformed to stylistic trends current in the Ottoman period, including full leather bindings bearing embossed pendant designs, floral patterns, and borders.

Finally, the modern period witnessed the continuation of the Ibadi manuscript tradition well into the nineteenth and twentieth centuries. The preference for unsewn text-blocks in the Mzab and possibly in Egypt reflects the practice of lending individual quires for the purpose of reading or copying. The widespread availability of the printed editions of the *Kitab al-siyar* and *Kitab al-jawahir*, however, means that manuscript copies of those works virtually disappeared at the end of the nineteenth century. By contrast, the other three prosopographical works continued to be copied well into the twentieth century. This, along with the combination of printed and handwritten materials in the same volumes, suggests that while printing did have an impact on Ibadi manuscript culture it did not suddenly supplant it.

The image of the Ibadi manuscript tradition from the Middle Period up to the twentieth century that emerges from this survey serves as a fitting complement to the process of the construction and maintenance of the Ibadi tradition over these same centuries. The previous chapters have demonstrated that the construction of the written network over the course of the Middle Period responded to circumstances particular to the Ibadi community in the Maghrib while at the same time reflecting broader changes to the religious, political, economic, and linguistic contexts in which Ibadis lived. In the same way, Ibadi manuscript culture and practices from the Middle Period to the twentieth century at once reflects the localized practices of Ibadi communities and the broader historical trends in the Arab-Islamic manuscript tradition up through the twentieth century.

Conclusion: (Re)inventing an Ibadi Tradition

***

This book began with my arrival at the first annual conference of the Ibadi Books of Siyar in 2014. One year after that conference, on 30 October 2015, I walked into the Hôtel Acropole in Les Berges du Lac in Tunis to attend its second meeting. Once again, specialists in Ibadi Islam came together from across the region and from Oman to discuss the Ibadi prosopographical tradition. This time, however, one book had been chosen as the focus of the conference: the *Kitab al-siyar* by Abu al-ʿAbbas al-Shammakhi. This struck me as a fitting choice for the first in what promised to be a series of compiler-specific conferences. Al-Shammakhi's book marked the end of the tradition of prosopography in the Middle Period, and so it made sense to begin with this most comprehensive version of the written network.

By that time I had spent over a year visiting libraries in Algeria, Tunisia, France, Italy, Ukraine, and Poland searching for copies of the *siyar* texts. These collections ranged from formal archives to university and cultural association libraries to stacks of hundreds of loose folios in someone's house. This experience left me keenly aware of an incredible modern network of Ibadi scholars, institutes, and associations that have been working diligently over the past couple of decades to document, catalog, preserve, and curate collections of Ibadi manuscripts across the Mediterranean region. Ibadi institutes and organizations in Algeria, Tunisia, and Libya fashion themselves as the preservers of the Ibadi tradition in the Maghrib. Over the past several years they have sought to do so through the creation of these libraries as well as private schools and clubs of different kinds.[1]

As a result, by the time I entered that hotel lobby in Tunis, I had a sense of the conference's place in a much bigger trend in the reimagining of Ibadi history underway in Northern Africa and beyond. The group that organized the conference, Jamʿiyyat Jarba al-Tawasul (Association Djerba Ettawasol), was one of those new Ibadi associations to have appeared in the past several years. In addition to organizing conferences, Ettawasol publishes a glossy color magazine addressing historical, religious, and social topics relevant to the Ibadi community, and runs a weekend school and lecture series at its headquarters in downtown Tunis just beside the Bibliothèque Nationale de Tunisie. This conference was at the core of several projects to construct a new, transnational identity for a global Ibadi network. What better symbol to use than the texts of the Ibadi prosopographical tradition of the Middle Period, which in the eyes of contemporary Ibadis had sought to do something very similar?[2]

As I noted at the beginning of the book, contemporary Ibadis are claiming a historical continuity in drawing that straight line between the modern Ibadi community and those of the scholars of the past. In many ways, this marks a further step in the elaboration of the "discursive tradition" of Ibadi Islam, to borrow Talal Asad's phrase, that has been the focus of this book.[3] But in other ways, the Ibadi community and its tradition are not only "imagined," in Benedict Anderson's well-known sense of the term, but are also *invented.* Eric Hobsbawm wrote that

> the peculiarity of "invented traditions" is that the continuity with [a historic past] is largely factitious. In short, they are responses to novel situations which take the form of reference to old situations ... It is the contrast between the constant change and innovation of the modern world and the attempt to structure at least

[1] In many ways, this is part of the trend that Augustin Jomier has discussed in his work on the invention of Ibadi "heritage" and "community" in twentieth-century Algeria. See Augustin Jomier, "*Un réformisme islamique dans l'Algérie coloniale: oulémas ibadites et société du Mzab (c. 1880–c.1970)*" (Ph.D. thesis, Université du Maine, 2015); cf. Augustin Jomier, "Iṣlāḥ ibāḍite et intégration nationale: vers une communauté mozabite ? (1925–1964)," *Revue des mondes musulmans et de la Méditerranée* 132 (2012): 175–95.

[2] For more on the Jamʿiyyat al-Tawāṣul (Ettawasol), its publications, and cultural activities see: www.ettawasol.net (accessed 5 February 2018).

[3] Talal Asad, *The Idea of an Anthropology of Islam* (Washington, D.C.: Center for Contemporary Arab Studies, Georgetown University, 1986).

some parts of social life within it unchanging and invariant, the makes the "invention of tradition" so interesting for historians.[4]

This book has shown what this modern invention of an Ibadi tradition overlooks through its vision of unchanging historical continuity: the conflict and change experienced by Ibadi communities in Northern Africa over nearly a millennium. In other words, inventing Ibadi Islam in the present means forgetting how the Ibadi tradition was invented and reinvented time and time again in the past. It is the process of constructing the Ibadi tradition and constantly maintaining it in response to changing circumstances that I have sought to trace in this book.

I have argued that in the eleventh century Ibadi scholars in the Maghrib began in earnest to construct a religious tradition through the formation of a written network. With the compiling of each new iteration, the written network expanded and refined the boundaries of the Ibadi community through the inclusion or exclusion of individuals. These texts drew connections among scholars, bringing them into the same community and marking its limits. Even those scholars whose lives were separated from one another by hundreds of years or thousands of kilometers could be linked through their stories appearing together in the same prosopography.

This was an iterative process, unfolding over several centuries. In each case, the Ibadi prosopographies reflected the historical contexts and changing circumstances that produced them. The first work of *siyar*, the *Kitab al-sira* (Chapter 2), initiated the tradition with its lament that the Ibadis and their history risked disappearing altogether in the eleventh century. This resulted from two centuries of increasing political, religious, and linguistic marginalization in Northern Africa. The *Kitab al-sira* succeeded in overcoming this threat of disappearance by linking the compiler's eleventh-century contemporaries with a tradition of the Ibadi Imams in both Basra and Tahart. The leadership of the scholars replaced the leadership of the Imam in what the *Kitab al-sira* presented as a seamless and inevitable progression of events. The connections among those authors made up the first written network of the prosopographical tradition. When visualized, this network draws clear connections among different historical periods and demonstrates the centrality of a small group of individuals as hubs connecting hundreds of other nodes in the community.

The move toward formalization continued through the twelfth and thirteenth centuries, as the *Siyar al-Wisyani* (Chapter 3) and the *Kitab*

[4] Eric Hobsbawm, "Introduction: Inventing Traditions," in *The Invention of Tradition*, ed. Eric J. Hobsbawm and Terence Ranger (Cambridge: Cambridge University Press, 2015), 2.

al-tabaqat (Chapter 4) both expanded and refined the written network. These prosopographies integrated much of the material from the *Kitab al-sira*, but they also updated the membership roster by including new generations of Ibadi scholars from their compilers' lifetimes, and drew them inside the boundaries of the Ibadi tradition. Each of these works likewise reflected the contexts out of which they emerged. The *Siyar al-Wisyani* demonstrates the important role of manuscript books to help mark the boundaries of community and connect scholars across time and space in the twelfth-century Maghrib. This composite text also reveals the increasingly defined role of the *ʿazzaba* as Ibadi scholars began to assume positions of religious and political leadership.

The *Kitab al-tabaqat* marked a new stage in the prosopographical tradition in terms of both language and content. Al-Darjini's work formalized the chronological structure of the community and the role of the *ʿazzaba*. His careful revision of the *Kitab al-sira* and supplement to it mirror the development of Arabic as a language of scholarship among Ibadis in the Maghrib, a change that reflects broader demographic transformations in the region. Lastly, his attention to biographies of scholars from specific regions of the Maghrib stems in part from the increasingly marginal position occupied by Ibadis there by the thirteenth century.

Al-Barradi's *Kitab al-jawahir* (Chapter 6) took the tradition a step further by taking a step backward, extending the written network back to the very beginnings of Islam. In bookending the history of Islam with the life of the Prophet Muhammad and the history of the Ibadi Rustamid dynasty, al-Barradi's work established a connection between the western and eastern communities, and recast the history of the Ibadis as the history of Islam itself. Likewise, the book list that belongs to the manuscript tradition of the *Kitab al-jawahir* links the two spheres of Ibadi history by bringing together their two corpora of texts.

The final iteration of the medieval Ibadi prosopographical tradition, al-Shammakhi's *Kitab al-siyar* (Chapter 7), brought together all the work of his predecessors into a great compilation of biographies and anecdotes. Network analysis of the relationships among the individuals appearing in the text revealed that al-Shammakhi's work provides a kind of broad outline of Ibadi communities and their history. Writing in the late fifteenth/early sixteenth century, al-Shammakhi's work likewise reflected the position of the Ibadis in the Maghrib, in which they found themselves a small minority. Although not a large community, the Ibadis of al-Shammakhi's time were no less mobile than their predecessors. This brought them into contact with the ideas and books of their Muslim coreligionists as never before.

This last point highlights another feature of the prosopographical tradition: the ever-increasing importance of manuscript books and manuscript culture to Ibadi communities of the Middle Period and beyond (Chapters 5 and 9). The availability of paper and leather in the Maghrib, and the manuscript culture for which these commodities laid the foundation, played a key role in allowing for the construction of the written network of the Ibadi tradition. Although there were Maghribi centers of paper production by the eleventh century, broader historical trends would suggest that paper used in Ifriqiya and Tripolitania in that earlier period would have come originally from Egypt or farther east. Nevertheless, the Ibadi prosopographies of the twelfth and thirteenth centuries suggest that, regardless of where it was coming from, paper was quickly becoming part of everyday life, and was readily available in the region.

The earliest extant copies of the prosopographies provide material evidence for a sea change in the history of paper and manuscript production in Northern Africa by the fourteenth century, however. Following the development of superior paper-production techniques in the Italian Peninsula in the thirteenth century, Italian paper came to dominate the market in the Maghrib where Ibadis lived. Watermarks carried by extant copies of the prosopographies suggest that this near-monopoly lasted from the Middle Period up through the beginning of the twentieth century. Paper of good quality was thus made readily available to Ibadi communities throughout Northern Africa through merchants in Mediterranean coastal cities such as Tunis and Tripoli, where paper could then be moved in caravans farther south into the Sahara. This was especially true for Saharan Ibadi communities in the Mzab valley from the sixteenth century onward, when that region became an intellectual hub and center of textual production.

Shortly thereafter, Ibadis established the Wikalat al-Jamus in Cairo, which served as a hub for manuscript production and circulation for the next four centuries. Like Tunis and Tripoli, Cairo also functioned as a center for the distribution of large quantities of European papers, evidenced by European watermarks in manuscript copies of the Ibadi prosopographies from the seventeenth to the early twentieth centuries. The lives of three exemplary scholars—Saʿid al-Baruni, Salim b. Yaʿqub, and Abu Ishaq Atfayyish—also demonstrated how the paths of paper and manuscript circulation overlapped with the orbits of Ibadi scholars and students, who moved among different hubs of intellectual activity in the centuries following the end of the prosopographical tradition. It was these orbits of people and books that helped maintain the prosopographical tradition throughout the early modern period. Manuscripts and the people who produced and used them were constantly on the move, connecting centers such as the Mzab, Jerba, the Jebel Nafusa, and Cairo. This remained the case all the way up to the late nineteenth century, when the prosopographies made their way to Ibadi printing presses in Cairo. Early lithographs of the *Kitab al-siyar* and the *Kitab al-jawahir* were produced in tandem with an ongoing manuscript tradition that transmitted the prosopographies well into the mid-twentieth century.

When the doors of the Wikalat al-Jamus finally closed in the 1950s, the manuscripts retraced the same circuits out of Cairo. The private libraries of those historic hubs such as Jerba, the Jebel Nafusa, and the Mzab valley today house copies of the prosopographies whose paratexts testify to their long journey from Egypt. But the manuscripts of the Wikalat al-Jamus are also symbolic of another important stage in the expansion of the Ibadi tradition outside Northern Africa. That many of the manuscripts of the Wikalat al-Jamus ultimately came into the possession of the current Grand Mufti of Oman, Shaykh Ahmad al-Khalili, is no coincidence. Already by the nineteenth century with the advent of Ibadi print houses the two historical spheres of Ibadis in the east and the west had begun to construct a sense of a global community. The nineteenth and twentieth centuries witnessed a broader attempt at a rapprochement not only between Ibadis and their Sunni coreligionists but also between Ibadis from the Maghrib and their confrères in the east.

Since its inception in the eleventh century the Ibadi prosopographical tradition has constructed and maintained the boundaries of the Ibadi community in Northern Africa. Each new iteration of the tradition redrew and further refined the contours of this religious community, adapting to changing political circumstances in the Maghrib and expanding its limits to bring in new scholars from more recent generations. This history of the construction of this written network emphasizes the cumulative character of the formation of the Maghribi Ibadi tradition. As the networks of people and places described in the tradition demonstrate, it took a tremendous amount of effort (and ink and paper) to create the prosopographical tradition and maintain it from the eleventh to the sixteenth centuries. This book has also demonstrated that maintenance in response to change continued well beyond the end of the late medieval prosopographical tradition. The sixteenth to twentieth centuries proved equally crucial to the maintenance of the community's boundaries and the survival of its history. In these later centuries, the continual circulation of scholars and books—moving along orbits connecting different hubs of Ibadi intellectual activity—allowed for the preservation of the tradition.

Finally, another theme to which I have consistently returned throughout the book has been the ways in which Ibadis have constructed and maintained their tradition in response to other communities. In many ways, the Ibadi tradition formed in dialogue with other Muslim traditions in Northern Africa and western Asia both in the Middle Period and afterwards. It is my hope that the model developed here for understanding the formation and maintenance of a religious tradition could prove useful to the study of other Muslim communities. Drawing inspiration from their Sunni coreligionists in northern Africa and beyond, the Ibadis cannot have been the only community to have constructed and maintained their tradition with the help of two complementary networks, one written and one human.

***

But the story is not over yet for the Ibadis. This process of tradition construction and maintenance continues today in a variety of forms. One has been the wave of Ibadi cultural associations, libraries, clubs, schools, and academic conferences in the Maghrib referred to at the opening of this chapter. The "Ibadi Books of *Siyar*" conference has continued to be held annually. Following the 2015 focus on al-Shammakhi's *Kitab al-siyar*, the 2016 conference theme was al-Darjini's *Kitab al-tabaqat*. The event took place in the town of Nafta, just near al-Darjini's home town. This brought Ibadis from both Northern Africa and Oman together, commemorating in this symbolic space the tradition of al-Darjini being asked by the Maghribi *'azzaba* to compose his book for an Omani audience. In 2017 these ties were further reinforced when the conference returned to Tunis with a comparative theme of the *siyar* in Oman. At the time of writing, another conference was set to be held in late-2018 in Jerba on the theme of the *Kitab Ibn Sallam*.

A second, related, way in which the process of tradition building and maintenance has continued has been another series of academic conferences organized by the Omani Ibadi community. Since 2010 the Omani Ministry of Endowments and Religious Affairs has financed an international annual conference of Ibadi and Omani Studies. These annual conferences have brought together specialists in Ibadi studies from across the globe with the effect of creating for the first time a space in which European, North American, Asian, and Northern African academics come together and discuss the state of the field. Unlike the Ettawasol conferences in Tunisia, which are held exclusively in Arabic, the Ibadi Studies conferences use English as the primary medium (with presentations in

French and Arabic, on occasion). Of course, these meetings and their subsequent publications carry the added benefit of allowing the Ministry to help shape the conversation and historiography on the Ibadi communities of both east and west. Like their Maghribi equivalents, these conferences comprise a diverse group of scholars from both spheres, and symbolically link the two regions and making a claim to their communal and historical ties. In this way, contemporary Ibadis are not entirely wrong in seeing this process of construction and maintenance of communal boundaries and identity as the heir to the prosopographical tradition.[5]

The Omani-funded conferences carry the added benefit of acknowledging the often-overlooked impact on the field of Ibadi studies from those outside the community: each conference convenes in a different location that served as the institutional home of a European orientalist or other non-Ibadi scholar who worked on Ibadi studies. The influence of these orientalist scholars of the nineteenth and twentieth centuries on the study of Ibadism remains in need of study, especially the relationship between the production of colonial knowledge on Ibadi communities in Oman and the Maghrib by French, Italian, and British scholars and officials of the colonial era.[6]

These and many other avenues for exploration and research surrounding the Ibadi prosopographical corpus remain to be followed. My aim here has not been to offer an exhaustive account of the contents of these works or a comprehensive history of the events and scholars they describe. I have instead sought to demonstrate that these texts do not make up not an assortment of biographical and historical works belonging to similar genres, but instead constitute a textual corpus and a cumulative tradition of prosopography—a written network. The goal of that written network, achieved only over many centuries through active construction and maintenance in response to change, was to draw the boundaries of the Ibadi community and in the process to construct and to maintain an Ibadi tradition in Northern Africa.

[5] The annual conference website is updated regularly at the start of each year: www.ibadi-studies.org (accessed 5 February 2018).

[6] Survey chapters on the impact of these different countries on the field of Ibadi studies were published in some of the recent volumes resulting from the Ibadi Studies conferences funded by the Omani Ministry of Endowments and Religious Affairs. Critical reflection on the production of colonial knowledge about Ibadis and its relationship with power, however, remains to be done. See collected papers in Reinhard Eisener, ed., *Today's Perspectives on Ibadi History and the Historical Sources, Studies on Ibadism and Oman 7* (Hildesheim: Georg Olms Verlag, 2015); Francesca, ed., *Ibadi Theology Rereading Sources and Scholarly Works.*

Appendix: Extant Manuscript Copies of the Ibadi Prosopographies

Note: Manuscripts marked with a (*) were identified after the conclusion of my research. I have included them here but they are not part of the network analysis presented in the book.

Type	Archive	Shelf Mark	Hijrī Date	Common-Era Date
		***Kitāb al-sīra wa-akhbār al-aʾimma* (al-Wārjalānī)**		
Microfilm	دار الكتب [المصرية]	9030 Ḥāʾ	١٥ جمادى الأولى سنة ١٣٠٢	2 March 1885
Manuscript	مكتبة الحاج مسعود بابكر	27 بابكر	unknown	unknown
Manuscript	مكتبة الحاج صالح لعلي	001 دغ	[early fourteenth century?]	[early nineteenth century?]
Manuscript	مكتبة الإستقامة	[الجزانة الأولى] 120	[second half of the tenth century?]	[sixteenth century?]
Digital facsimile	مكتبة آل فضل	015 د غ	٥ ذو القعدة ٨٨٣ هـ	1/29/1479
Manuscript	مكتبة الحاج صالح لعلي	035 م	first half of the thirteenth century	early nineteenth century
Manuscript	مكتبة الإستقامة	118 (*al-khizāna al-ūlā*)	الأربعاء ٤ ذي القعدة ٩٨٢ هـ	15 February 1575
Manuscript	مكتبة الحاج صالح لعلي	186 م	الأربعاء ٢٨ شعبان ٩٥٧ هـ	10 September 1550
Photocopy	مكتبة إيروان	10 مص	١١ ذو القعدة ١٣٨٤ هـ	15 March 1965
Manuscript	مكتبة القطب	2 ث	رجب ١٣١٠	November/December 1897
Manuscript	University of Leiden (the Netherlands)	Or. 14.005	[thirteenth century?]	[nineteenth century?]
Manuscript	Archives Nationales d'Outre Mer (Aix-en-Provence, France)	7APOM/12	fourteenth century	1950–56
Manuscript	مكتبة آل يدر	45	1343	1924

Photographed copy	Ivan Franko National University of Lviv	1055 I	[980?]	[late sixteenth century?]
Manuscript	Ivan Franko National University of Lviv	1054 II	١٠ صفر ١٣٤٥	1926
Manuscript	Ivan Franko National University of Lviv	1085 II	[thirteenth century?]	[nineteenth century?]
Manuscript	Ivan Franko National University of Lviv	1088 II–II.5	[thirteenth century?]	[nineteenth century?]
Photocopy	Institute of Oriental Studies, Jagiellonian Library	Depozyt 1.23	*terminus ante quem* 1349–50	*terminus ante quem* 1931
Photocopy	Institute of Oriental Studies, Jagiellonian Library	Depozyt 1.15	*terminus ante quem* 1349–50	*terminus ante quem* 1931
Photocopy	Institute of Oriental Studies, Jagiellonian Library	No. 16 [see notes]	*terminus ante quem* 1349–50	*terminus ante quem* 1931
Photocopy	Institute of Oriental Studies, Jagiellonian Library	Depozyt 1.26	*terminus ante quem* 1349–50	*terminus ante quem* 1931
Manuscript	Centre de littérature et de linguistique arabes (CNRS)	None	*terminus ante quem* 1342	*terminus ante quem* 26 March 1924
Manuscript	Centre de littérature et de linguistique arabes (CNRS)	None	٢٠ ربيع الأول ١٣٤٥	26 March 1924
Manuscript	مكتبة الشيخ سالم بن يعقوب	93	unknown	unknown
		Kitāb siyar al-Wisyānī		
Manuscript	مكتبة الحاج صالح لعلي	001 دغ	[thirteenth century?]	[late nineteenth/early twentieth century?]
Manuscript	مكتبة الحاج صالح لعلي	186 م	[956?]	[1549?]
Manuscript	مكتبة الحاج صالح لعلي	186 م	الجمعة ٢٣ شعبان ٩٥٦ هـ	15 September 1549

(cont.)

Type	Archive	Shelf Mark	Hijrī Date	Common-Era Date
Manuscript	مكتبة الحاج صالح لعلي	001 دغ	[thirteenth–fourteenth century?]	[late nineteenth/early twentieth century?]
Manuscript	مكتبة الحاج سعيد محمد	16 دغ	late twelfth/early thirteenth century	early to mid-nineteenth century
Manuscript	مكتبة آل يدر	45	1343	1924
Manuscript	مكتبة الحاج مسعود بابكر	27 بابكر	[second half of the tenth century?]	[mid-to-late sixteenth century?]
Manuscript	المكتبة البارونية (جربة)	69	eleventh century	mid-seventeenth century
Photocopy	مكتبة القطب	11 ث	١٥ رمضان ١٣٣٨	3 June 1920
Photocopy	مكتبة إيروان	23 [م]ص	fourteenth century	1 June 1973
Manuscript	Institute of Oriental Studies, Jagiellonian Library	Depozyt 1.26	unknown	[*terminus ante quem* 1931]
Manuscript	مكتبة الشيخ سالم بن يعقوب	113 ح	unknown	unknown
Microfilm	دار الكتب [القاهرة]	9112 ح	[?]١١٩٦	[1781–82?]
		***Kitāb ṭabaqāt mashāyikh al-maghrib* (al-Darjīnī)**		
Manuscript	Bibliothèque nationale de Tunisie	A-MSS-03606	unknown	[1820–60]
Manuscript	مكتبة الحاج صالح لعلي	035 م	[first half of the thirteenth century?]	nineteenth century
Manuscript	مكتبة الإستقامة	[الجزانة الأولى] 120	second half of the tenth century	sixteenth century

Manuscript	مكتبة إيروان	70	الإثنين ٢٢ جمادى الأول ١٢١٨ هـ	9 September 1803
Manuscript	مكتبة عمي سعيد	52	unknown	unknown
Manuscript	مكتبة الحاج سعيد محمد	26	عشية الأربعاء ٩ صفر ١١٨٠ هـ	6 July 1767
Manuscript	مكتبة الشيخ حمو بابا وموسى (مكتبة جمعية عمي سعيد)	حدغ 81	later twelfth/early thirteenth century	eighteenth–nineteenth century
Manuscript	مكتبة الشيخ حمو بابا وموسى (مكتبة جمعية عمي سعيد)	حدغ 98	[thirteenth century?]	[eighteenth/nineteenth century?]
Manuscript	الخزانة العامة (مكتبة جمعية عمي سعيد)	م 63	[ninth–tenth century?]	[sixteenth–seventeenth century?]
Manuscript	مكتبة الحاج صالح لعلي	م 034	الجمعة ٢٩ جمادى الأولى ١١٨٩ هـ	27 July 1775
Digital facsimile	مكتبة الإستقامة	الخزانة الثانية : أ 99	[ninth/tenth century?]	[fifteenth/sixteenth century?]
Manuscript	مكتبة إيروان	68	٢٠ ربيع الثاني ١٢٨٣ هـ	31 August 1866
Manuscript	مكتبة عمي سعيد	11	[twelfth century?]	[eighteenth century?]
Manuscript	المكتبة البارونية (جربة)	80	ذو الحجة ١١٧٤ هـ	1 July 1761
Manuscript	مكتبة القطب (بني يسجن الجزائر)	ث 8	٧ صفر ٧٥٨	28 January 1357
Manuscript	المكتبة البارونية (جربة)	81	[tenth century?]	[sixteenth century?]
Microfilm	دار الكتب [القاهرة]	ح 10418	جمادى الأول ٩٩٦	1 April 1588
Manuscript	Archives Nationales d'Outre Mer (Aix-en-Provence, France)	7APOM/3	[N/A]	1950–57 [see notes]
Manuscript	مكتبة الشيخ سالم بن يعقوب	س 14	١١ رمضان ١٣٥٧	4 November 1938

(cont.)

Type	Archive	Shelf Mark	Hijrī Date	Common-Era Date
Glass photographic sheets	Ivan Franko National University of Lviv	1056 I (2)	[٧ صفر ٧٥٨]	[28 January 1357]
Black and white photos of MS	Ivan Franko National University of Lviv	1056 I (2)	٧ صفر ٧٥٨	[28 January 1357]
Manuscript	Ivan Franko National University of Lviv	1088 II–II.4	[thirteenth century?]	[nineteenth century?]
Photocopy	Institute of Oriental Studies, Jagiellonian Library	Depozyt 1.13	١٩ شعبان ١٣٤١	6 April 1923
Photocopy	Institute of Oriental Studies, Jagiellonian Library	Depozyt 1.16	[1192?]	[1778?]
Manuscript	مكتبة الشيخ سالم بن يعقوب	97	unknown	unknown
Manuscript	مكتبة الشيخ سالم بن يعقوب	74	unknown	unknown
Manuscript	مكتبة الشيخ سالم بن يعقوب	65	[nineteenth century?]	[mid- to late fifteenth century?]
Manuscript*	Rare Books and Manuscript Library, Columbia University	X89.7 Ab92	[thirteenth century?]	[nineteenth century?]
		Kitāb al-jawāhir al-muntaqāt **(al-Barrādī)**		
Manuscript	المكتبة البارونية	73	حول رمضان ١٠٩١	1 October 1680
Manuscript	Bibliothèque nationale de Tunisie	A-MSS-024493	unknown	[nineteenth century?]
Manuscript	مكتبة الحاج سعيد محمد	د غ 23	tenth century	mid-to-late sixteenth century

Digital facsimile	مكتبة الإستقامة	118 [الخزانة الأولى]	عصر يوم الخميس ٥ ذي القعدة ٩٨٢ هـ	16 February 1575
Manuscript	مكتبة إيروان [الجزائر]	80	unknown	[early to mid-nineteenth century?]
Manuscript	مكتبة إيروان [الجزائر]	66	١٩ رمضان ١٢٩٠	10 November 1873
Manuscript	مكتبة آت خالد [الجزائر]	124 م	السبت ٢٨ ذو القعدة ١١٨٦ هـ	20 February 1773
Manuscript	مكتبة الحاج سعيد محمد [الجزائر]	28	late twelfth century	late eighteenth century
Manuscript	مكتبة الحاج سعيد محمد [الجزائر]	38	الأحد ٢٤ صفر ١١٥٣ هـ	20 May 1740
Manuscript	مكتبة الإستقامة	[الخزانة الأولى] 88	شعبان ١١٩٢ هـ	1 September 1778
Manuscript	مكتبة الإستقامة	[الخزانة الثانية] 35	صحى يوم الخميس ٢٤ جمادى الثانية ١٣٠٣ هـ	30 March 1886
Manuscript	مكتبة إيروان	70	unknown	[nineteenth century?]
Digital facsimile	مكتبة الإستقامة	[الخزانة الأولى] 67	عشية الأربعاء ٢ ربيع الثاني ١٢٢٩ هـ	24 March 1814
Manuscript	المكتبة البارونية (جربة)	72	unknown	[seventeenth century?]
Manuscript	المكتبة البارونية (جربة)	82	[tenth century?]	[sixteenth century?]
Manuscript	Università degli Studi di Napoli L'Orientale	MS ARA 93	[thirteenth century?]	[mid-nineteenth century?]
Manuscript	Università degli Studi di Napoli L'Orientale	None	صفر ١١٨٨	1 April 1774
Microfilm	دار الكتب [القاهرة]	8456 ح	٢٣ ربيع الأول ١١٣٢	1720

(cont.)

Type	Archive	Shelf Mark	Hijrī Date	Common-Era Date
Manuscript	مكتبة الشيخ سالم بن يعقوب		آخر جمادى الأول ١١٦٦	(late) March 1753
Manuscript	مكتبة القطب	ث 1	رمضان ١٠٩٠	1 October 1679
Photocopy	Institute of Oriental Studies, Jagiellonian Library	Sygn. Depozyt 1.2	twentieth century	[*terminus ante quem* 1931]
Manuscript	مكتبة الشيخ سالم بن يعقوب	95	unknown	unknown
		***Kitāb al-siyar* (al-Shammākhī)**		
Manuscript	Bibliothèque nationale de Tunisie	A-MSS-22257	جمادى الثاني ١١١٠	1 December 1698
Manuscript	الخزانة العامة (مكتبة جمعية عمي سعيد)	م 18	صبيحة الأربعاء ١ جمادى الأول ١١٦٣	8 April 1750
Manuscript	مكتبة الحاج صالح لعلي	م 032	الإثنين ٢١ شوال ١٢٩٧هـ	26 September 1880
Manuscript	مكتبة الحاج صالح لعلي	م 036	السبت ١٠ شعبان ١٢٠٤ هـ	12 April 1790
Manuscript	مكتبة آل يدر	79	٢٩ ربيع الأول ١٢٨٣ هـ	11 August 1866
Manuscript	مكتبة الشيخ أحمد بن حمد الخليلي	139	*terminus ante quem* 1125	*terminus ante quem* eighteenth century
Manuscript	مكتبة الشيخ حمو بابا وموسى (مكتبة جمعية عمي سعيد)	حدغ 100	[second half of the thirteenth century?]	[nineteenth century?]
Manuscript	الخزانة العامة (مكتبة جمعية عمي سعيد)	د غ 195	unknown	[late seventeenth/early eighteenth century?]
Manuscript	مكتبة الإستقامة	الخزانة الثانة: أ/130	[1115?]	[1703–04?]
Manuscript	المكتبة البارونية (جربة)	70	[eleventh century?]	[seventeenth century?]

Manuscript	Università degli Studi di Napoli L'Orientale	MS ARA 30	جمادى الأول ١١٨٧	1 August 1773
Microfilm	دار الكتب [القاهرة]	8591 ح	جمادى الاول سنة ١١٣٩	1 September 1736
Manuscript	Bibliothèque nationale de Tunisie	A-MSS-15349	ليلة الأربعا ٢٥ من ربيع الأول ١٠٦٢	6 March 1652
Manuscript	مكتبة الحاج مسعود بابكر	[none]	الاثنين ٥ صفر ١١٣٢ هـ	17 December 1719
Manuscript	مكتبة آت خالد	109 م	١٦ ذو الحجة ١١٧٨	5 June 1765
Manuscript	مكتبة الإستقامة	75	[twelfth–thirteenth century?]	[eighteenth–nineteenth century?]
Manuscript	Ivan Franko National University of Lviv	1084 II	unknown	[nineteenth century?]
Manuscript	Ivan Franko National University of Lviv	1083 II	[1282?]	[1865?]
Photocopy	Institute of Oriental Studies, Jagiellonian Library	[unknown]	١٥ شعبان ١١١٩	10 November 1707
Printed image from microfilm	دار الكتب [القاهرة]	769 تاريخ	٢٧ ذو الحجة ١١٧٩	5 June 1766
Manuscript	مكتبة الشيخ سالم بن يعقوب	96	١٢٤٤ هـ	1 September 1828
Manuscript	مكتبة الشيخ سالم بن يعقوب	5	unknown	unknown
Manuscript	مكتبة الشيخ سالم بن يعقوب	5	unknown	unknown
Manuscript	مكتبة الشيخ سالم بن يعقوب	5	unknown	unknown
Manuscript	مكتبة الشيخ سالم بن يعقوب	5	unknown	unknown
Manuscript	مكتبة الشيخ سالم بن يعقوب	41 ق	[thirteenth century?]	[nineteenth century?]
Manuscript*	Association pour le sauvegarde de l'île de Djerba	MS 013 [4]	[eleventh century?]	[seventeenth century?]

Bibliography

ʿAbd al-Ḥalīm, Rajab Muḥammad. *al-Ibāḍiyya fī Miṣr wa-ʾl-Maghrib wa-ʿalāqātuhum bi-Ibāḍiyyat ʿUmān wa-ʾl-Baṣra*. al-Sīb: Maktabat al-Ḍāmirī, 1990.

Abū Madyan. *The Way of Abū Madyan: Doctrinal and Poetic Works of Abū Madyan Shuʿayb ibn al-Ḥusayn al-Anṣārī (c. 509/1115–16–594/1198)*. Edited by V. Cornell. Cambridge: Islamic Texts Society, 1996.

Abun-Nasr, Jamil M. *A History of the Maghrib in the Islamic Period*. Cambridge: Cambridge University Press, 1987.

Aillet, Cyrille. "A Breviary of Faith and a Sectarian Memorial: A New Reading of Ibn Sallām's Kitāb (3rd/9th Century)." In *Ibadi Theology: Rereading Sources and Scholarly Works*, edited by Ersilia Francesca, 67–82. Hildesheim: Georg Olms Verlag, 2015.

ed. "L'ibāḍisme, une minorité au cœur de l'islam." *Revue du monde musulman et de la Méditerranée* 132 (2012): 13–36.

"Tāhart et les origines de l'imamat rustumide." *Annales Islamologiques* 45 (2011): 47–78.

Aillet, Cyrille, Patrice Cressier, and Sophie Gilotte, eds. *Sedrata, histoire et archéologie d'un carrefour du sahara médiéval à la lumière des archives inédites de Marguerite Van Bercham*. Collection de la Casa de Velázquez 161. Madrid: Casa de Velázquez, 2017.

Aillet, Cyrille, and Sophie Gilotte. "Sedrata: l'élaboration d'un lieu de mémoire." *Revue du monde musulman et de la Méditerranée* 132 (2012): 91–114.

Aillet, Cyrille, and Muḥammad Ḥasan. "The Legal Responsa Attributed to Aflaḥ b. ʿAbd Al-Wahhāb (208–58/823–72): A Preliminary Study." In *Ibadi Jurisprudence: Origins, Developments, and Cases*, edited by Barbara Michalak-Pikulska and Reinhard Eisener, 137–46. Hildesheim: Georg Olms Verlag, 2015.

Amara, Allaoua. "Entre le massif de l'Aurès et les oasis: apparition, évolution et disparition des communautés ibâḍites du Zāb (VIIIe–XIVe siècle)." *Revue des mondes musulmans et de la Méditerranée* 132 (2012): 115–35.

"La malikisation du Maghreb central (III/Vie–IX/XIIe siècle)." In *Dynamiques religieuses et territoires du sacré au Maghreb médiéval: éléments d'enquête*, edited by Cyrille Aillet and Bull Tuil Leonetti, 25–50. Madrid: Estudios Árabes Islámicos. Consejo Superior de Investigaciones Científicas, 2015.

"Remarques sur le recueil ibāḍite–wahbite Siyar al-Mashāyikh: retour sur son attribution." *Andalus-Maghrib* 15 (2008): 31–40.

Anderson, Lisa. "Nineteenth-Century Reform in Ottoman Libya." *International Journal of Middle East Studies* 16, no. 3 (1984): 325–48.

Asad, Talal. *The Idea of an Anthropology of Islam*. Washington, D.C.: Center for Contemporary Arab Studies, Georgetown University, 1986.

Baadj, Amar S. *Saladin, the Almohads and the Banū Ghāniya: The Contest for North Africa (12th and 13th Centuries)*. Leiden; Boston: Brill, 2015.

Bābāʿammī, Muḥammad Ṣāliḥ Nāṣir, ed. *Muʿjam aʿlām al-ibāḍiyya (Dictionnaire des hommes illustres de l'Ibadisme, les hommes du Maghreb)*, vol. II. Beirut: Dār al-Gharb al-Islāmī, 2000.

Baghṭūrī, Muqrīn b. Muḥammad al-. *Siyar mashāyikh nafūsa*. Edited by Tawfīq ʿIyād al-Shuqrūnī [online edition]. Tawalt, 2009: www.tawalt.com/wp-content/books/tawalt_books/siyar_nafousa/siyar_nafousa.pdf.

Baḥḥāz, Ibrāhīm b. Bakīr. *al-Dawla al-rustamīyya*. Algiers: Maṭbaʿat Lāfūmīk, 1985.

Baḥḥāz, Ibrāhīm b. Bakīr, ed., *Fihris makhṭūṭāt khizānat Dār al-Talāmīdh (Irwān)*. Ghardaia: Muʾassasat al-Shaykh ʿAmmī Saʿīd, 2009.

al-Bakrī, ʿAbdallāh b. ʿAbd al-ʿAzīz b. Muḥammad. *al-Masālik wa-ʾl-mamālik*, vol. II. Beirut: Dār al-Kutub al-ʿIlmīyya, 2003.

Barabási, Albert-László, and Eric Bonabeau. "Scale-Free Networks." *Scientific American* 288, no. 5 (2003): 50–59.

Bargaoui, Sami. "(Ne plus) Être ibadhite dans la régence de Tunis: un processus de démarquage confessionnel à l'époque moderne," [forthcoming].

al-Barrādī, Abū al-Qāsim b. Ibrāhīm. *al-Jawāhir al-muntaqāt fī itmām mā akhalla bihi Kitāb al-ṭabaqāt*. Cairo: al-Maṭbaʿa al-Bārūniyya, 1884.

al-Bārūnī, Saʿīd, ed. *Fihris makhṭūṭāt maktabat al-Bārūnī bi-Jarba*. Tunis: n.p., 1998.

Bastian, M., S. Heymann, and M. Jacomy. "Gephi: An Open Source Software for Exploring and Manipulating Networks," 2009: https://gephi.org/publications/gephi-bastian-feb09.pdf.

Bekri, Chikh. *L'Algérie aux IIe/IIIe siècles (VIIIe/IXe): quelques aspects méconnus du Royaume Rostémide (144–296/761/2–908/9)*. Paris: Éditions Publisud, 2004.

Blondel, Vincent D., Jean-Loup Guillaume, Renaud Lambiotte, and Etienne Lefebvre. "Fast Unfolding of Communities in Large Networks." *Journal of Statistical Mechanics: Theory and Experiment* no. 10 (2008): 1–12.

Bloom, Jonathan. *Paper before Print: The History and Impact of Paper in the Islamic World*. New Haven: Yale University Press, 2001.

Brett, Michael. "The Diplomacy of Empire: Fatimids and Zirids, 990–1062." *Bulletin of the School of Oriental and African Studies, University of London* 78, no. 1 (2015): 149–59.

Ibn Khaldun and the Medieval Maghrib. Aldershot: Ashgate/Variorum, 1999.

"Ifriqiya as a Market for Saharan Trade from the Tenth to the Twelfth Century AD." *Journal of African History* 10, no. 3 (1969): 347–64.
"Islam and Trade in the 'Bilad al-Sudan', Tenth–Eleventh Century AD." *Journal of African History*, 24, no. 4 (1983): 431–40.
"Muslim Justice under Infidel Rule: The Normans in Ifriqiya, 517–55 H/1123–1160 AD." *Cahiers de Tunisie* 43 (1991): 325–68.
The Rise of the Fatimids: The World of the Mediterranean and the Middle East in the Fourth Century of the Hijra, Tenth Century CE. Leiden; Boston: Brill, 2001.
Briquet, Charles-Moïse. *Les filigranes: dictionnaire historique des marques du papier dès leur apparition vers 1282 jusqu'en 1600. A facisimile of the 1907 ed. with supplementary material contributed by a number of scholars*, 4 vols. Amsterdam: Paper Publications Society, 1968.
De la valeur des filigranes du papier comme moyen de déterminer l'âge et la provenance de documents non datés. Geneva: Impr. Romet, 1892.
Brugnatelli, Vermondo. "D'une langue de contact entre berbères ibadites." In *Berber in Contact: Linguistic and Socio-Lingusitic Perspectives*, Berber Studies 22, edited by Mena Lafkioue and Vermondo Brugnatelli, 39–52. Cologne: Rüdiger Köppe Verlag, 2008.
Brunschvig, Robert. *La Berbérie Orientale sous les Hafsides des origines à la fin du XVième siècle*, 2 vols. Paris: Maisonneuve, 1940.
Buʿajīla, Najya. *al-Islām al-khārijī*. Beirut: Dār al-Ṭalīʿa, 2006.
al-Būjadīdī, ʿAlī. "al-Shaykh Sālim b. Yaʿqūb: ḥayāt rajul wa-tajribat jīl." *Majallat al-ḥayāt* 12 (2012): 170–82.
Bulliet, Richard W. *The Patricians of Nishapur: A Study in Medieval Islamic Social History*. Cambridge, MA: Harvard University Press, 1972.
Būrās, Yaḥyā. "al-Ḥayāt al-fikriyya bi-minṭaqat mizāb fi-l-qarnayn 9–10 [AH]/15–16 [CE]." *El-Minhāj: dawriyya ʿilmiyya mutakhaṣṣiṣa fī makhṭūṭāt al-ibāḍiyya wa-Wādī Mīzāb fī wathāʾiqihā al-arshīfiyya* 2 (2013): 96–131.
Chamberlain, Michael. *Knowledge and Social Practice in Medieval Damascus, 1190–1350*. Cambridge; New York: Cambridge University Press, 1994.
Chapoutot-Remadi, Mounira. "Abū Yazīd al-Nukkārī." *Encyclopedia of Islam*, Third Edition, 2013.
Cherifi, Brahim. "La Ḥalqa des ʿazzāba: un nouveau regard sur l'histoire d'une institution religieuse ibāḍite." *Bulletin of the Royal Institute for Inter-Faith Studies* 7, no. 1 (2005): 39–68.
Cook, Michael. *Early Muslim Dogma: A Source-Critical Study*. Cambridge; New York: Cambridge University Press, 1981.
Cooperson, Michael. "Biographical Literature." In *The New Cambridge History of Islam*, vol. IV: *Islamic Cultures and Societies to the End of the Eighteenth Century*, edited by Robert Irwin, 458–73. Cambridge; New York: Cambridge University Press, 2010.
Classical Arabic Biography: The Heirs of the Prophets in the Age of al-Maʾmūn. Cambridge; New York: Cambridge University Press, 2010.
Cornell, Vincent J. *Realm of the Saint: Power and Authority in Moroccan Sufism*. Austin: University of Texas Press, 1998.

Crone, Patricia. *Medieval Islamic Political Thought*. Edinburgh: Edinburgh University Press, 2005.

Crone, Patricia, and Fritz Zimmermann, eds. *The Epistle of Sālim Ibn Dhakwān*. New York: Oxford University Press, 2001.

Cuperly, Pierre. *Introduction à l'étude de l'ibāḍisme et de sa théologie*. Algiers: Office des publications universitaires, 1984.

Custers, Martin H. "Catalog of Waqf-Books in Wikālat Al-Baḥḥār (Jāmūs)" [unpublished document given to author via e-mail], 2016.

Ibāḍī Publishing Activities in the East and in the West, c. 1880–1960s: An Attempt to an Inventory, with References to Related Recent Publications. Maastricht: n.p., 2006.

al-Ibāḍiyya: A Bibliography, 3 vols. Maastricht: Universitaire Pers, 2006.

al-Ibāḍiyya: A Bibliography, 2nd edition, 3 vols. Hildesheim: Georg Olms Verlag, 2016.

al-Darjīnī, Aḥmad ibn Saʿīd. *Kitāb ṭabaqāt al-mashāʾikh bi-ʾl-Maghrib*. Edited by Ibrāhīm Ṭallay, 2 vols. Constantine: n.p., 1974.

Déroche, François, Annie Berthier, and M. I Waley. *Islamic Codicology: An Introduction to the Study of Manuscripts in Arabic Script*. London: al-Furqān, 2006.

Djaabiri, Farhat. *ʿAlāqāt ʿUmān bi-shimāl Ifrīqiyā*. Muscat: al-Maṭābiʿ al-ʿĀlamiyya, 1991.

Niẓām al-ʿazzāba ʿind al-ibāḍiyya bi-Jarba (L'Organisation des azzaba chez les ibadhites de Jerba). Tunis: Institut National d'Archéologie et d'Art, 1975.

Doumerc, Bernard. "Les relations commerciales entre Djerba et la République de Venise à la fin du Moyen-Âge." In *Actes du Colloque sur l'histoire de Jerba*, 36–45. Tunis: Institut national d'archéologie et d'art, 1982.

Venise et l'émirat hafside de Tunis 1231–1535. Paris; Montreal: L'Harmattan, 1999.

Eisener, Reinhard, ed. *Today's Perspectives on Ibadi History and the Historical Sources*. Studies on Ibadism and Oman 7. Hildesheim: Georg Olms Verlag, 2015.

Ennami, Amr Khalifa. "A Description of New Ibadi Manuscripts from North Africa." *Journal of Semitic Studies* 15, no. 1 (1970): 63–87.

Faroqhi, Suraiya N. "Demography and Migration." In *The New Cambridge History of Islam, vol. IV: Islamic Cultures and Societies to the End of the Eighteenth Century*, edited by Robert Irwin (New York: Cambridge University Press, 2010), 306–31.

Ferhat, Halima. "Le livre instrument de savoir et objet de commerce dans le Maghreb médiéval." *Hespéris-Tamuda* 32 (1994): 53–62.

Fierro, Maribel. "The Almohads and the Ḥafṣids." In *The New Cambridge History of Islam*, vol. II: *The Western Islamic World: Eleventh to Eighteenth Centuries*, ed. Maribel Fierro, 66–105. Cambridge: Cambridge University Press, 2010.

Fihris makhṭūṭāt khizānat muʾallafāt al-shaykh al-ʿallāma Amuḥammad b. Yūsuf Aṭfayyish al-Yasjanī al-shahīr bi-ʾl-quṭb. Ghardaia: Maktabat al-Quṭb, 2013.

Francesca, Ersilia. "Early Ibāḍī Jurisprudence: Sources and Case Law." *Jerusalem Studies in Arabic and Islam* 30 (2005): 231–63.

"The Formation and Early Development of the Ibāḍī Madhhab." *Jerusalem Studies in Arabic and Islam* 28 (2003): 260–77.

ed. *Ibadi Theology: Rereading Sources and Scholarly Works*. Hildesheim: Georg Olms Verlag, 2015.

Fuʾād Sayyid, Amīn. *Dār al-Kutub al-Miṣriyya: tārīkhuhā wa-taṭawwuruhā*. Cairo: Maktabat al-Dār al-ʿArabiyya lil-Kitāb, 1996.

Gacek, Adam. *Arabic Manuscripts: A Vademecum for Readers*. Leiden; Boston: Brill, 2009.

Gaiser, Adam. "The Kharijites and Contemporary Scholarship." *History Compass* 7, no. 5 (2009): 1376–90.

Muslims, Scholars, Soldiers: The Origins and Elaboration of the Ibāḍī Imamate Traditions. Oxford: Oxford University Press, 2010.

Shurat Legends, Ibadi Identities: Martyrdom, Asceticism, and the Making of an Early Islamic Community. Columbia, S.C.: University of South Carolina Press, 2016.

"Slaves and Silver across the Strait of Gibraltar: Politics and Trade between Umayyad Iberia and Khārijite North Africa." *Medieval Encounters* 19, nos. 1–2 (2013): 41–70.

Gephi: An Open Source Software for Exploring and Manipulating Networks (version 0.9.2), 2018. https://gephi.org.

Ghazal, Amal N. *Islamic Reform and Arab Nationalism: Expanding the Crescent from the Mediterranean to the Indian Ocean (1880s–1930s)*. London; New York: Routledge, 2010.

"The Other Frontiers of Arab Nationalism: Ibadis, Berbers, and the Arabist–Salafi Press in the Interwar Period." *International Journal of Middle East Studies* 42, no. 1 (2010): 105–22.

Goffart, Walter. "Rome's Final Conquest: The Barbarians." *History Compass* 6, no. 3 (2008): 855–83.

Goitein, Shelomo Dov. *A Mediterranean Society: The Jewish Communities of the Arab World as Portrayed in the Documents of the Cairo Geniza*, 6 vols. Berkeley: University of California Press, 1967–93; vol. I: *Economic Foundations* (1999).

Görke, Andreas, and Konrad Hirschler, eds. *Manuscript Notes as Documentary Sources*. Beirut: Orient-Institut, 2012.

Gouja, Mohamed. "Kitāb al-Siyar d'Abū al-Rabīʿ Sulaymān al Wisyānī (Vie–XIIème) étude, analyse et traduction fragmentaire." Ph.D. thesis, Université de Paris I, 1984.

Gräberg di Hemsö, Jakob. "Prospetto del commercio di Tripoli d'Affrica e della sue relazioni con quello dell' Italia. Articolo 1." In *Antologia* 27: 79–99. Florence: Gabinetto scientifico e letterario di G. P. Vieusseux, 1827.

Hafsi, Ibrahim. "Recherches sur le genre Tabaqat dans la littérature arabe [1]." *Arabica* 23 (1976): 227–65.

"Recherches sur le genre Tabaqat dans la littérature arabe [2]." *Arabica* 24 (1977): 1–41.

"Recherches sur le genre Tabaqat dans la littérature arabe [3]." *Arabica* 24 (1977): 150–86.

Halevi, Leor. "Christian Impurity versus Economic Necessity: A Fifteenth-Century Fatwa on European Paper." *Speculum* 83, no. 4 (2008): 917–45.

Hall, Bruce S., and Charles C. Stewart. "The Historic 'Core Curriculum' and the Book Market in Islamic West Africa." In *The Trans-Saharan Book Trade: Manuscript Culture, Arabic Literacy and Intellectual History in Muslim Africa*, edited by Graziano Krätli and Ghislaine Lydon, 109–74. Leiden; Boston: Brill, 2011.

Halm, Heinz. *The Empire of the Mahdi: The Rise of the Fatimids*. Translated by Michael Bonner. Leiden; New York: Brill, 1996.

Hassen, Mohamed. "Peuplement et organisation du territoire dans une région d'implantation ibāḍite: le Jebel Demmer dans le sud-est de l'Ifrīqiya." *Revue des mondes musulmans et de la Méditerranée* 132 (2012): 137–54.

Heawood, Edward. *Watermarks Mainly of the 17th and 18th Centuries*. Hilversum: Paper Publications Society, 1950.

Hills, Richard L. "Early Italian Papermaking: A Crucial Technical Revolution." In *Produzione e Commercio Della Carta e Del Libro Secc. XIII–XVIII*, edited by Simonetta Cavaciocchi, 73–97. Florence: Le Monnier, 1992.

Hirschler, Konrad. *The Written Word in the Medieval Arabic Lands: A Social and Cultural History of Reading Practices*. Edinburgh: Edinburgh University Press, 2012.

Hirschler, Konrad. "Reading Certificates (samāʿāt) as a Prosopographical Source: Cultural and Social Practices of an Elite Family in Zangid and Ayyubi Damascus." In *Manuscript Notes as Documentary Sources*, ed. Andreas Görke and Konrad Hirschler, 73–92. Beirut: Orient-Institut, 2012.

Hobsbawm, Eric J., and Terence Ranger, eds. *The Invention of Tradition*. Cambridge: Cambridge University Press, 2015.

Hoffman, Valerie J. "The Articulation of Ibādī Identity in Modern Oman and Zanzibar." *The Muslim World* 94, no. 2 (2004): 201–16.

The Essentials of Ibāḍī Islam. Syracuse: Syracuse University Press, 2012.

"Historical Memory and Imagined Communities: Modern Ibāḍī Writings on Khārijism." In *Historical Dimensions of Islam: Essays in Honor of R. Stephen Humphreys*, edited by James E. Lindsay and Jon Armajani, 185–200. Princeton: Darwin Press, 2009.

Hopkins, J. F. P, and Nehemia Levtzion. *Corpus of Early Arabic Sources for West African History*. Cambridge; New York: Cambridge University Press, 1981.

Horden, Peregrine, and Nicholas Purcell. *The Corrupting Sea: A Study of Mediterranean History*. Oxford; Malden, MA: Blackwell, 2000.

Hunter, Dard. *Papermaking: The History and Technique of an Ancient Craft*. New York: Dover Publications, 1943.

Ibn Bakīr al-Ḥājj Saʿīd, Yūsuf. *Tārīkh Banī Mzāb: dirāsa ijtimāʿiyya wa-iqtiṣādiyya wa-siyasiyya*. 3rd edition Ghardaia: n.p., 2014.

Ibn Ḥawqal, Abū al-Qāsim. *Kitāb ṣūrat al-arḍ*. Edited by Michael J. de Goeje. 2nd edition, Bibliotheca Geographorum Arabicorum. Leiden: Brill, 1939.

Ibn al-Ṣaghīr. *Akhbār al-aʾimma al-rustumiyyīn*. Edited by Muḥammad Nāṣir and Ibrāhīm b. Bakīr Baḥḥāz. Beirut: Dār al-Gharb al-Islāmī, 1986.

Chronique d'Ibn Saghir sur les imams rostemides de Tahert. Translated by Gustave-Adolphe de Calassanti-Motylinski. Paris: E. Leroux, 1907.

Ibn Sallām al-Ibāḍī. *Kitāb fīhi bad' al-islām wa-sharā'i' al-dīn*. Edited by Werner Schwartz and Sālim b. Ya'qūb. Beirut: Dār Iqra', 1986.
Idris, Hady Roger. *La Berbérie Orientale sous les Zirides*, 2 vols. Paris: Maisonneuve, 1962.
Iṭfayyish, Abū Isḥāq Ibrāhīm, ed. *al-Minhāj: majalla 'ilmiyya siyāsiyya ijtimā'iyya niṣf shariyya* (Cairo, 1925–30).
Jacques, Kevin. "Arabic Islamic Prosopography: The Tabaqat Genre." *In Prosopography Approaches and Applications: A Handbook*, 387–414. Oxford: Occasional Publications, 2007.
Authority, Conflict, and the Transmission of Diversity in Medieval Islamic Law. Leiden; Boston: Brill, 2006.
Jomier, Augustin. "Iṣlāḥ ibāḍite et intégration nationale: vers une communauté mozabite? (1925–1964)." *Revue des mondes musulmans et de la Méditerranée* 132 (2012): 175–95.
"Un réformisme islamique dans l'Algérie coloniale: oulémas ibadites et société du Mzab (c. 1880–c.1970)." Ph.D. thesis, Université du Maine, 2015.
Julien, Charles-André. *Histoire de l'Afrique du Nord: des origines à 1830*. Paris: Payot & Rivage, 1994.
Kenney, Jeffrey. *Muslim Rebels: Kharijites and the Politics of Extremism in Egypt*. Oxford; New York: Oxford University Press, 2006.
Knysh, Alexander D. *Ibn 'Arabi in the Later Islamic Tradition: The Making of a Polemical Image in Medieval Islam*. Albany: State University of New York Press, 1999.
Islamic Mysticism: A Short History. Leiden: Brill, 2010.
Kościelniak, Krzysztof. "The Contribution of Prof. Tadeusz Lewicki (1906–1992) to Islamic and West African Studies." *Analecta Cracoviensia: Studia Philosophico-Theologica Edita a Professoribus Cracoviae*. 44 (2012): 241–55.
Laroui, Abdallah. *L'histoire du Maghreb: un essai de synthèse*. Casablanca: Centre Culturel Arabe, 1995.
Lewicki, Tadeusz. "L'état nord-africain de Tahert et ses relations avec le Soudan occidental à la fin du VIIIe et au IXe siècle." *Cahiers d'études africaines* 2, no. 8 (1962): 513–35.
Les ibadites en Tunisie au Moyen Âge. Rome: Angelo Signorelli, 1958.
"Mélanges berbères-ibadites." *Revue des Études Islamiques* 3 (1936): 267–85.
"Notice sur la chronique ibāḍite d'ad-Darjīnī." *Rocznik Orientalistyczny* 11 (1936): 146–72.
Lewinstein, Keith. "The Azāriqa in Islamic Heresiography." *Bulletin of the School of Oriental and African Studies, University of London* 54, no. 2 (1991): 251–68.
"Making and Unmaking a Sect: The Heresiographers and the Ṣufriyya." *Studia Islamica*, no. 76 (1992): 75–96.
Love, Paul M. Jr. "The Colonial Pasts of Medieval Texts in Northern Africa: Useful Knowledge, Publication History, and Political Violence in Colonial and Post-Independence Algeria." *Journal of African History* 58, no. 3 (2017): 445–63.

"Djerba and the Limits of Rustamid Power: Considering the Ibāḍī Community of Djerba under the Rustamid Imāms of Tāhert (779–909CE)." *al-Qantara* 33, no. 2 (2012): 297–323.
"Écouter le conte d'un manuscrit: penser avec une copie d'une chronique ibadite de la bibliothèque Barouni à Djerba." *Études et Documents Berbères* 35–36 (2016): 301–13.
"Ibāḍī Manuscripts in the Bibliothèque Nationale de Tunisie: Descriptions, Watermarks, and Implications." *Journal of Islamic Manuscripts* 7 (2016): 1–35.
"The Sālim Bin Ya'qūb Ibāḍī Manuscript Library in Jerba, Tunisia: A Preliminary Survey and Inventory." *Journal of Islamic Manuscripts* 8 (2017): 257–80.
"The Sufris of Sijilmasa: Towards a History of the Midrarids." *Journal of North African Studies* 15, no. 2 (2010): 173–88.
"Writing a Network, Constructing a Tradition: The Ibadi Prosopographical Corpus in Medieval Northern Africa (11th–16th C.)." Ph.D. thesis, University of Michigan, 2016.
Mackeen, Mohamed. "The Rise of al-Shādhilī (d. 656/1256)." *Journal of the American Oriental Society* 91 (1971): 479–80.
Madelung, Wilferd. "Abd Allāh Ibn Ibāḍ and the Origins of the Ibāḍiyya." In *Authority, Privacy and Public Order in Islam: Proceedings of the 22nd Congress of L'Union Européenne des Arabisants et Islamisants*, edited by E. Michalak-Pikulska and A. Pikulski, 52–57. Leuven: Peeters, 2006.
"The Authenticity of the Letter of 'Abd Allāh b. Ibāḍ to 'Abd al-Malik." Edited by Cyrille Aillet. *Revue des mondes musulmans et de la Méditerranée* no. 132 (2012): 37–43.
Masson, Paul. *Histoire des établissements et du commerce français dans l'Afrique barbaresque (1560–1793) (Algérie, Tunisie, Tripolitaine, Maroc)*. Paris: Hachette, 1903.
McDougall, James, and Judith Scheele, eds. *Saharan Frontiers: Space and Mobility in Northwest Africa*. Bloomington: Indiana University Press, 2012.
Meouak, Mohamed. *La langue berbère au Maghreb médiéval: textes, contextes, analyses*. Leiden; Boston: Brill, 2015.
Minawi, Mostafa. *The Ottoman Scramble for Africa: Empire and Diplomacy in the Sahara and the Hijaz*. Stanford: Stanford University Press, 2016.
Motylinski, Adolphe. "Bibliographie du Mzab: les livres de la secte abadhite." *Bulletin de Correspondance Africaine* 3 (1885): 15–72.
Muṣlaḥ, Aḥmad. *al-Waqf al-jarbī fī Miṣr wa-dawruhu fī 'l-tanmiya al-iqtiṣādiyya wa-'l-ijtimā'iyya wa-'l-thaqāfiyya min al-qarn al-'āshir ilā 'l-qarn al-rābi' 'ashar al-hijrīyayn (Wikālat al-Jāmūs namūdhajan)*. Kuwait: al-Amāna al-'Āmma lil-Awqāf, 2012.
Newman, Mark. *Networks*. Oxford: Oxford University Press, 2010.
Noth, Albrecht, and Lawrence Conrad. *The Early Arabic Historical Tradition: A Source-Critical Study*. Translated by Michael Bonner. Princeton: Darwin Press, 1994.
Nu'mān ibn Muḥammad, Abū Ḥanīfah. *Founding the Fatimid State: The Rise of an Early Islamic Empire: An Annotated English Translation of al-Qāḍī*

al-Nu'mān's Iftitāḥ al-Da'wa. Translated by Hamid Haji. London: I. B. Tauris, 2006.
Omant, Henri Auguste, ed. *Missions archéologiques françaises en Orient aux XVIIe et XVIIIe siècles: documents publiés par H. Omont*. Paris: Imprimerie Nationale, 1902.
Ould-Braham, Ouahmi. "The Case of the Kitāb al-Siyar of Wisyānī (Sixth H/XII Century AD) and its Various Manuscript Copies." In *Today's Perspectives on Ibadi History and the Historical Sources*, edited by Reinhard Eisener, 161–76. Hildesheim: Georg Olms Verlag, 2016.
"Une chronique Ibāḍite à textes berbères: le complexe Kitāb al-siyar de Wisyānī." *Études et Documents Berbères* 29–30 (November 2010): 311–44.
"Pour une étude approfondie d'une source historique médiévale: une chronique ibāḍite à textes berbères (VIe H/XIIe siècle)." *Études et Documents Berbères* 33 (2014): 7–26.
Oussedik, Fatma. "The Rise of the Baba Merzug: Diaspora, Ibadism, and Social Status in the Valley of the Mzab." in *Saharan Frontiers: Space and Mobility in Northwest Africa*. Edited by James McDougall and Judith Scheele. Bloomington: Indiana University Press, 2012, 93–108.
Petry, Carl. *The Civilian Elite of Cairo in the Later Middle Ages*. Princeton: Princeton University Press, 1981.
Poncet, Jean. "Encore à propos des hilaliens: la 'mise au point' de R. Idris." *Annales* 23, no. 3 (1986): 600–62.
"Le mythe de la catastrophe hilalienne." *Annales ESC* 22 (1967): 1099–1120.
Prevost, Virginie. "'Abd al-Raḥmān ibn Rustum al-Fārisī: une tentative de biographie du premier imam de Tāhart." *Der Islam* 86, no. 1 (2011): 44–64.
L'aventure ibāḍite dans le Sud tunisien, VIIIe–XIIIe siècle: effervesence d'une région méconnue. Helsinki: Academia Scientiarum Fennica, 2008.
"La chaussée d'al-Qanṭara, pont entre Djerba et le continent." *Lettres Orientales* 11 (2006): 165–88.
"Les enjeux de la bataille de Mānū (283/896)." *Revue des mondes musulmans et de la Méditerranée* 132 (2012): 75–90.
"La formation des réseaux ibadites nord-africans (VIIIe–XIIe siècles)." In *Espaces et réseaux en Méditerranée (Vie–XVIe siècles)*, vol. II, 167–86. Paris: Éditions Bouchène, 2010.
"Genèse et développement de la ḥalqa chez les ibāḍites maghrébins." In *Les scribes et la transmission du savoir*, ed. Christian Cannuyer, Acta Orientalia Belgica 19, 109–24. Brussels: Société belge d'études orientales, 2006.
"L'ibadisme berbère: la légitimation d'une doctrine venue d'orient." In *La légitimation du pouvoir au Maghreb médiéval*, edited by Annliese Nef and Élise Voguet, 55–74. Madrid: Casa de Velázquez, 2011.
Les Ibadites: de Djerba à Oman, la troisième voie de l'Islam. Turnhout: Brepols, 2010.
"L'influence de l'état rustumide dans le Sud Tunisien." *Acta Orientalia* 68 (2007): 113.
"Majmāj et les sept savants: la création du Dīwān al-ʿazzāba." *Acta Orientalia* 73 (2012): 35–58.

"La renaissance des ibadites wahbites à Djerba au Xe siècle." *Folia Orientalia* 40 (2004): 171–91.

"Une tentative d'histoire de la ville ibadite de Sadrāta." *Mélanges de la Casa de Velázquez* 38, no. 2 (2008): 129–47.

Raymond, André. "Tunisiens et Maghrébins au Caire au dix-huitième siècle." *Les cahiers de Tunisie* 7, no. 26–27 (1959): 335–71.

Reif, Stefan Clive, and Shulamit Reif, eds. *The Cambridge Genizah Collections: Their Contents and Significance*. Cambridge: Cambridge University Press, 2002.

Robinson, Chase F. *Islamic Historiography*. Cambridge; New York: Cambridge University Press, 2003.

Rouighi, Ramzi. *The Making of a Mediterranean Empire: Ifriqiya and Its Andalusis, 1200–1400*. Philadelphia: University of Pennsylvania Press, 2011.

Rubinacci, Roberto. "Bibliografia degli scritti di Roberto Rubinacci." In *Studi arabo-islamici in onore di Roberto Rubinacci nel suo settantesimo compleanno*, XIII–IX. Naples: Universitario Orientale, 1985.

"Il 'Kitāb al-Jawāhir' di al-Barrādī." *Annali dell'Istituto Universitario Orientale di Napoli* 4 (1952): 95–110.

"La professione di fede di al-Gannawuni." *Annali di Istituto Orientale di Napoli* 14 (1964): 552–92.

Al Salimi, Abdulrahman. "Identifying the Ibadi/Omani Siyar." *Journal of Semitic Studies* 55, no. 1 (2010): 115–62.

"Themes of the Ibadi/Omani Siyar." *Journal of Semitic Studies* 54, no. 2 (2009): 475–514.

Sālim b. Yaʿqūb. *Tārīkh jazīrat jarba wa- ʿulamāʾihā*. Tunis: Cérès Éditions, 2009.

Savage, Elizabeth. "Berbers and Blacks: Ibadi Slave Traffic in Eighth-Century North Africa." *Journal of African History* 33, no. 2 (1992): 351–68.

A Gateway to Hell, a Gateway to Paradise: The North African Response to the Arab Conquest. Princeton: Darwin Press, 1997.

"Survival through Alliance: The Establishment of the Ibadiyya." *Bulletin of the British Society for Middle Eastern Studies* 17, no. 1 (1990): 5–15.

Scheper, Karin. *The Technique of Islamic Bookbinding: Methods, Materials and Regional Varieties*. Leiden; Boston: Brill, 2015.

al-Shammākhī, Abū al-ʿAbbās Aḥmad b. Saʿīd. *Kitāb al-siyar*. Cairo: al-Maṭbaʿa al-Bārūniyya, 1883.

Kitāb al-siyar. Edited by Muḥammad Ḥasan, 3 vols. Beirut: Dār al-Gharb al-Islāmī, 2009.

Stock, Brian. *The Implications of Literacy: Written Language and Models of Interpretation in the Eleventh and Twelfth Centuries*. Princeton: Princeton University Press, 1983.

Ṭālibī, ʿAmmār. *Ārāʾ al-khawārij al-kalāmiyya: al-mūjaz li-Abī ʿAmmār ʿAbd al-Kāfī al-Ibāḍī*, vol. II. Algiers: Al-Sharika al-Waṭaniyya li-l-Nashr, 1978.

al-Tanāwatī, Abū ʿAmmār ʿAbd al-Kāfī. *Siyar Abī ʿAmmār ʿAbd al-Kāfī*. Edited by Masʿūd Mazhūdī. Oman: Maktabat al-Ḍāmirī, 1996.

Tijānī, Abū Muḥammad ʿAbdallāh b. Muḥammad b. Aḥmad al-. *Riḥlat al-Tijānī*. Tunis: Dār al-ʿArabiyya li-ʾl-Kitāb, 1981.

Timani, Hussam S. *Modern Intellectual Readings of the Kharijites*. New York: P. Lang, 2008.

Touati, Houari. "Écriture et commerce dans le Sahara précolonial." *Studia Islamica* 107 (2012): 122–31.

Valls i Subirà, Oriol. *Paper and Watermarks in Catalonia*. Amsterdam: Paper Publication Society, 1970.

Velkov, Asparuch. *Les filigranes dans les documents ottomans: trois croissants*. Sofia: Éd. "Texte – Trayanov," 1983.

Walz, Terence. "The Paper Trade of Egypt and the Sudan in the Eighteenth and Nineteenth Centuries and Its Re-Export to the Bilād as-Sūdān." In *Trans-Saharan Book Trade: Manuscript Culture, Arabic Literacy and Intellectual History in Muslim Africa*, edited by Graziano Krätli and Ghislaine Lydon, 73–107. Leiden; Boston: Brill, 2011.

Wansbrough, John E. "The Decolonization of North African History." *Journal of African History* 9, no. 4 (1968): 643–50.

Lingua Franca in the Mediterranean. Richmond: Curzon Press, 1996.

al-Warjalānī, Abū Yaʿqūb Yūsuf b. Ibrāhīm. *al-Jāmiʿ al-ṣaḥīḥ musnad al-Imām al-Rabīʿ b. Ḥabīb b. ʿUmar al-Azdī al-Baṣrī*. Edited by Maḥmūd ʿAyrān. Damascus: al-Maṭbaʿa al-ʿUmūmiyya, 1968.

al-Warjalānī, Abū Zakarīyāʾ Yaḥyā ibn Abī Bakr. *Kitāb al-sīra wa-akhbār al-aʾimma*. Edited by ʿAbd al-Raḥmān Ayyūb. Tunis: Dār al-Tūnisiyya li-l-Nashr, 1985.

Wilkinson, John. "Ibadi Hadith: An Essay on Normalization." *Der Islam* 62 (1985): 231–59.

Ibāḍism: Origins and Early Development in Oman. Oxford: Oxford University Press, 2010.

al-Wisyānī, Abū al-Rabīʿ Sulaymān. *Kitāb siyar al-Wisyānī*. Edited by ʿUmar b. Luqmān Būʿaṣbāna, 3 vols. Muscat: Wizārat al-Turāth wa-ʾl-Thaqāfa, 2009.

Index

Other titles in the series

Agricultural Innovation in the Early Islamic World: The Diffusion of Crops and Farming Techniques, 700–1100, Andrew M. Watson
Muslim Tradition: Studies in Chronology, Provenance and Authorship of Early Hadith, G. H. A. Juynboll
Social History of Timbuktu: The Role of Muslim Scholars and Notables 1400–1900, Elias N. Saad
Sex and Society in Islam: Birth Control before the Nineteenth Century, B. F. Musallam
Towns and Townsmen of Ottoman Anatolia: Trade, Crafts and Food Production in an Urban Setting 1520–1650, Suraiya Faroqhi
Unlawful Gain and Legitimate Profit in Islamic Law: Riba, Gharar and Islamic Banking, Nabil A. Saleh
Men of Modest Substance: House Owners and House Property in Seventeenth-Century Ankara and Kayseri, Suraiya Faroqhi
Roman, Provincial and Islamic Law: The Origins of the Islamic Patronate, Patricia Crone
Economic Life in Ottoman Jerusalem, Amnon Cohen
Mannerism in Arabic Poetry: A Structural Analysis of Selected Texts (3rd Century AH/9th Century AD–5th Century AH/11th Century AD), Stefan Sperl
The Rise and Rule of Tamerlane, Beatrice Forbes Manz
Popular Culture in Medieval Cairo, Boaz Shoshan
Early Philosophical Shiism: The Ismaili Neoplatonism of Abu Ya'qub Al-Sijistani, Paul E. Walker
Indian Merchants and Eurasian Trade, 1600–1750, Stephen Frederic Dale
Palestinian Peasants and Ottoman Officials: Rural Administration around Sixteenth-Century Jerusalem, Amy Singer
Arabic Historical Thought in the Classical Period, Tarif Khalidi
Mongols and Mamluks: The Mamluk–Ilkhanid War, 1260–1281, Reuven Amitai-Preiss
Knowledge and Social Practice in Medieval Damascus, 1190–1350, Michael Chamberlain
The Politics of Households in Ottoman Egypt: The Rise of the Qazdağlis, Jane Hathaway
Hierarchy and Egalitarianism in Islamic Thought, Louise Marlow
Commodity and Exchange in the Mongol Empire: A Cultural History of Islamic Textiles, Thomas T. Allsen
State and Provincial Society in the Ottoman Empire: Mosul, 1540–1834, Dina Rizk Khoury
The Mamluks in Egyptian Politics and Society, Thomas Philipp and Ulrich Haarmann (eds.)
The Delhi Sultanate: A Political and Military History, Peter Jackson
European and Islamic Trade in the Early Ottoman State: The Merchants of Genoa and Turkey, Kate Fleet

The Ottoman City between East and West: Aleppo, Izmir, and Istanbul, Edhem Eldem, Daniel Goffman, and Bruce Masters
The Politics of Trade in Safavid Iran: Silk for Silver, 1600–1730, Rudolph P. Matthee
The Idea of Idolatry and the Emergence of Islam: From Polemic to History, G. R. Hawting
A Monetary History of the Ottoman Empire, Şevket Pamuk
Classical Arabic Biography: The Heirs of the Prophets in the Age of al-Ma'mun, Michael Cooperson
Empire and Elites after the Muslim Conquest: The Transformation of Northern Mesopotamia, Chase F. Robinson
Poverty and Charity in Medieval Islam: Mamluk Egypt, 1250–1517, Adam Sabra
Culture and Conquest in Mongol Eurasia, Thomas T. Allsen
Christians and Jews in the Ottoman Arab World: The Roots of Sectarianism, Bruce Masters
Arabic Administration in Norman Sicily: The Royal Diwan, Jeremy Johns
Law, Society and Culture in the Maghrib, 1300–1500, David S. Powers
Revival and Reform in Islam: The Legacy of Muhammad al-Shawkani, Bernard Haykel
Tolerance and Coercion in Islam: Interfaith Relations in the Muslim Tradition, Yohanan Friedmann
Guns for the Sultan: Military Power and the Weapons Industry in the Ottoman Empire, Gábor Ágoston
Marriage, Money and Divorce in Medieval Islamic Society, Yossef Rapoport
The Empire of the Qara Khitai in Eurasian History: Between China and the Islamic World, Michal Biran
Domesticity and Power in the Early Mughal World, Ruby Lal
Power, Politics and Religion in Timurid Iran, Beatrice Forbes Manz
Postal Systems in the Pre-Modern Islamic World, Adam J. Silverstein
Kingship and Ideology in the Islamic and Mongol Worlds, Anne F. Broadbridge
Justice, Punishment and the Medieval Muslim Imagination, Christian Lange
The Shiites of Lebanon under Ottoman Rule, 1516–1788, Stefan Winter
Women and Slavery in the Late Ottoman Empire, Madeline Zilfi
The Second Ottoman Empire: Political and Social Transformation in the Early Modern World, Baki Tezcan
The Legendary Biographies of Tamerlane: Islam and Heroic Apocrypha in Central Asia, Ron Sela
Non-Muslims in the Early Islamic Empire: From Surrender to Coexistence, Milka Levy-Rubin
The Origins of the Shi'a: Identity, Ritual, and Sacred Space in Eighth-Century Kufa, Najam Haider
Politics, Law, and Community in Islamic Thought: The Taymiyyan Moment, Ovamir Anjum
The Power of Oratory in the Medieval Muslim World, Linda G. Jones
Animals in the Qur'an, Sarra Tlili

The Logic of Law Making in Islam: Women and Prayer in the Legal Tradition, Behnam Sadeghi

Empire and Power in the Reign of Süleyman: Narrating the Sixteenth-Century Ottoman World, Kaya Şahin

Law and Piety in Medieval Islam, Megan H. Reid

Women and the Transmission of Religious Knowledge in Islam, Asma Sayeed

The New Muslims of Post-Conquest Iran: Tradition, Memory, and Conversion, Sarah Bowen Savant

The Mamluk City in the Middle East: History, Culture, and the Urban Landscape, Nimrod Luz

Disability in the Ottoman Arab World, 1500–1800, Sara Scalenghe

The Holy City of Medina: Sacred Space in Early Islamic Arabia, Harry Munt

Muslim Midwives: The Craft of Birthing in the Premodern Middle East, Avner Giladi

Doubt in Islamic Law: A History of Legal Maxims, Interpretation, and Islamic Criminal Law, Intisar A. Rabb

The Second Formation of Islamic Law: The Hanafi School in the Early Modern Ottoman Empire, Guy Burak

Sexual Violation in Islamic Law: Substance, Evidence, and Procedure, Hina Azam

Gender Hierarchy in the Qur'an: Medieval Interpretations, Modern Responses, Karen Bauer

Intellectual Networks in Timurid Iran: Sharaf al-Din ʿAli Yazdi and the Islamicate Republic of Letters, Ilker Evrim Binbaş

Authority and Identity in Medieval Islamic Historiography: Persian Histories from the Peripheries, Mimi Hanaoka

The Economics of Ottoman Justice: Settlement and Trial in the Sharia Courts, Metin Coşgel and Boğaç Ergene

The Mystics of al-Andalus: Ibn Barrajan and Islamic Thought in the Twelfth Century, Yousef Casewit

Muhammad's Heirs: The Rise of Muslim Scholarly Communities, 622–950, Jonathan E. Brockopp

The First of the Modern Ottomans: The Intellectual History of Ahmed Vasif, Ethan Menchinger

Non-Muslim Provinces under Early Islam: Islamic Rule and Iranian Legitimacy in Armenia and Caucasian Albania, Alison Vacca

Women and the Making of the Mongol Empire, Anne F. Broadbridge

Slavery and Empire in Central Asia, Jeff Eden

Christianity in Fifteenth-Century Iraq, Thomas A. Carlson

Child Custody in Islamic Law: Theory and Practice in Egypt since the Sixteenth Century, Ahmed Fekry Ibrahim

Ibadi Muslims of North Africa: Manuscripts, Mobilization, and the Making of a Written Tradition, Paul M. Love Jr.

For EU product safety concerns, contact us at Calle de José Abascal, 56–1°,
28003 Madrid, Spain or eugpsr@cambridge.org.

www.ingramcontent.com/pod-product-compliance
Ingram Content Group UK Ltd.
Pitfield, Milton Keynes, MK11 3LW, UK
UKHW020328140625
459647UK00018B/2065
* 9 7 8 1 1 0 8 4 5 9 0 1 3 *